GUIDE TO
BIRDS OF THE
SALTON SEA

D1478851

GUIDE TO BIRDS OF THE SALTON SEA

Barbara W. Massey and Richard Zembal

Arizona-Sonora Desert Museum

*The publisher gratefully acknowledges
the financial support of the*

JiJi Foundation

Arizona-Sonora Desert Museum Press
2021 North Kinney Road
Tucson, Arizona 85743
asdmpress@desertmuseum.org
www.desertmuseum.org

ISBN 1-886679-21-5

Printed in Canada

Book and Cover Design by Theresa Reindl Bingham
Photographs © Peter L. Knapp
Bird Illustrations © Narca Moore-Craig
Maps by Ken Althiser

DEDICATION

With pleasure and gratitute we dedicate this book to Dr. Charles Collins, recently retired after 33 years of teaching ornithology at California State University, Long Beach. Charlie introduced us to the Salton Sea and its birds in the 1970s and has since done likewise for several generations of graduate students in his field ornithology classes. Thank you, Charlie, for this and many other good things.

TABLE
OF
CONTENTS

List of Illustrations xi

Map: Orientation to Site Locations xv

Acknowledgments xiii

Introduction xvii
> Sources of Information xix
> Where to Access the Database xxi
> How to Use This Book xxii
> Abbreviations xxii

The Place 1

The Vegetation 5

The Birds 7
> Status 10
> Occurrence 10
> Census Results 10

Site Chapters 15
> Alamo River Delta 17
> The Avenues (76, 79, 81, 84 Avenues) 21
> Bombay Beach 27
> Fig Lagoon 31
> Finney Lake 35
> Johnson Street 41
> Obsidian Butte 45
> Ramer Lake 51
> Red Hill County Park 55

Salton Sea State Recreation Area
(North Beach Marina, Headquarters, Salt Creek) 59
Sonny Bono National Wildlife Refuge -
Headquarters area, Rock Hill 65
Sonny Bono National Wildlife Refuge -
Unit 1 (plus Poe Road) 69
West Side (Desert Shores,
Salton Sea Beach, Salton City) 73
Whitewater River Delta   79
Wister Unit - State Imperial Wildlife Area   83

Additional Sites 91
Hayes Street 91
United States Naval Test Base   92
Westmorland Eucalyptus Grove   93

Cumulative Tables 94
Summation of Species Seen on Counts at all Sites 94
Monthly Occurrence of Species on Counts 106

Nocturnal Roosting 117
Counts 118
Roosts   121

Nesting 125
Waterbirds 127
Ducks 129
Others 129

Species Accounts   131

Rare Species Seen during the Count Period 185

Species of Concern 189

Plant List 191

Literature Cited 193

About the Participants 197

Southwest Birding Opportunities for the Ecotourist 203

Index to Species Accounts 207

Appendix: Chapter Tables 209
    Alamo River Delta 210
    the Avenues 216
    Bombay Beach 224
    Fig Lagoon 228
    Finney Lake 233
    Johnson Street 240
    Obsidian Butte 246
    Ramer Lake 252
    Red Hill County Park 259
    Salton Sea Recreation Area 264
    Sonny Bono National Wildlife Refuge-Headquarters 271
    Sonny Bono National Wildlife Refuge-Unit 1 277
    West Side 282
    Whitewater River Delta 287
    Wister Unit-State Imperial Wildlife Area 293

List
of
Illustrations
by Narca Moore-Craig

Black Skimmer iii

American Avocet xvii

Northern Harrier 17

Magnificent Frigatebird 21

Northern Shoveler 27

Abert's Towhee 31

Marsh Wren 35

Black Skimmer 41

Eared Grebe 45

Tree Swallow 51

Chilean Flamingo 55

Ruddy Duck 59

Gull-billed Tern 65

White Pelican 69

Ring-billed Gull 73

Doule-crested Cormorant 79

Snow Goose 83

White-faced Ibis 117

Red-winged Blackbird 125

Peregrine Falcon 131

Clapper Rail 189

Acknowledgments

It is a pleasure to thank all those who helped us with this book. First on the list are the censusers who committed to a 2 year period of regular treks to the sea. They are all acknowledged in the chapters. Several in particular were always willing to pinch hit at short notice. Paul Jorgensen comes readily to mind; he censused Finney and Ramer Lakes, Red Hill, and Wister Unit in addition to the State Recreation Area, which was his regular beat. Bob Miller took over Finney and Ramer Lakes for Barbara Massey in 1999 when she moved to Oregon, and Wister Unit (south portion) for Mark Wimer when he moved to Maryland.

We turned to Alan Harper for help with a computer program that would accommodate the huge database we were collecting. He devised a wonderful program in Filemaker Pro that allowed us to sort data in many useful ways.

El Dorado Audubon was of enormous help, not only acting as fiduciary for the grants, but contributing generously from its own budget to further the project. Several other Audubon chapters answered our appeal for funding, including Los Angeles, Laguna Hills, Santa Monica, and Santa Clara. Financial support also came from the JiJi Foundation, Homeland Foundation and the Will J. Reid Foundation. Their grants helped pay expenses for monthly censusing trips to the Salton Sea by participants from Los Angeles and San Diego, the bird sketches, and some of the publication costs.

The plant list was the work of Pat Flanagan in consultation with Larry Hendrickson, both of the San Diego Natural History Museum.

The maps were produced by the Salton Sea Database Program of The Redlands Institute, for which we thank Tim Krantz and Ken Althiser.

Two reviewers read the manuscript and provided valuable suggestions. Charlie Collins, who was not given a week to enjoy his retirement from California State University, Long Beach before receiving the manuscript for review, provided helpful advice and comments, as he has done for us for the past 30 years. Dr. Stephen Russell also reviewed the manuscript and recommended changes that have resulted in a better book.

Narca Moore-Craig did the bird sketches that so enliven the text; Peter Knapp is the photographer who captured the magic of the sea and its birds.

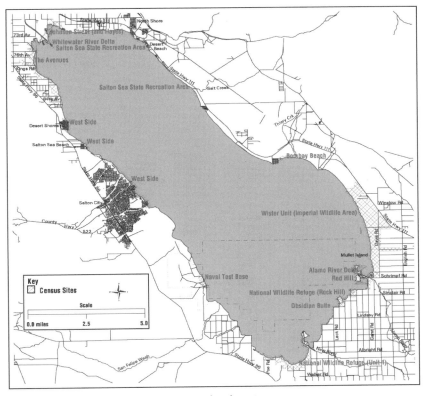

Orientation to Count Site Locations: 12 shoreline sites

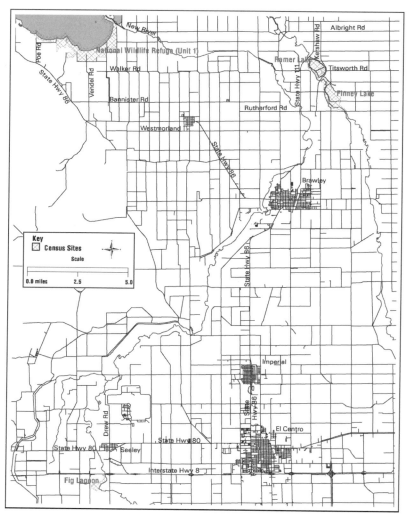

Orientation to Count Site Locations: 3 inland sites

Introduction

The Salton Sea as we know it today is the result of an engineering miscalculation. It is undoubtedly the largest body of water ever created by accident, but is only the latest manifestation of a lake in the Salton Sink. The marks of an ancient shoreline are clearly visible high on the cliffs on the northwest shore, evidence of Lake Cahuilla, which occupied the basin until about 300 years ago. It was born of the dynamics of the lower Colorado River, existed for decades at a time, then went dry until the river roamed again.

The history of today's Salton Sea makes astonishing reading. In 1905 a cut was made in the west bank of the Colorado River below Yuma to introduce more water into an irrigation canal that ran from the river to the Imperial Valley. The canal was only a few years old but already siltation had severely impaired its functionality, and it was hoped that increasing the flow would solve this problem. However, the amount of water that would roar down the river during heavy storms in the watershed was not factored into the equation; and heavy storms did indeed occur. The cut allowed flood waters to follow a straighter course to lower elevations than did the river channel, and the river was unintentionally diverted northward into the Salton Sink. When the flow finally slowed enough to be dammed in 1907 there was a body of water we now know as the Salton Sea. All of the sea and much of the surrounding land in the sink are below sea level; in 1998 the sea's surface was minus 227 feet. The water was expected to evaporate in a few years, as had other, smaller floods in the sink. Instead, the water level rose significantly, due primarily to irrigation runoff from the vast agricultural operations in the Imperial and Coachella Valleys. A recent book, Salt Dreams (deBuys & Myers 1999), was the source of most of this information; it gives an engrossing account of the creation and subsequent history, both human and natural, of the sea.

Fish apparently arrived with the first influx of Colorado River water. In 1908 a field biologist exploring the sea noted an abundance of fishes and identified carp, Colorado perch and catfish (Grinnell 1908). Later, California Department of Fish and Game introduced croaker, orange mouth corvina and sargo to enhance fishing; all have thrived. Tilapia was also introduced to control algae, and dominates the fish fauna today.

This rich food base attracted fish-eating birds from the beginning, and the abundance and diversity of birds found here today makes the sea a site of regional and national importance. It provides a wintering home for hundreds of thousands of water-associated birds, including approximately 90% of the western population of American White Pelicans, 90% of the North American population of Eared Grebes, and 49% of the North American population of Ruddy Ducks (Tetra Tech Inc. 2000). It has a resident population of waterfowl, shorebirds, herons, egrets and rails, including the endangered Yuma Clapper Rail. It is a breeding site for several migratory species that are uncommon in California, such as Fulvous Whistling-Duck and Gull-billed Tern.

But there is a dark side, for the sea today is an impending ecological disaster. Because it is a sink with no outflow, the continual addition of salts and nutrients from agriculture and human settlements in the surrounding drainages have caused severe hyper-salinity, eutrophy, and pollution. These conditions threaten to devastate the fish populations, and thus the birds, and a catastrophe of major proportions is close at hand. Indeed, the huge die-offs of fish and birds in the 1990s were a prelude to what lies ahead. The problems grew well beyond handling by local or regional agencies and the federal government finally has now become involved. In 1998 the 105th Congress passed H.R. 3267, providing millions of dollars to fund research projects that might offer technical solutions. Several are now being tested. A thorough and readable account of the problems and their proposed solutions is found in Salt Dreams (deBuys & Myers 1999).

Despite the significance of the Salton Sea to the avifauna of western United States, there are no books and very few articles about bird use. The most useful publication is a recent report by Point Reyes Bird Observatory (PRBO), the result of a year's study (1999) of the abundance and distribution of waterbirds (Shuford *et. al.* 2000).

We had two reasons for writing this book, both driven by the precarious future of the sea as a bird haven. One was to create a database of bird distribution and occurrence around the sea. The other was to guide birding enthusiasts who wish to visit but have no means of knowing where, when, or how to do so.

Sources of Information

Censuses

Fifteen sites were chosen around the sea. Based on what was already known about bird use, we decided to cover the entire southeast shoreline from Poe Road east to the north boundary of the Wister Unit of the State Imperial Wildlife Area, and the northwest shoreline from 84th Avenue east to Johnson Street. These areas were subsequently shown to be of highest density and most importance for birds (Shuford *et. al.* 2000). In addition we chose in-between sites on the east and west shores to sample bird use in areas not usually visited. Measurements by Ken Althiser of Redlands Institute, based on Geographic Information System (GIS) maps of the sea, gave us an estimate of the extent of coverage by the counts. It was approximately 55 - 60% of the shoreline.

We had no difficulty finding volunteers to cover the sites. Interest in, and concern for, birds of the Salton Sea is widespread among professional and amateur birdwatchers in southern California. Counts were generally done in the early morning and took 2 - 4 hours to complete.

Data collection was designed to cover a 2-year period. Starting in January 1998, we planned to do a monthly count at 12 sites around the Salton Sea and 3 more in the Imperial Valley. In the 2nd year the counts were taken bimonthly. The count period was to be the last full week of every month and its bracketing weekends, 9 days in all. The usual time of day for the counts was to be early morning. After the counts began there were exceptions to every aspect of the plan, because the censusers (most of them busy, professional people living in coastal cities) had to juggle their schedules to manage the long distances and time required to get to the sea. Not all sites received the same coverage; the number of counts per site ranged from 11 to 19. On some occasions, multiple counts were done at several sites on the same day, and occasionally a count was outside the designated period by 1 to 3 days. Withal, the coverage was adequate to compile a database of impressive dimensions that reflects avian use of the sea and its surroundings over a 2-year period.

Christmas Counts

Since the first Audubon Christmas Counts in 1965 (Salton Sea [north] 1966), this annual event has provided data on wintering birds. The south-end count, centered at the Sonny Bono National Wildlife Refuge Headquarters, embraces the New and Alamo River mouths and the Wister Unit of the State Imperial Wildlife Area. The north-end count, centered at the Whitewater River Delta, reaches south to Desert Shores and north into the Coachella Valley.

Other sources

The PRBO report (Shuford *et. al.* 2000) provided data for 1999 that supplemented ours, particularly about nesting colonies.

Nocturnal roost counts

Counts at night roosts were done each month in 1998 at Ramer and Finney Lakes, Fig Lagoon and Sunbeam Lake, all of which had permanent water. Other known roosts were monitored intermittently.

The duck clubs - D & K, Osterkamp, Wilderness and "Keystone" - had water in their ponds only during the hunting season, and as they dried the birds relocated. The birds also moved to other sites for no apparent reason. When they abandoned a night roost we did too.

See the section on "Nocturnal Roosts" for detailed information on roosts and roosting.

Rare bird sightings

Monthly counts give an overall view of distribution and seasonality but do not necessarily include rare birds, which may be missed if present for only a few days. Fortunately the sea is a favored location for rare-bird enthusiasts and is visited regularly by some of the best birders in southern California. For many years sightings of unusual birds at the Salton Sea have been included in the Southern Pacific Coast Region section in Audubon Field Notes/North American Birds. In addition, sightings of rare birds have been posted on the internet at CALBIRD (www.calbird@kiwi.net). A weekly summary of southeastern California is available also by e-mail from San Bernardino Valley Audubon Society. We have included sightings from these sources for 1998-1999 in the section "Rare Species seen during the Count Period".

Where to Access the Database

The database is in Filemaker Pro for MacIntosh and contains close to 14,000 entries. It is housed at the San Diego Museum of Natural History (Ornithology Department) and the Salton Sea Database Program of The Redlands Institute, University of Redlands. It can be accessed by anyone with a scientific interest in its contents.

How to Use this Book

The book has two major approaches:

Site chapters

If you want to take a birdwalk there is a chapter on each of the census sites; choose the one you wish to visit and read about it. Each site chapter has a brief description of the area and its vegetation, directions for getting there, a section on the birdlife, and a table listing the birds seen on the counts, their abundance and seasonality.

Maps of the Salton Sea on pages xv and xvi shows all the sites covered in site chapters. Each chapter has a map showing the trail and some helpful landmarks. The book does not include field identification; it is designed to be used in conjunction with one of the many available field guides.

Species accounts

Alternatively, if you visit the Salton Sea wanting to see a certain bird you can read about it in the chapter called "Species Accounts" first and learn where and when you are most likely to find it, then turn to the pertinent site chapter(s) to become familiar with the chosen walk(s). The "Species Accounts" section covers all the species seen on the counts, giving frequency of occurrence, seasonality, sites where they were seen, and comments, if appropriate.

Abbreviations

The use of acronyms and other shortcuts can be annoying, but if the proper name is as long as some in this book, it can be a just as annoying to see it over and over again. We have decided to stay with the full names of places mentioned infrequently, and abbreviate names that are used many times. Here is a list.

Abbreviation	Full name
Alamo	Alamo River Delta
the Avenues	76th, 79th, 81st, 84th Avenues combined
BLM	United States Bureau of Land Management
BR	United States Bureau of Reclamation
CDFG	California Department of Fish and Game
N.E.S.S.	North end of the Salton Sea (Riverside County)
NWR	Sonny Bono National Wildlife Refuge
NWRHq	Sonny Bono National Wildlife Refuge Headquarters, Rock Hill
PRBO	Point Reyes Bird Observatory
Red Hill	Red Hill County Park (plus Hazard Unit of NWR)
S.E.S.S.	South end of the Salton Sea (Imperial County)
SSSRA	Salton Sea State Recreation Area (North Shore Marina, State Park Headquarters, and Salt Creek)
Unit 1	Sonny Bono National Wildlife Refuge, Unit 1 (plus Poe Road)
USFWS	United States Fish and Wildlife Service
West Side	3 sites on the west shore combined: Salton City, Salton Sea Beach, and Desert Shores
Whitewater	Whitewater River Delta
Wister Unit	Wister Unit of State Imperial Wildlife Area

We hope you will enjoy using this book as much as we enjoyed preparing it. It attempts to give a broad perspective on the birds of the Salton Sea. Knowing what has been seen, and where and when, should provide a basis for detecting changes as they occur.

THE
PLACE

The Salton Sea lies in the Colorado Desert in south-eastern California. Its long axis is in a northwest-south-east direction. Three rivers flow into it: the Whitewater arises in the San Bernardino Mountains, comes down through the Coachella Valley, and empties into the north end; the Alamo and New Rivers flow into the south end from Mexico. There is no outlet. None of the rivers, however, provides significant amounts of water to the sea; most of that comes from the numerous irriga-tion drainage ditches that pepper the shores.

Flatlands surround the sea, but more narrowly in the north where there are close mountain ranges: the Chocolate Mountains on the east, the Orocopias on the north and the Santa Rosas on the west. These arid ranges change hues throughout the day and create a backdrop of subtle desert colors against the also-changing blues and grays of the sea. The flatlands edging the sea broad-en as one travels south and the mountains become a ghostly backdrop. Much of the arid-land vegetation that once grew along the shore has been replaced by intensive agriculture, settlements, and duck ponds, particularly along the northwest and southeast shores. The Coachella Valley, with its orchards, grape vines and fish farms, lies to the north; the Imperial Valley, with its vast fields of crops, to the south. Several major highways follow the perimeter of the sea, and dirt roads perpendicular to them provide access to the shore.

The sea's dimensions in 1998 were approximately 36 by 15.5 miles; its elevation minus 227 feet; the average depth 31 feet. The approximate salinity was 44,000 - 45,000 parts per million; salinity of seawater is approximately 35,000 parts per million (deBuys & Myers 1999). It is a basin of very little rain, the average annual precipitation is 2.5 inches. It is hot, with more than 110 days per year exceeding 100 degrees Fahrenheit.

A few rocky mounds jut from the salt flats and shallow waters along the southern shores, notably Red Hill, Rock Hill and Obsidian Butte. Mullet Island off the southeast shore serves as a major nesting site for the Double-crested Cormorant.

The water level has fluctuated over the years, sometimes with disastrous consequences for real estate and other ventures. In the early 1960s, Salton City on the west shore was the site of a small real estate boom and one of the attractive come-ons was a yacht club and marina. After a sharp rise in water level the boom went bust, and the yacht club and other shoreline structures became partially submerged derelicts, favored subjects for many a photographer. The NWR, a 37,600 acre wildlife area established in 1930 on the southeast shore, also suffered major loss of land from immersion. Today only 1,785 acres remain above water.

Bird use of the sea and the Imperial Valley has multiplied and diversified over the years. The entire sea serves as bird habitat; one cannot stand on any part of the shore in winter without seeing rafts of Eared Grebes and Ruddy Ducks bobbing on the water. But the greatest concentrations are along the northwest shore in the vicinity of the Whitewater River Delta and the southeast shore from the New River Delta east to the north end of the Wister Unit. The valley itself, with its rotationally flooded agricultural fields, attracts large flocks of foraging waterbirds and shorebirds.

In addition to the NWR there are several agency-owned areas around the sea. The Wister Unit, a large acreage on the southeast shore, was acquired by the state in 1956 and is administered by CDFG. The SSSRA, established on the east shore in 1955, is administered by California State Parks Department. The now-defunct Naval Test Base on the western shore is currently under two federal agencies - BR and BLM. There are also numerous private duck clubs in the Imperial Valley with diked ponds that are flooded during the winter months. And while all of these areas provide much-needed habitat for water-associated birds, all except the SSSRA allow waterfowl hunting, and areas that offer year-round refuge to birds are in scant supply.

THE VEGETATION

The Salton Sink, an arid desert landscape with hyper-saline soils, is sparsely vegetated by desert scrub except along the water channels. Along the edge of the sea the vegetation has been greatly impacted by human activities. The sea covers approximately 381 square miles of the lowest elevations in the sink; agriculture, human settlements and other disturbances along the shores have eliminated much of the shoreline desert scrub. Some of the least impacted patches can be found on the northwestern and western shores, such as the Naval Test Base, and on the extremely arid western shore (e.g. SSSRA). The common plants are arrowweed (*Pluchea sericea*), iodine bush (*Allenrolfea occidentalis*), quailbush (*Atriplex lentiformis*), salt grass (*Distichlis spicata*), and screwbean mesquite (*Prosopis pubescens*), which grows locally and is usually festooned with mistletoe (*Phoradendron californicum*).

Tamarisk trees, also called salt cedar, are exotics from Eurasia that were introduced several centuries ago into southwestern communities for their fast growth and the welcome shade they provided. Unfortunately they proved invasive and have replaced many of the native riparian species. The seedlings of *Tamarix chinensis* apparently arrived with the Colorado River water and thrived from the beginning; *T. aphylla* was planted for windbreaks. Around the sea they now dominate the landscape, lining the ditches and river channels, and thriving in the towns and settlements. They have outcompeted native trees and shrubs in riparian corridors, offering few compensations; their use as wildlife habitat is minimal compared to native trees (Hunter *et. al.* 1988).

The irrigation runoff ditches and many of the duck ponds have stands of cattail Typha spp. and bulrush (*Scirpus* spp.), some of them dense enough to support marsh birds. Common reed (*Phragmites communis*) and giant reed (*Arundo donax*) also grow in wet places.

The Whitewater River once flowed freely into the sea, forming a riparian corridor through the Coachella Valley. The delta is now confined within a channel and the native vegetation has been severely invaded by tamarisk. There are few cottonwoods Popolus fremontii or willows Salix sp. remaining. Even so, the most bird-friendly riparian habitat around the sea is found here. Desert scrub flanks the riparian corridor.

THE
BIRDS

From the first, the sea attracted birds. Waterbirds in great flocks were noted in 1906, while the sea was still filling (James 1911). In 1908 Joseph Grinnell, an ornithologist whose writings on the distribution of birds in California and Baja California are classics of ornithological literature, took a boat trip on the sea. He saw flocks of Eared Grebes and small numbers of Common Loons, Western Grebes, Ring-billed Gulls and Caspian Terns. All except the loon are common at the sea today. He also found 3 species of waterbirds nesting on two islands in the southern part of the sea. On Echo Island he estimated 1000 pairs of breeding American White Pelicans, and on nearby Pelican Island found 147 Double-crested Cormorant and 7 Great Blue Heron nests (Grinnell 1908). Although his landmarks are not referent to present day locations, one of them was quite certainly Mullet Island, where cormorants continue to nest. The others were presumably submerged under rising sea levels. He also noted herons and cormorants roosting on partially submerged snags and telephone poles, just as they do today.

In May 1927 two ornithologists set out by boat to investigate a report of Gull-billed Tern nesting somewhere at the sea. They found 500 nests on 3 undesignated islands (Pemberton 1927). Since this species was previously known only as a seabird nesting along the Atlantic and Gulf coasts, there was much speculation as to how it found and adapted to an inland lake. An estimated 450 pairs of White Pelicans were also found breeding. And although there was no mention of Double-crested Cormorant, many other species were seen including White-faced Ibis, Fulvous Whistling-Duck, and Roseate Spoonbill, one of which was collected!

Today, all habitats that are bird-friendly are well occupied. The open waters of the sea support rafts of Eared Grebes and Ruddy Ducks most of the year, in numbers so vast they cannot be counted accurately and must be estimated. White Pelicans also float on the open waters over the entire sea, and many species of ducks raft close to shore. The sand bars at the deltas attract flocks of gulls and pelicans; the ubiquitous snags of trees that drowned when the water rose are usually festooned with cormorants, herons, and egrets. The shoreline provides foraging habitat for shorebirds and roosting areas for gulls. Ponds are plentiful just inland, particularly along the southeast shore. Most are managed for hunting but also host large numbers of Black-necked Stilts, American Avocets, gulls, and terns along with the ducks. Where they are very shallow and filled with cattails they attract bitterns and rails, and provide nesting habitat for species such as Red-winged and Yellow-headed Blackbird, Marsh Wren and Common Yellowthroat. Riparian areas, although both limited in acreage and degraded in quality, provide habitat for resident passerines (Black Phoebe, Verdin, Abert's Towhee, Song Sparrow) and attract migrants. The agricultural fields in the Imperial and Coachella Valleys host large flocks of foraging Cattle Egrets, White-faced Ibis, and Ring-billed Gulls all year round; and Snow Geese, Sandhill Cranes and Mountain Plovers in winter.

The nesting scene is dominated by waterbirds, and nesting colonies provided quite spectacular birding experiences. At Ramer Lake in 1998 approximately 10,000 Cattle Egret nests crowded the snag field in the south pond. At the north end of the sea, 75 Great Blue Heron nests were scattered in the snags off Johnson Street in 1998. The comings and goings of 10,000 Double-crested Cormorants at the colony on Mullet Island could be seen from shore at Alamo and Wister Unit. Some passerines also nested colonially, such as Cliff Swallow and Red-winged

Blackbird. Others, while not colonial, were abundant in marsh habitat, like Marsh Wren and Common Yellowthroat at Finney and Ramer Lakes.

The nocturnal roosts are another stellar feature for those looking for exciting and aesthetic bird experiences. Cattle Egret and White-faced Ibis at Ramer Lake, Snow Geese at Unit 1, and Sandhill Crane at Keystone are several of the highlights (see section on "Nocturnal Roosting"). A simultaneous roost count in January 1999 tallied more than 38,000 birds at 9 sites. Watching and listening to hundreds of birds fly in against a darkening sky in long V formations is a thrilling experience.

In winter the sea is crowded with waterfowl, most of which move north to Canada and Alaska to breed. Banding of waterfowl has been conducted for many years by personnel of the NWR. Recently a map showing the location of banding recoveries in North America was completed by the Salton Sea Database Program of Redlands Institute, using data from the United States Geological Survey (USGS) Bird Banding Laboratory. There have been recoveries in all states west of the Mississippi River, and in Alaska and Hawaii. There is also a dense pattern of recoveries in southwestern Canada. These data are preliminary and will be developed further and made available to those interested by the Redlands Institute.

The abundance of birds at the Salton Sea is unparalleled regionally. Nesting colonies of 5,500 pairs of Double-crested Cormorants and 10,000 Cattle Egrets; roosting flocks of 17,000 Cattle Egrets and 8,000 White-faced Ibis; rafts of 5,000 Eared Grebes on the open water—all are regular occurrences. Even the die-offs have reached astonishing levels, such as the 150,000 Eared Grebes that succumbed to unknown causes in 1992.

To balance this largesse, there are the exciting appearances of rare birds, usually in the form of one transient individual (see section on "Rare species seen during the Count Period"). The sea both meets the bird seeker's expectations and offers unexpected bonuses for those who search out rare birds.

The most recent checklist cites nearly 400 species seen at the Salton Sea and its environs since records have been kept (Shuford *et. al.* 1999). The majority are waterbirds, but a surprising number of passerines have been observed during migration (Shuford *et. al.* 2000).

Status

Bird use of the Salton Sea falls generally into 3 categories:

1) **Residents**. Birds that are present year-round and that breed locally. More than 60 species are in this category.

2) **Migrants**. Birds that spend a part of their year at the sea. They fall into several subcategories.
    a) **Wintering birds**. This is the largest group and includes species that number in the thousands, such as Eared Grebe, Snow Goose, and Ruddy Duck. Others come in small numbers, arrive much later, and stay only a few months. The Sandhill Crane is one example.
    b) **Summer arrivals**. Birds that come north to breed, such as Fulvous Whistling-Duck, Gull-billed Tern, Lesser Nighthawk, and Western Kingbird.
    c) **Transients**. Birds that stop over during spring and/or fall migration, such as Common Tern, Brant, Wilson's Warbler, and Black-headed Grosbeak.

3) **Visitors**. Birds that are seen occasionally, such as Surf Scoter and Sage Sparrow; or seasonally such as Wood Stork, Laughing Gull, and Black Tern. Species that are present year-round but do not breed are categorized as year-round visitors, such as American White Pelican, Black-bellied Plover, Willet, and Ring-billed Gull.

Occurrence

Occurrence is an assessment of abundance of a species within the habitat. Such terms as "common" and "fairly common" are defined and used on check-lists. They attempt to estimate not only how many birds may be seen but whether they are regular or erratic in occurrence. A list of terms and their definitions as used in the "Species Accounts" is given at the beginning of that section.

Census results

Two hundred twenty-nine species were seen on the counts; their occurrence at the count sites is shown in the table entitled "Summation of Species Seen on the Counts at all Sites" (page 94). Species are noted as present or absent for each site.

Difficulty in differentiating Long-billed Dowitchers from Short-billed Dowitchers led us to pool them into the category Dowitcher spp. even though the great majority of dowitchers at the sea is reportedly the Long-billed. Similarly, Snow Geese could be difficult to tell from less frequently seen Ross's Geese in the flocks in which they occur; they were called White Geese when identification was uncertain.

Twenty-five species were seen at all sites. Seventeen were residents: Double-crested Cormorant, Great Blue Heron, Great Egret, Snowy Egret, Redhead, Ruddy Duck, American Kestrel, American Coot, Killdeer, Black-necked Stilt, American Avocet, Caspian Tern, Black Phoebe, Say's Phoebe, Verdin, Song Sparrow, and Great-tailed Grackle. Eight were year-round visitors (non-breeding residents): Eared Grebe, Turkey Vulture, Northern Shoveler, Green-winged Teal, Western Sandpiper, Dowitcher spp., Ring-billed Gull and Forster's Tern.

Forty-one species were seen at only one site; many were migrants making a stopover en route north, but some were out-of-range birds making unexpected appearances: Common Loon, Greater White-fronted Goose, Mute Swan, Eurasian Wigeon, Greater Scaup, American Golden-Plover, Baird's Sandpiper, Little Gull, Lesser Black-backed Gull, Sabine's Gull, Least Tern, Spotted Dove, Red-naped Sapsucker, Eastern Phoebe, and Plumbeous Vireo.

The greatest diversity was at Wister Unit, where 163 species were logged. Wister was the largest site, and had enough habitat diversity to attract more species of upland birds than any other site, in addition to its host of waterbirds. Other sites with large numbers of species were the Avenues (142), Finney Lake (133), Ramer Lake and NWRHq (128), and Whitewater (127).

The presence or absence of species throughout the year is shown in the table entitled "Monthly Occurrence of Species on Counts" on page 106. Sixty-six species were present in every month, about evenly divided between residents and year-round (non-breeding) visitors. Not all of the resident birds were seen monthly; local species such as Burrowing Owl, Anna's Hummingbird, and Bewick's Wren were scarce at the count sites because of habitat limitations. Autumn brought species such as Snow Goose, Ruby-crowned Kinglet, and White-crowned Sparrow, that arrived in September and October and stayed until late spring. Spring migration, often a signal event in the California deserts, was muted at the Salton Sea. May was the best month, but usually only a few species were seen at a few sites. Only once did a mixed wave of warblers pass through during a count - at Finney Lake in May (see chapter on Finney Lake for details). Summer saw the arrival of species that came north to breed such as Fulvous Whistling-Duck, Gull-billed Tern, Black Skimmer, White-winged Dove, and Ash-throated Flycatcher. These birds arrived in March and April and were generally gone by September.

The number of individuals per count was far greater from September through March than the rest of the year, reflecting the long-known fact that the Salton Sea is a winter haven for waterbirds. Species diversity, however, did not fluctuate very much, although it was slightly higher in May when the migrants came through on their way north, and most wintering species were still represented by at least small populations. The table below shows the number of individuals (rounded off) and species on monthly counts in 1998:

Monthly Counts in 1998

Month	Number of individuals/count	Number of species/count
January	101,000	141
February	128,100	128
March	105,300	130
April	66,550	141
May	26,580	147
June	34,700	127
July	63,700	129
August	67,700	116
September	93,000	140
October	111,900	125
November	125,600	135
December	140,000	122

The most abundant species was the Eared Grebe. For 6 months of the year (November - April) its numbers were more than double the next contender.

In winter months there were 19 species with tallies higher than 1000 individuals per count. They were (in descending order) Eared Grebe, Snow Goose, Ruddy Duck, Northern Shoveler, Ring-billed Gull, American White Pelican, American Coot, Double-crested Cormorant, Cattle Egret, American Wigeon, Green-winged Teal, American Avocet, Dowitcher spp., Herring Gull, Pintail, California Gull, White-faced Ibis, Lesser Scaup and Black-necked Stilt.

In summer there were 6 species with numbers greater than 1000 per count. Four were nesting species (Double-crested Cormorant, Cattle Egret, Black-necked Stilt, and American Avocet); two were year-round (non-breeding) visitors (American White Pelican and Ring-billed Gull).

Both the setting and the birding experience of the Salton Sea are wonderfully unique. The contrasts afforded by this sea in the desert - between the dry, sparse desert scrub with its largely crepuscular or nocturnal fauna and the huge expanse of open water with its teeming birdlife, all under one vast desert sky - burn into one's memory. Birding the sea is unforgettable. If you have a fraction of the delight that we experienced in doing the fieldwork for this book, you will be lucky indeed.

SITE
CHAPTERS

The 15 count sites are covered in alphabetical order in the following section. To find the location of a site, refer to the maps of the Salton Sea on pages xv and xvi. Each chapter includes directions on how to get there, a brief description of the trail and the vegetation, a detail map of the site, and a discussion of birds seen on the counts. A table of occurrence for each site can be found in the Appendix. Page references to the appropriate tables are given in each chapter.

Plants and birds are identified by their common names. Scientific names of plants may be found in the back of book under "Plant List," in alphabetical order by family. Scientific names of birds are found in the "Species Accounts." All lists of birds are in American Ornithologists' Union checklist order (see American Ornithologists' Union 1998).

ALAMO RIVER DELTA

Fieldwork: Kathy Molina, Kennon Corey
Table of Occurrence: Barbara Massey
Text: Barbara Massey

The Alamo River Delta does not meet one's preconceived ideas of what a delta should be; the actual watercourse has been channeled and diked, as have most of the waterways at the Salton Sea. However, the river mouth is the major feature of this important east-side site, hence the name.

Driving Directions

Coming from the north, go south along Highway 111 on the east side of the sea past the town of Niland approximately 2.3 miles to Schrimpf Road. Turn right (west) on Schrimpf and go to Davis Road (about 3.5 miles) where the counts began. From the south the turnoff is approximately 1.5 miles north of Sinclair Road. The count area was along Davis Road from Schrimpf north to Noffsinger, all along the west side. The east side is salt barrens.

Before (or after) driving Davis Road it is an excellent idea to view the delta from the end of Garst Road. To do this, turn off Highway 111 on Sinclair where there is a sign to the Sonny Bono NWR. Go west on Sinclair to Garst, then north on Garst to the end. Garst makes a sharp turn west to Red Hill Marina but do not take it. Go straight over the bridge that spans the Alamo River

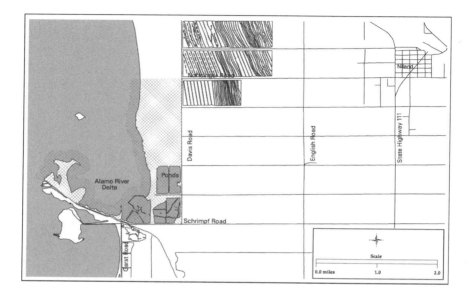

and park. Ahead lie the ponds and sand bars of the delta that are too far to see from Davis Road.

Site description and Vegetation

From the beach at the north end of Garst Road there is a good overview of the outermost ponds and the sea. The sand bars and shallows with their flocks of pelicans, gulls, and shorebirds are well seen from there. A spotting scope is a great asset in visualizing the flocks of American White Pelicans that often roost on the sand bars, and the exotic flamingos that sometimes mingle with them.

To get from the beach to the intersection of Davis and Schrimpf Roads it is necessary to backtrack to Sinclair, turn east and go back to Highway 111, then go north to Schrimpf Road and take a left (west) to Davis Road. The count site embraced all the diked ponds, sand bars, and open sea west of Davis Road between Schrimpf and Noffsinger. The ponds off Davis Road are large and heavily used by waterfowl and shorebirds. It is possible to drive out some of the dikes but caution must be exercised. The dirt tracks are narrow and some do not have turnarounds. Walking is a better method of viewing the area.

A very interesting geologic feature lies at the corner of Davis and Schrimpf Roads on the east side. A series of active mud volcanoes erupt from a salt pan, forming warm pools at their bases. Their gurgles and grunts are incongruous and intriguing sounds in the otherwise silent landscape. They are well worth a visit. The picturesque remains of a resort and spa can be found farther north on Davis Road.

The vegetation is unremarkable. Tamarisks line the dikes along with arrowweed and iodine bush. Giant reed grows vigorously in the drainage ditches.

Birds

Counts were done every month in 1998; in January, May, July, September, and November 1999; and in January 2000. During these 18 counts 109 species were seen (see table on page 210). The number of species per count ranged from 27 to 60 with September the month of highest species diversity.

The delta was notable for waterbirds. American White Pelican, Double-crested Cormorant, Great Blue Heron, Great Egret, Ruddy Duck, American Coot, Black-bellied Plover, Black-necked Stilt, American Avocet, Marbled Godwit, Western Sandpiper, and Ring-billed Gull were present on all, or almost all, counts, and usually in very large numbers. It was a good place to find Laughing Gulls in spring and summer; only at Wister Unit were they seen more often. Flocks of Green-winged Teal and Northern Shoveler foraged in the shallow waters of the ponds in winter. In addition to the resident Black-necked Stilt and American Avocet, the shallows also attracted hosts of migrating shorebirds, with Western Sandpiper leading in numbers (approximately 5,700 in March, 10,600 in July). Large numbers of Long-billed Curlews were often in the area (541 in September 1999). American Coots were more abundant here than anywhere else around the sea. It was a preferred site for Stilt Sandpipers, seen on 7 counts, particularly in winter. Snowy Plovers nested on the salt flats here in the largest numbers found anywhere at the sea.

At the bridge over the Alamo River on Garst Road, debris often piled up, forming a floating raft where a Western Grebe was observed making a nesting attempt. In the adjacent marsh Yuma Clapper Rails were heard occasionally.

Raptors frequented the area, particularly Osprey, American Kestrel, and Peregrine Falcon, this last species often sitting in one of the dead tree snags on the shoreline. A Merlin was seen twice.

Resident passerines were surprisingly well represented, despite the paucity of bird-friendly upland habitat. Black Phoebe, Verdin, Marsh Wren, Common Yellowthroat and Song Sparrow were all found along the edges of the ponds where there was vegetation. A few Loggerhead Shrikes were resident along the barrens on the east side of Davis Road.

Unusual sightings

The delta was one of two places where Wood Storks were seen in summer, the other site was Wister Unit. They were typically seen either at the end of Garst Road or at the corner of Schrimpf and Davis Roads.

Flamingos could occasionally be picked out among the White Pelican flocks, but were too far away to be identified to species. A trio of Mute Swans was present in July 1999. A Black-throated Sparrow, seen in August 1998, was found elsewhere only at the Naval Test Base.

The Avenues

Fieldwork: Chet McGaugh
Text and Table of Occurrence: Barbara Massey

Between the towns of Mecca and Desert Shores on the northwest shore, a series of dirt roads lead east from State Highway 86 to the edge of the sea. They are numbered from north to south, and counts were done at 76th, 79th (Kings Road), 81st, and 84th Avenues. Much of the land between the highway and the shore has been converted to agricultural use, and the process is continuing. There is little native scrub remaining. Highway 86 is being rerouted closer to the shore from 82nd Avenue north, but according to the California Department of Motor Vehicles, access will be available to all roads that were there before construction. The current county road map does not show this change; we hope there will be a new one shortly.

Coverage of this important section of the shoreline fell below the standard set for the counts. Two counts (April and September) were missed in 1998, important months for migrants. In 1999 only the January count was patterned after the previous ones. Subsequent counts were done by PRBO and their protocol was different from ours. The data were pooled for the 4 sites; the schedule was every third month (April, August and November) instead of in alternate months; and the counts excluded Eared Grebe, American White Pelican, Double-crested Cormorant, all ducks and geese, and all upland birds except for raptors. There was no count in January 2000.

Narca

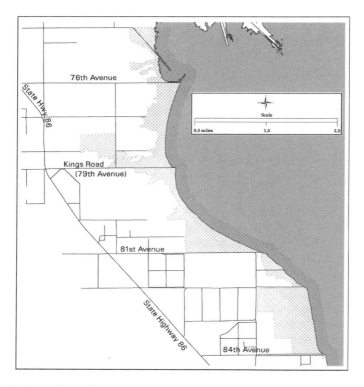

Withal, the data from the Avenues do not match up well with the rest of the sites. But because the area is large and of great importance as bird habitat, we have included it, with the above caveats.

In the table on page 216, data from all 4 avenues were pooled for seasonal occurrence, with individual columns for each avenue to show where each species was seen. The comments give the range of numbers for each species with the month of highest and lowest numbers.

Counts for 1998 (January, February, March, May, June, July, August, October and December) and January 1999 (a total of 10) were tallied separately for the 4 sites. The pooled data from the PRBO counts in 1999 were used where appropriate—for seasonality and numbers of individuals, but not for occurrence at the individual avenues. The comments column in the occurrence table acknowledges 13 counts when the PRBO data were usable, and 10 when they were not.

Birds (summary for the 4 avenues)

One hundred forty-two species were seen at the Avenues. The usual waterbirds and shorebirds that frequent the sea were seen in all seasons and at all 4 avenues: Eared Grebe, American White Pelican, Double-crested Cormorant, Great Blue Heron, Great Egret, Snowy Egret, Green Heron, White-faced Ibis, Northern Shoveler, Northern Pintail, Ruddy Duck, American Coot, Killdeer, Black-necked Stilt, American Avocet, Greater Yellowlegs, Least Sandpiper, Ring-billed Gull, California Gull, Caspian and Forster's Tern. Osprey were always present and in greater numbers than at any other site; American Kestrel was the other regularly seen diurnal raptor. Upland birds seen in all seasons and at all avenues were Common Ground-dove, Greater Roadrunner, Black Phoebe, Verdin, Marsh Wren, Northern Mockingbird, Song Sparrow and House Finch. In the appropriate season White-winged Dove, Belted Kingfisher, Western Kingbird, American Pipit, Yellow-rumped Warbler, and White-crowned Sparrow were present.

Several species were seen at the Avenues and not elsewhere on the counts: White-tailed Kite, Greater Scaup, Spotted Dove, Eastern Phoebe, Scott's Oriole, and Lawrence's Goldfinch. This distinction does not mean that they could occur only here, but rather indicates their rarity around the sea. Unusual species seen here and at only one other site were Magnificent Frigatebird, Red-shouldered Hawk and Black Scoter.

Individual Avenues

76th Avenue

Driving Directions

From Highway 195 (or the new Highway 86), exit east onto 76th Avenue (marked by a street sign across from Oasis School on Highway 195). Follow the dirt road to the shore (approximately 1 mile). Four-wheel drive is not usually necessary but could be essential after rain—admittedly a rare occurrence at the sea.

Site Description and Vegetation

The count area included the shoreline and the open sea, plus the little remaining native desert scrub along the road to the sea, including arrowweed and quail bush. An irrigation runoff ditch that parallels the road has patches of cattail and sedge, with dense tamarisk on the berms. At the shore, one looks east across the sea past a line of partially submerged power poles, north over shallow water to the sand bars and snags between 76th Avenue and the Whitewater River Delta, and south over a large salt pan.

Birds

Large flocks of American White Pelicans often roosted on the sand bars to the north. On one count in March, a trio of Chilean Flamingos was observed (see "Species Accounts - Non-native Species" for details). Double-crested Cormorants and Great Blue Herons festooned the branches of the partially drowned snags at all seasons, and Great Blue Herons nested on the old power poles. The salt pan on the south side was a favored roosting site for Ring-billed and California Gulls. Shorebirds frequented the shoreline and sandbars. Marsh Wren, Common Yellowthroat and Song Sparrow were frequently in the marsh vegetation in the irrigation ditch.

The only sightings of Chilean Flamingo, White-tailed Kite, Sage Thrasher, and Scott's Oriole were at 76th Avenue; and Magnificent Frigatebird and Black Scoter were seen at only one other site.

The snags in the shallow waters between 76th Avenue and Whitewater River Delta have long been used for nesting. In 1999 there were 4 species: Great Blue Heron (139 nests), Great Egret (82 nests), Snowy Egret (48 nests), and Black-crowned Night-Heron (23 nests) (Shuford *et. al.* 2000).

79th Avenue (Kings Road)

Driving Directions

Exit east onto 79th Avenue (the street sign says Kings Road) from Highway 86. Follow the dirt road to where it forks at a drainage ditch;

take the right (south) fork to the shore (less than 2 miles). Four-wheel drive is not necessary.

Site Description and Vegetation

The count area included the shoreline and the open sea, plus what little native desert scrub remained. The vegetation is similar to that at 76th Avenue, with the addition of fields of salt grass dotted with screwbean mesquite on the north side. The runoff ditch has stands of cattails dense enough to host marsh birds. At the sea's edge there is open water ahead and salt pan north and south. A line of power poles stands in the water and has many old Great Blue Heron nests in its arms.

Birds

Several species were recorded here and nowhere else around the sea; Greater Scaup, Eastern Phoebe, and Lawrence's Goldfinch were each seen once.

81st Avenue

Driving Directions

Exit east onto 81st Avenue (marked by a street sign) from Highway 86 approximately 0.7 mile south of the turnoff for 79th Avenue. Follow the dirt road to the shore (less then 2 miles). The last quarter mile is more a track than a road.

Site Description and Vegetation

Native vegetation is present from new Highway 86 to the shore. An irrigation runoff ditch has marsh vegetation and tamarisk as at the other avenues. Fields of salt grass interspersed with the desert scrub lie on the north side. At the sea's edge there is a beach on the north side that is heavily laden with driftwood. On the south shore drowned snags both on shore and out in the water provide roosting habitat for waterbirds.

Birds

The only sighting of a Spotted Dove was made here. Two pairs of Great Blue Herons nested in 1999 (Shuford *et. al.* 2000).

84th Avenue

Driving Directions

Exit east onto 84th Avenue (marked by a street sign) from Highway 86 about 1.0 mile south of the turnoff for 79th Avenue. Follow the dirt road to the shore (less than 2 miles).

Site Description and Vegetation

The dirt road is lined almost to the shore with agricultural enterprises, including citrus groves, vineyards, date palm groves and fish farms. The road forks at the start of an irrigation runoff ditch about 0.5 mile from the sea. The right fork is traversable, it is maintained because of the cultivated fields. Just before the shore there is a salt-encrusted pond on the north side, a favorite haunt of ducks and shorebirds. At the shore one looks north over a beach and south to a large grove of snags—a roost for cormorants and herons.

Birds

This site offered a close look at waterbirds and shorebirds that used the pond. By staying inside a vehicle, one could be very near to several species of waterfowl, as well as White-faced Ibis, Black-necked Stilt and American Avocet. Virginia Rail, Common Moorhen, Marsh Wren and Common Yellowthroat were seen and heard in the marsh vegetation in the ditch. No one-of-a-kind sightings were made here.

BOMBAY BEACH

Fieldwork and Text: Kennon Corey
Table of Occurrence: Barbara Massey

Bombay Beach was selected as a census site because of its location (about equidistant from SSSRA and Wister Unit), not for its renown as bird habitat. The eastern shore has sparse scrub vegetation and lacks the deltas and embayments that enhance the sea for birds on the northwest and southeast shores. Nevertheless it was found to host more species and larger numbers of individuals than anticipated.

Driving Instructions

Bombay Beach is on the east shore. The turnoff from Highway 111, marked by a big 'welcome' sign, is approximately 17 miles north of Niland and 16 miles south of the SSSRA. Turn off and take the first left, which is 1st Street. At the end of 1st Street, several dirt roads continue into the scrub paralleling the shoreline for 100 - 200 meters before heading northeast away from the Sea. It is possible to park along these dirt roads, but do not get stuck in the mud! Walk through the scrub and sometimes muddy soil south to the shoreline and head east away from Bombay Beach; the shoreline runs east-west here.

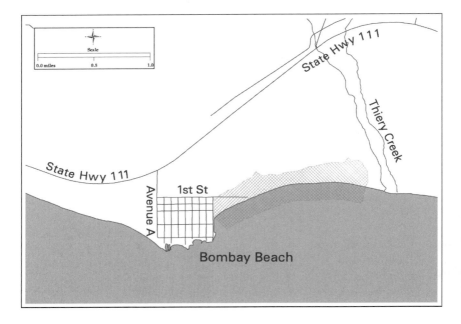

Site Description and Vegetation

Although adjacent to a mobile home settlement on the eastern shore, the shoreline where the counts were done has not been much disturbed. The walk is approximately 1 mile along the shore. Inland, there are shallow ponds used by duck hunters in season (take care and call the CDFG for precise hunting season dates). There were birds all along the shore, in the ponds, and on the sea, with a large concentration in a cove about 1 mile down the shore. The vegetation is almost a monoculture of iodine bush intermixed with a small amount of bush seepweed.

Birds

Counts were done only in 1998. They were conducted every month except October; 76 species were seen on these 11 counts (see table on page 224). The number of species per count ranged from 13 - 40 with May the month of highest species diversity.

The large ponds adjacent to the sea were perhaps the biggest attraction; they supported great numbers of Redhead, Green-winged Teal,

Northern Shoveler and other ducks; as well as several species of shore-birds, terns, and phalaropes. Coyotes were twice observed running along the edge of these ponds, apparently seeking any unsuspecting or injured birds.

The shoreline provided a great opportunity for observing Snowy Plover, Western Sandpiper, Least Sandpiper, Savannah Sparrow, and American Pipit at close range. A large group of White Pelicans often loafed along the shoreline at the end of the transect away from Bombay Beach.

The scrub appeared to be prime nesting habitat for Lesser Nighthawks. Twenty-nine individuals were observed in July, some foraging over the scrub areas and some being flushed from the shrubs. An eggshell fragment found in the scrub confirmed nesting. Other frequently observed upland birds included Abert's Towhee and Song Sparrow.

Unusual sightings

A Parasitic Jaeger was observed chasing gulls and terns over the ponds in August; a Bank Swallow was flushed from the dense vegetation along the shoreline in July. Common Goldeneyes were seen twice in winter immediately offshore along with huge rafts of Eared Grebes.

There is enough diversity of habitat—beach, brackish ponds, scrub, and open sea—to support many more species, and the site deserves further attention by birders.

FIG LAGOON

Fieldwork and Text: Doug Julian
Table of Occurrence: Barbara Massey

Fig Lagoon is a part of the vast irrigation system of the Imperial Valley. It was constructed by the Imperial Irrigation District in the aftermath of tropical storm Kathleen in 1976. Fig Drain was badly damaged by runoff from that storm. During reconstruction the drain outlet was enlarged to create an evaporation pond in the New River channel. Its purpose was to reduce runoff into the Salton Sea. As a by-product of the change, the 80 acre lagoon attracts many species of wildlife including waterfowl and other birds.

Driving directions

Fig Lagoon is located between Derrick and Drew Roads just south of Interstate 8 near the town of Seeley. Exit Interstate 8 at Drew Road. Turn south and drive 1.5 miles to Diehl Road. Turn west on Diehl and drive 1 mile to Derrick Road. Turn north on Derrick and drive 1.3 miles to the lagoon which is on the east side of the road. There is a parking area on the bluff overlooking the lagoon at its northwest corner.

Trail description and vegetation

Dirt roads on the bluff allow both walking and driving; best viewing is from the north and west sides. You can also drive around the lagoon on the south and east sides at the water level, but 4-wheel drive may be necessary when traversing from the bluff to the lower level

31

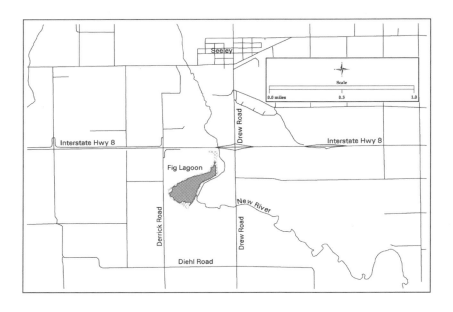

because the road sometimes turns into deep fine dust.

The vegetation at the water's edge consists of cattails and reeds which host a variety of herons, bitterns and rails. The surrounding area has palo verde, honey mesquite, tamarisk and quail bush which attract song birds. There are also agricultural fields in the immediate area which draw a large variety of birds.

Birds

Counts were done January through October 1998; January, May, July, September, and November 1999; and January 2000. Eighty-six species were seen on these 15 counts (see table on page 228). There were 19 to 37 species per count with March the month of highest diversity.

Water-associated birds seen in all seasons included Pied-billed Grebe, Western Grebe, Double-crested Cormorant, Great Blue Heron, Great Egret, Snowy Egret, Cattle Egret, Green Heron, Black-crowned Night-heron, Cinnamon Teal, Ruddy Duck, American Coot, Black-necked Stilt and Marsh Wren.

The vegetation around the lagoon hosted a number of upland birds.

Frequently seen were Mourning Dove, Greater Roadrunner, Black Phoebe, Verdin, Yellow-rumped Warbler, Abert's Towhee, and Red-winged Blackbird.

Spring migrants included Western Wood-Pewee, Willow Flycatcher, Western Kingbird, Orange-crowned Warbler, Yellow Warbler, and Wilson's Warbler.

Several species of birds of prey were seen during the counts. Northern Harrier and American Kestrel were present in all seasons; others seen occasionally were Osprey, Cooper's Hawk, Red-tailed Hawk, and Merlin.

Gulls and terns were attracted to the lagoon and nearby fields. The most common gull was Ring-billed Gull. Forster's Tern foraged in the lagoon in all seasons.

A few of the birds seen on the counts were uncommon or rare to the sea: Common Loon, Surf Scoter, Heermann's Gull and Mountain Bluebird. Although no accidentals were seen during the counts there have been a few such sightings during the past few years: Red-throated Loon, Yellow-crowned Night-heron, Roseate Spoonbill, Magnificent Frigatebird, Neotropic Cormorant, Rose-breasted Grosbeak, and Long-tailed Duck.

Fig Lagoon was a year-round night roost for several species; Great and Snowy Egret, Cattle Egret and White-faced Ibis used it regularly (see the chapter on "Nocturnal Roosting").

FINNEY LAKE

Fieldwork: Barbara Massey,
Richard Zembal, Bob Miller, Paul Jorgensen
Text and Table of Occurrence: Barbara Massey

Finney and Ramer Lakes were formed by diverting water from the Alamo River to create ponds for hunting. Owned by two baseball players, Ed Finney and Fred Ramer, they were sold to the state in the early 1930s and are now part of the State Imperial Wildlife Area administered by the CDFG (headquartered at the Wister Unit). Finney Lake consists of two large ponds separated by a dike. The water is "fresh," meaning not salty, but is of poor quality.

It was created primarily for hunting and fishing but has become good habitat for water-associated birds.

Driving Directions

Finney Lake is southeast of the Salton Sea between the towns of Calipatria and Brawley. To reach the lake from the north take Highway 111 to Albright Road, turn left and go 0.4 mile, then right onto Kershaw Road for approximately 2 miles. A sign will indicate a left on Titsworth Road, then the next right leads by dirt road into the Finney Lake parking and camping area. From the south take Highway 111 out of Brawley and turn right on Rutherford Road (about 4 miles). Take the next left onto Kershaw (just past the railroad crossing) and drive north to Titsworth (see above).

There is a southern entrance off Rutherford shortly

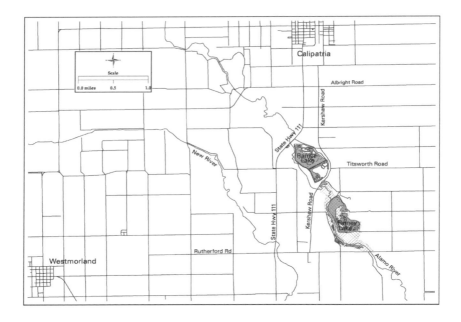

east of Kershaw. A dirt road winds through the whole complex of ponds and arrives ultimately at the north entrance.

Trail description and vegetation

The bird counts began at the north end; the first stop was on Kershaw Road at the bridge over the Alamo River under which a Cliff Swallow colony bred in spring. Just north of the bridge a pond with many drowned snags hosted ducks, wading birds and shore birds. Instead of going north to Titsworth you can take a right onto the first dirt road (unmarked) north of the pond, which leads to the lake and is lined with quail bush, tamarisk, arrowweed, and eucalyptus that provide habitat for upland birds. Just before the campground an abandoned orchard and several large eucalyptus trees around unused CDFG buildings attract migratory passerines along with an occasional out-of-range bird.

Finney Lake is south (right) of the CDFG buildings, and the count continued around the large northernmost pond. The usual coverage was by foot, although in the summer months it was more comfortable to drive. The walk was approximately 2 miles long and took about 2 hours.

The lake shore and the dikes between the ponds are heavily vegetated with tamarisk. The dikes are usually traversable by car except when infrequent storms turn them into slick mud. Dense stands of cattails form islands in the ponds and provide cover and nesting habitat for many water birds. Arrowweed, quail bush and tamarisk dominate the uplands.

Birds

Counts were done every month in 1998; in January, May, June, July, September, and November 1999; and in January 2000. During these 19 counts 133 species were seen (see table on page 233). The number of species per count ranged from 36 to 70 with May the month of the highest species diversity.

Water-associated birds seen year-round included Pied-billed Grebe, Western and Clark's Grebe, Double-crested Cormorant, Great Blue Heron, Great and Snowy Egret, Green Heron, Black-crowned Night-Heron, White-faced Ibis, Mallard, Cinnamon Teal, Ruddy Duck, Common Moorhen, American Coot, Killdeer, Black-necked Stilt, Marsh Wren and Common Yellowthroat.

Many of these species nested at Finney Lake and among those documented were Pied-billed Grebe, Western Grebe, Clark's Grebe, Green Heron, Cinnamon Teal, Ruddy Duck, Common Moorhen, American Coot, Killdeer, Marsh Wren, and Common Yellowthroat. The sighting of a Western Grebe with a chick in November was evidence of unusually late nesting. In the freshwater marsh vegetation Marsh Wrens nested in abundance; in June 1998 there were 69 males singing territorially in the lake reeds. Red-winged Blackbirds also nested densely in cattails and reeds in the smaller, brackish ponds. Yuma Clapper Rail and Sora were present during the breeding season and presumed to be nesting.

Fulvous Whistling-Duck bred in the dense cattail marshes; a brood of ten chicks was seen with their parents in July 1999.

Vegetation around the lake edges provided habitat for resident upland birds. Frequently seen species included Mourning Dove, Black Phoebe, Verdin, Cactus Wren, Black-tailed Gnatcatcher, Common Yellowthroat, Abert's Towhee, Song Sparrow, Red-winged Blackbird, and Great-tailed Grackle, all of which were either documented as nesting or in residence during the breeding season and presumed to be nesting. Yellow-rumped Warbler and White-crowned Sparrow were common winter visitors. Crissal Thrasher, an uncommon bird at the Salton Sea, was seen at only 4 sites; breeding at Finney Lake was documented when a pair was observed feeding a juvenile in July 1998.

Upland birds that came to breed in summer included White-winged Dove, Lesser Nighthawk, Western Kingbird, Cliff Swallow, Yellow-breasted Chat and Bullock's Oriole. A colony of Cliff Swallows nested under the bridge over the New River on Kershaw Road in May 1998.

Migratory song birds were uncommon, and seen more in spring than in fall, as was also true in the nearby Anza-Borrego Desert (Massey 1998). Waves of migrants were rare, but were very exciting when seen. Bob Miller observed a mixed flock one day in May 1999. It was composed of flycatchers (Western Wood-Pewee, Willow Flycatcher, Pacific-slope Flycatcher, and Ash-throated Flycatcher), Warbling Vireos, warblers (Orange-crowned, Yellow, Black-throated Gray, Townsend's, Hermit, and Wilson's Warblers, and Yellow-breasted Chat), a Western Tanager and a Lazuli Bunting. There were more than 100 birds in the flock.

Formerly, Finney Lake was a popular nesting site and nocturnal roost for White-faced Ibis and Cattle Egret. But during 1998 they were usually seen flying over Finney to roost at Ramer Lake. On two occasions in the fall of 1998, however, large numbers of ibis did roost at Finney— 3400 in September and 450 in October (see "Nocturnal Roosting").

Unusual sightings

A juvenile Magnificent Frigatebird circled overhead in August 1998. An Inca Dove was seen once in September 1998. Bank Swallow was a rare species on the counts; 10 were seen on an April visit. A California Thrasher was observed for 15 minutes vocalizing from the top of a tamarisk at the north end in May 1998. This species was out of range at the Salton Sea, but the bird's appearance and vocalizations made identification quite secure (see "Species Accounts"). A Lucy's Warbler was observed in July 1998. Although this species was within its range, its preferred habitat (mesquite, cottonwood) is in short supply around the Salton Sea. It was not seen elsewhere during the counts. A Black-throated Magpie Jay was perched in a eucalyptus one May morning in 1998; presumably an escaped bird, it was also seen once at Fig Lagoon (see "Species Accounts - Nonnative Species").

JOHNSON STREET

Fieldwork: Richard Zembal, Barbara Massey
Text and Table of Occurrence: Barbara Massey,
Richard Zembal

Johnson Street is recommended, along with Whitewater, for a good view of the northwest shore of the Salton Sea. Its sandy beach, drowned snag forest just offshore, and man-made ponds inshore all provide habitat for a multiplicity of water-associated birds.

Driving Directions

Driving south on Highway 111, the turnoff is just a few miles south of the town of Mecca. On approach, a sign indicates the turnoff, which is a dirt road on the right (south). Take the dirt road approximately 2 miles to the shore, where it is obvious that you cannot drive any farther.

Trail description and vegetation

An unvegetated drainage ditch runs along the dirt road on the west side and empties into the sea. Desert pupfish can be seen in the clear shallows, and big tilapia defend nests close to the sea. Desert scrub and tamarisk provide what sparse vegetation there is along the road. A few mesquite tussocks farther west provide habitat for passerines. Near the end of the road the ditch becomes a dense cattail marsh. Just short of the sea there are sever-

al large ponds on the east side that belong to a duck club and attract waterfowl in winter. They are diked and the dikes can be walked. (A warning about the salt-encrusted mud that must be traversed to reach the ponds—it can be treacherous.) The shore on the east side of the road curves into a bay and its shallow waters and numerous snags provide good waterbird habitat. This 'snaggery' is one of the major waterbird nesting areas.

Offshore there is a flat-topped, man-made structure that once had some other use, but is now partially submerged and provides nesting habitat for Gull-billed Tern and Black Skimmer.

Birds

Counts were done monthly in 1998; in January, March, April, May, July, and November of 1999; and in January 2000. On these 19 counts we saw 117 species (see table on page 240). The number of species per count ranged from 36 to 58; April, July, August and September were the months of greatest species diversity. A varied waterfront (snags, sand bars, mud flats, shallow waters) supported a large variety of water birds.

Present on all counts were Eared Grebe, Double-crested Cormorant, Great Blue Heron, Snowy Egret, Ruddy Duck, American Coot, Killdeer, Black-necked Stilt, Ring-billed Gull, Marsh Wren and Great-tailed Grackle. Eared Grebe flocks rafted on the open water; Double-crested Cormorant, Great Blue Heron, Great and Snowy Egret perched in the branches of drowned trees; shorebirds foraged on the sandbars; and ducks used the shallow waters for feeding and resting.

This site was particularly good for waterfowl. Twenty species were seen during the count period, including several of infrequent occurrence like Blue-winged Teal, Canvasback and Surf Scoter. There were many close inshore, feeding in the shallows and easily viewed, especially with a spotting scope.

The ponds adjacent to the shore provided quiet water for many water-associated birds. Herons and egrets, ducks, shore birds, gulls, terns and swallows used them regularly. Marsh Wrens and Yellow-headed Blackbirds nested in the cattails. Redheads were common in winter. A few Snowy Plovers nested on the salt flats in the dry pond at the sea edge on the west side.

Offshore, the snags provided nesting habitat for Double-crested Cormorant, Great Blue Heron, Great Egret, Snowy Egret and Black-crowned Night-Heron. Nest building began in April and by July there were many juveniles in evidence. In 1998 approximately 50 Cattle Egrets nested in addition to the above list but did not return in 1999. The artificial island provided nesting habitat for Gull-billed Terns and Black Skimmers, one of two breeding sites for these birds at the sea. Both these species are seasonal at the sea, arriving to breed in April and gone by September.

Unusual sightings

A Prairie Falcon was seen in November 1998, one of 4 sightings on the counts. Two Fulvous Whistling-Ducks flew over in September. One or two Least Bitterns frequented the ponds in summer, and were more readily seen in the cattails here than at most other sites where they occurred. Johnson Street was also one of the better sites for seasonal viewing of the flocks of Black Terns that visited the sea in summer.

OBSIDIAN BUTTE

Fieldwork: John Fitch, Clarann Levakis
Table of Occurrence: Barbara Massey
Text: John Fitch

Coverage at this site included the ponds east of Obsidian Butte, the butte and its shoreline, and the area southwest to the intersection of Young and Kornbloom Roads. Obsidian Butte is a small, rocky hill of volcanic glass. It is being quarried and is slowly disappearing. Along the route are one large and two small ponds and a drainage canal with cattails and tamarisk. The road curves around the north side of the butte along the shoreline; on the south side, in addition to the drainage canal, there are agricultural fields and a thermal generating plant.

Driving directions

Obsidian Butte is just west of NWRHq. From Highway 86 at the town of Westmorland, take Forrester Road north, jog right at Walker to Gentry and continue north to McKendry, approximately 9.5 miles in all, 0.5 mile short of Sinclair). Turn west on McKendry, which is a dirt road, and follow it about 1 mile; it crosses an irrigation ditch beyond which are ponds on both sides. The route then follows an unnamed dirt road around the butte, across a dike, and along the shoreline to Lack Road. It then turns right at Lindsey Road and follows the shoreline to Young and Kornbloom.

Trail description and vegetation

The bird counts started at the north east end of the route at Obsidian Butte. The dominant vegetation here is a mix of iodine bush and quail bush.

The shoreline along the sea is made up of sandy beach and a rock sea wall used by fishermen.

The large pond south of the butte is shallow and composed of a mud and salt substrate. A fence crosses it on an east-west line, and provides perches for gulls and terns. There is scattered scrub vegetation along the north and west shore.

The road crosses a dike between the pond and the sea, then turns west. On the sea side of this turn is a sandy beach with several large dead trees. Driving west, a drainage canal is on the left. It is choked with cattails and lined with tamarisk along its periphery.

The road turns south, passing the thermal plant. A large dead tree on the right provide a much-used roost for raptors and cormorants. The first of the small ponds is at the corner of Lindsey and Lack. A sandy beach with large saltbush separates it and the second pond from the sea. They both contain numerous dead trees.

The agricultural fields grew alfalfa primarily, but were bare much of the time. The drainage canal between the road and the fields holds cattails, saltbush and tamarisk, and was flooded most of the year. The farmer has removed most of the vegetation along these channels.

The route is about 5 miles long, and took about three hours to bird. Birding was mostly drive and stop. We walked along the two small ponds and the area around Obsidian Butte.

It should be noted that along the west facing shoreline it was best to stay in a vehicle during windy weather, as waves could wash over the road. The resulting foul smelling, glazed donut effect was not comfortable. But it was also a sharp evocation of the polarized, ugly and beautiful nature of the Salton Sea.

Birds

Counts were done February through December 1998; February, May, July, September and November in 1999; and in January 2000. During the 17 counts, 112 species were seen (see table on page 246). The number of species per count ranged from 35 to 62 with March the month of the highest species diversity.

The main features on this route were the shoreline and the sea. The common birds using the open water were Eared Grebe, Double-crested Cormorant, Brown and White Pelican, California and Ring-billed Gull, and Caspian Tern. During the winter, several species of ducks were present, including Ruddy Duck, Mallard and Northern Pintail. The shore was a good place to practice identifying immature gulls, always a challenge to bird enthusiasts. One could observe a wide range of plumages at close range.

The large pond along the shoreline was frequented year-round by Black-necked Stilt, American Avocet, Forster's Tern, Pied-billed Grebe, California and Ring-billed Gull, American Coot and Great Blue Heron. In winter, shorebirds seen regularly were Killdeer, Greater Yellowlegs, Lesser Yellowlegs, Wilson's Phalarope, Willet, Western Sandpiper, and

Least Sandpiper. Yellow-footed and Herring Gulls were present in small numbers most months. The road around Obsidian Butte was closed during the breeding season, when Brown Pelicans attempted to nest along an offshore rocky spit. Also seen on this spit were Heermann's Gull and Brant. Black Tern, Laughing Gull and Bonaparte's Gull visited the large pond in season.

The large dead tree by the thermal plant was a roosting site for Peregrine Falcon and Osprey.

The rock and scrub habitat around Obsidian Butte was the best place around the sea to find the large-billed race of the Savannah Sparrow during the winter. A few Lesser Nighthawks nested in spring and summer; Mourning Doves were present all year but in much larger numbers in spring and summer. Black-necked Stilts also nested. Their flop-on-the-ground-and-scream displays were quite comical and very distracting. Gull-billed Terns paid no heed, however, and took many stilt chicks.

The two small ponds, the drainage canal and their associated vegetation held many species of water-associated birds, including Black-crowned Night-Heron, Green Heron, Great and Snowy Egret, and many species of ducks. Yellow-rumped Warbler, Song Sparrow, Red-winged Blackbird, and Great-tailed Grackle were common upland species. Pied-billed Grebe, Cinnamon Teal, Common Moorhen, American Coot, Song Sparrow, Abert's Towhee and Black Phoebe nested around the ponds; while Common Yellowthroat and Yellow-headed and Red-winged Blackbird nested in the reeds of the canal.

Birds commonly using the agricultural fields were Great Blue Heron, Great Egret, Snowy Egret, Cattle Egret, White faced Ibis, Red-winged Blackbird and Mourning Dove. A pair of Ring-necked Pheasants was seen on one occasion. Western Kingbird and Black Phoebe nested on poles and other structures on the edges of the fields. The thermal plant was notable (in a sense) as the only place on the route to see House Sparrow and European Starling.

Migratory species were few except for swallows; 4 species (Barn, Cliff, Rough-winged and Tree) came through in good numbers every year.

Nesting was confirmed for Pied-billed Grebe, Brown Pelican, Cinnamon Teal, Common Moorhen, American Coot, Killdeer, Black-necked Stilt, California Gull, Lesser Nighthawk, Black Phoebe, Western Kingbird, Verdin, European Starling, Song Sparrow, Red-winged

Blackbird, Yellow-headed Blackbird, and Great-tailed Grackle. Probable nesters included Green Heron, Morning Dove, Common Yellowthroat, Abert's Towhee and House Sparrow.

Although several nesting attempts were made by the endangered Brown Pelican in 1998, none were successful; they did not breed successfully during the count period.

Unusual sightings

Horned Grebes were seen here 2 times and only once elsewhere during the counts. A Sabine's Gull was present in November 1998, the only one seen on the counts. Bushtit and Chipping Sparrow were seen once; Ruddy Turnstone, Virginia's Warbler and American Goldfinch were seen at only one other site. Other unusual species seen here (during the count period but not on the counts) were Neotropic Cormorant, Magnificent Frigatebird, Solitary Sandpiper, Ruff and Glaucous Gull (see "Rare Species seen during the Count Period").

RAMER LAKE

Fieldwork: Barbara Massey, Richard Zembal,
Bob Miller, Paul Jorgensen
Text and Table of Occurrence: Barbara Massey

Ramer and Finney Lakes were formed by diverting water from the Alamo River to create ponds for hunting. Owned by two baseball players, Ed Finney and Fred Ramer, they were sold to the state in the early 1930s and are now part of the State Imperial Wildlife Area administered by the CDFG (headquartered at the Wister Unit). Ramer Lake consists of two large ponds separated by a dike. There are drivable dirt roads on the dike and around the shoreline. The water is "fresh," meaning not salty, but is of poor quality. It was created primarily for hunting and fishing but has become good habitat for many water-associated birds.

Driving Directions

The lake is between the towns of Calipatria and Brawley. It is bounded on north and south by Albright and Rutherford Roads; east and west by Kershaw Road and Highway 111. It can be reached by a dirt road off Kershaw approximately 1.3 miles south of Calipatria or by a potholed paved road off Highway 111 also about 1.3 miles south of Calipatria. Both entrances have signs.

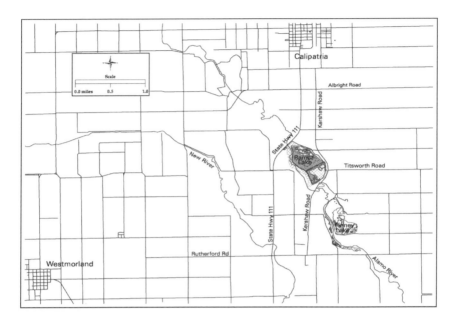

Trail description and vegetation

The bird counts encompassed both ponds and consisted of walking (or driving) around the ponds and across the central dike to count all the water birds, and checking the trees and shrubs surrounding the ponds for upland birds. The walk was approximately 2 miles long and took 2 to 3 hours.

Around the lake arrowweed, tamarisk, quail bush and iodine bush are the major upland plants. Common and giant reed grow in the ditches. Plantings around the unused CDFG buildings in the southeast corner include palms and a few native species (cottonwood, palo verde, mesquite).

Birds

Counts were done every month in 1998; in January, May, June, July, September, and November 1999; and in January 2000. During these 19 counts,128 species were seen (see table on page 252). The number of species per count ranged from 43 to 74 with May the month of the highest species diversity.

Resident water-associated birds present on most or all counts included Pied-billed Grebe, Western Grebe, Clark's Grebe, Double-crested Cormorant, Great Blue Heron, Great Egret, Snowy Egret, Green Heron, Black-crowned Night-Heron, White-faced Ibis, Mallard, Cinnamon Teal, Ruddy Duck, Common Moorhen, American Coot, and Marsh Wren. This site was very good for close-range differentiation of Western and Clark's Grebe, often seen in the same field of a spotting scope. Courtship between these two closely related species was also observed here (see "Species Accounts"). The Marsh Wren, more easily heard than seen, was often close at hand darting through the vegetation at the ponds' edges. Common Moorhen, another hard-to-see species, was frequently visible in the southeast corner of the south pond.

Resident upland birds seen frequently included Mourning Dove, Black Phoebe, Verdin, Common Yellowthroat, Abert's Towhee, Song Sparrow, and Great-tailed Grackle. Yellow-rumped Warbler and White-crowned Sparrow were common in winter.

Nesting waterbirds included Pied-billed Grebe, Western and Clark's Grebe, Double-crested Cormorant, Great Egret, Cattle Egret, Common Moorhen, American Coot, Killdeer, Black-necked Stilt, Marsh Wren, Common Yellowthroat, Red-winged Blackbird, and Yellow-headed Blackbird. Species of waterbirds that came for the summer, and presumably nested, were Least Bittern and Fulvous Whistling-Duck. Yuma Clapper Rail was heard only once but its secretive nature could have masked a larger presence.

Upland birds that came to breed included White-winged Dove, Lesser Nighthawk, Western Kingbird, Cliff Swallow, Yellow-breasted Chat and Bullock's Oriole. Crissal Thrasher probably nested, although not observed during the breeding season.

Migratory passerines were uncommon, and seen more often in spring than in fall.

One of the most interesting features of Ramer Lake was its use as a night roost. Monthly counts throughout 1998 tallied thousands of birds each time (see "Nocturnal Roosts"). Most were concentrated in the dead tree snags in the south pond, but occasionally the reeds in the north pond were also used. Cattle Egret and White-faced Ibis were the dominant species, followed by Double-crested Cormorant. There were usually small numbers of Great Egret, Snowy Egret and Black-crowned Night

Heron as well. Periodically, flocks of Ring-billed Gulls would roost in the north pond.

In spring, while continuing to serve as a roosting site, the snags of the south pond became a major nesting site for Cattle Egret and several other species. In late June 1998 the following nests could be seen from the central dike: 5 Double-crested Cormorant, 2 with chicks; 20 Great Egret, several with chicks; and 3,500 Cattle Egret, many with chicks. A few Snowy Egrets and White-faced Ibis also nested. In 1999 nesting was initiated, but the site was abandoned for unknown reasons. A huge nesting colony was subsequently found at Westmorland Eucalyptus Grove (see "Additional Sites"); presumably the relocation site for this colony.

The number of Cattle Egrets, White-faced Ibis and Double-crested Cormorants on the counts varied hugely, depending on whether the count was started at daylight when the birds were still roosting, or later in the morning. Roosting birds took off in waves early in the morning to feed throughout the valley, and a few hours after daylight they were almost all gone except when tending nests. Thus the range given in the table on page 252 for White-faced Ibis is 3 to 8,270. During the nesting season Cattle Egrets were present in large numbers throughout the day tending their young, but in other months there might be few or none.

Unusual sightings

A flock of Greater White-fronted Geese seen in January 2000, the only occurrence of this species on the counts. Inca Dove was seen once in May 1999. Ramer Lake was one of two sites where Fulvous Whistling-Ducks could be seen on the ground. They favored the south edge of the south pond. Another singular species was the Vermilion Flycatcher, seen in October 1998 and twice more that winter. A pair was again seen the following winter, indicating that it may be a recurrent winter visitor. Bank Swallow was rarely seen on the counts; a flock of 20 was observed here in September. A MacGillivray's Warbler was seen in May, the only one on the counts.

Red Hill County Park

Fieldwork: Barbara Massey, Carol Roberts
with assistance from Paul Jorgensen, Richard Zembal
Text and Table of Occurrence: Barbara Massey

Red Hill is a landmark along the southeast shore of the Salton Sea—a rocky outcrop that is indeed red, composed of
obsidian, pumice and other volcanic rocks.
It was being quarried during the count period.
The county park and marina are on the outcrop,
connected to the mainland by a
causeway.

Driving Directions

From the west side, take Highway 86 to
the town of Westmorland. Turn north on Forrester
Road, jog right at Walker to Gentry and continue north
to the end (approximately 7 miles) where it dead-ends at
Sinclair Road. Turn right on Sinclair and then take the
first left which is Garst Road (about 1 mile) and has a
sign for the county park. The roads beyond this point are
dirt, but easily traversed in a standard car, except after
the rare rainstorm.

If coming from the east side of the sea, turn off
Highway 111 onto Sinclair and head west approximately 4.5 miles to Garst.

Trail description and vegetation

The count area included Red Hill Marina County
Park and the ponds of the Hazard Unit (NWR) that are

adjacent to Garst Road. The site is bounded on the north side by the Alamo River Delta and by NWRHq on the south. The counts started about 0.5 mile along Garst where the shore of the sea appears on the west and the ponds of the Hazard Unit on the east. The road turns sharply west after approximately 1 mile and becomes a causeway that continues on to the county park and marina. At the point where the road reaches the county park a right fork leads to the park office from which one can see the shallows and sand bars that lie west of the Alamo River Delta, with their thousands of birds. An alternate road leads up over the red rocks to the campground and marina. A short hike up the rocky mound east of the campground allows a closer view of the sandbars. The road circles Red Hill and returns to the junction.

Observation was mostly from a car (in order to prevent the birds from flushing) with regular stops to use a spotting scope. The ponds along the right side of Garst are flooded only in the winter months; on the left side the open shallow waters and salt flats of the sea remain unchanged throughout the year.

The vegetation is unexceptional. The causeway is lined with tamarisk and iodine bush. A few ornamental trees and shrubs around the office and adjacent trailer park seem to attract mostly Great-tailed Grackles.

Birds

Counts were done February through December 1998; in January, March, July, September, and November 1999; and in January 2000; a total of 17. Ninety-two species were seen on these 17 counts (see table on page 259). The number of species per count ranged from 28 to 52 with October the month of highest diversity.

Waterbirds dominated the site. The flooded ponds were frequented by large numbers of herons, egrets, ducks, coots, and shore birds. Even in summer some of the ponds retained water, and post-breeding flocks of Gull-billed Terns, Black Terns and (occasionally) Black Skimmers were to be found there, roosting and foraging. The dikes that separated the ponds were a favorite day roost for ducks and gulls. Shore birds, gulls and pelicans were regularly seen on the salt flats at the edge of the sea. Rafts of Eared Grebes and Ruddy Ducks floated on the open water, and Double-Crested Cormorants perched in the drowned snags, creating elegant photo opportunities when the light was right. From the far end of Red Hill hundreds of roosting and preening White Pelican, Double-Crested Cormorant, and Ring-billed Gull could be seen on the sandbars.

Birds of prey were more common than anticipated. An American Kestrel was seen several times on the rocks of Red Hill; twice a Northern Harrier was seen coursing over the ponds; Osprey, Merlin, Peregrine Falcon and Prairie Falcon were each seen once in winter.

Land birds were in short supply, reflecting the paucity of upland habitat. Black Phoebe, Song Sparrow and Great-tailed Grackle were resident in small numbers; Yellow-rumped Warbler was a winter visitor; a few migrating swallows came through in season. A pair of Western Kingbirds nested in a power pole along the road in 1998.

Unusual sightings

Four Lesser Flamingos were seen in January among a flock of several hundred White Pelicans far out on a sandspit. With a spotting scope, one could easily pick out the brilliant pink birds among their white neighbors. Two species of flamingo have been resident at the Salton Sea for many years and were seen at both ends of the sea during the count period (see "Species Accounts - Nonnative species"). Mountain Plover was a rare species on the counts, although a regular forager in the agricultural fields of Imperial Valley. One was seen at Red Hill in March. The only Western Bluebird seen on the counts was here in March.

SALTON SEA STATE RECREATION AREA

Fieldwork and Text: Paul Jorgensen
Table of Occurrence: Barbara Massey

The shoreline along the northeast section of the Salton Sea is relatively barren as habitat for birds. What vegetation exists is mainly nonnative salt cedar growing to the water's edge. Fresh water is scarce. A few drowned trees off-shore provide roost sites for cormorants and nesting for herons; there are two small harbors and one creek mouth with a few acres of marsh. Absent are the many varied and bird-rich habitats found extensively in other sections of the sea, such as lakes, ponds, irrigation canals, large reed marshes, rivers, extensive drowned trees, mud flats and cultivated fields. Adjacent uplands are mostly disturbed areas comprised of a trailer park, state park facilities, large bare-ground parking and camping sites, and sparse saline desert scrub. Sea level has played a big role in bird habitats. Along the park-owned shoreline, rising waters and crumbling shoreline resulted in the need to grade new camping areas inland, with a net loss of sandy beach habitat.

Three birding spots along seven miles of the northeast

shore were covered: the privately-owned North Shore Marina with its abandoned hotel and yacht club; park headquarters and Varner Harbor, in the SSSRA, with its visitor center and active marina; and Salt Creek, a shoreline campground further south but within the SSSRA.

Driving Directions

All three spots are just west of Highway 111 and can be reached by driving south from the town of Mecca or north from Niland. The following directions are from north to south. North Shore Marina is about nine miles southeast of Mecca. Turn west (right) on Marina Drive and head towards the sea. Proceed to the two-story abandoned hotel overlooking the marina. To reach park headquarters and Varner Harbor, drive about 1.5 miles farther south on Highway 111 to the SSSRA. Turn west (right) at the well-signed park entry road and proceed left after the kiosk, heading south towards the headquarters building. The small harbor is immediately south of the headquarters building. Salt Creek is 6 miles south of headquarters along Highway 111; turn west (right) at the park sign onto the dirt road to Salt Creek Campground (undeveloped). Drive about 0.3 mile to the shore and walk north along the shoreline to the mouth of Salt Creek.

Site Description and Vegetation

North Shore Marina

The hotel/marina was a hot spot for tourism in the 1960s, including show business celebrities. By the early 1980s the yacht club was abandoned and the hotel declined soon after. Habitat consists of the sea itself, some man-made rock jetties, a sparsely vegetated shoreline and cultivated trees and shrubs around inhabited areas. There is no accessible fresh water source. Fortunately, birds don't know the marina is closed and a good number of waterbirds congregate in its shelter to roost and feed. During all-too-frequent fish die-offs, a northerly wind brings millions of dead talapia into the small harbor. Although unpleasant to humans this event is a big attraction to scavenging birds. A good place to view the many pelicans, grebes, herons, gulls and waterfowl is from a drive-up location just south of the hotel. Another vantage point is approximately 100 yards south at the foot of Desert Beach Drive. Looking to the far north along the salt cedar-lined shore with a scope, you can often see up to 6 species of egrets and herons roosting above the shore. Make sure to check both jetties for less-obvious smaller shore birds.

Park Headquarters and Varner Harbor

Habitats include the open beach; the calm, shallow waters of the harbor bordered with only a small stand of cattail or bulrush; a heavily brackish marsh of mixed salt cedar and a few reeds; dense lines of salt cedar at the sea's edge; and uplands of burrobush, saltbush, and boxthorn. Fresh water is absent. The beach is a mixture of sand and pulverized nonnative barnacles. The same conditions that bring dead fish into North Shore Marina also occur at Varner Harbor, providing a bonanza for gulls and other scavengers. You can park at the nearby campground and view birds from the patio area at the headquarters and visitor center, but the best vantage point is from the fishing jetty along the south side of Varner Harbor. As you drive out to the jetty, note the small marsh and dense backdrop of salt cedar just south of the road where rails, herons, marsh wrens, and grackles are among the birds found roosting or nesting. Be sure to look closely at birds loafing on the barrier beach which forms the harbor. This is where gulls and terns are most easily viewed. On your way out, consider stopping at the entry kiosk to check the area for land birds, especially during migration.

Salt Creek

The key feature of this site is the habitat created by Salt Creek, which is fed by springs to the east. The creek provides perennial standing water, usually as far east as the Highway 111 bridge, but is an intermittent stream at best. Vegetation is limited to salt cedar and salt-adapted small shrubs, such as burrobush and saltbush. Where the creek meets the sea there is an open backwater of a few acres or less, which is presumably salty or heavily brackish. A few reeds persist around the edges, backed by more dense salt cedar. A sand and shell berm usually forms a shoal, blocking surface creek flows from entering the sea unless there is heavy rain runoff. In winter, the ponded water at the creek mouth often has good numbers of ducks and gulls. Drive or walk south along the length of the shore of the undeveloped campground. This is a good area to scope for large flocks of grebes, pelicans, waterfowl and gulls. This beach is the only place where Snowy Plovers were seen. (Note: In an effort to restore native habitat, the State Department of Parks and Recreation is systematically removing salt cedar from the creek sides, from the shore east to beyond the Highway 111 bridge).

Birds

Counts were done every month in 1998; in January, March, May, July, September, and November 1999; and in January 2000. During these 19 counts, 116 species were seen (see table on page 264). The number of species per count ranged from 20 to 44 with May the month of highest diversity.

Most numerous and frequently encountered species were Eared

Grebe, American White Pelican, Double-crested Cormorant, Northern Shoveler, Ruddy Duck, Western Sandpiper, American Coot, Black-necked Stilt, Bonaparte's Gull, Ring-billed Gull, California Gull, Herring Gull, Caspian Tern, Rock Dove, European Starling, Brewer's Blackbird and Great-tailed Grackle. Eared Grebe was by far the most numerous with 26,680 on the count in Jan 2000. Next most numerous, also in January, were Ring-billed and California Gull with one day count highs of 1,760 and 1,570 respectively. birds unusual to the site were Clark's Grebe, Surf Scoter, Common Goldeneye, Yuma Clapper Rail, Snowy Plover, Thayer's Gull, Yellow-footed Gull, Glaucous-winged Gull, and Laughing Gull.

Relatively few geese, shorebirds or marsh birds were recorded, presumably because of lack of suitable habitat. Land birds were also poorly represented owing to poor habitat and the minimal amount of time spent searching uplands.

The amount of nesting habitat in the area was very limited for most water birds, and only a few of the potential nesting species were documented as breeders. Lack of native vegetation resulted in most species nesting in salt cedar; lack of open ground safe from predators, such as would be provided by islands, resulted in absence of ground-nesters. Those species observed breeding in the survey area included Great Blue Heron, Black-crowned Night Heron, Common Moorhen, American Coot, Killdeer, Black-necked Stilt, Rock Dove, Mourning Dove, Say's Phoebe, Verdin, Northern Mockingbird, European Starling, and Great-tailed Grackle. Probable breeders included Pied-Billed Grebe and Green Heron.

Unusual sightings

Birds seen here and not elsewhere on the counts were Lesser Black-backed Gull (January 2000) a flock of Cedar Waxwings (January 1998) and a female Summer Tanager (August 1999). The Lesser Black-backed Gull was the only out-of-range bird at SSSRA. Franklin's Gull was seen twice at SSSRA and only once elsewhere on the counts.

An observation worthy of further investigation was of Willow Flycatcher. Normally, the migrant subspecies, *Empidonax traillii brewsteri*, has moved north through this area by mid June. On 25 June 1998, two calling individuals were seen and heard, one in salt cedar just south of Varner Harbor and another 15 minutes later in salt cedar six miles away at Salt Creek. This is an exceptionally late date and, based on current information, equals or exceeds the latest date for this closely watched migrant in the southwest. The possibility exists that these birds were the resident subspecies *E. t. extimus*, known to nest in salt cedar elsewhere. The dense vegetation made it difficult to follow either bird closely, but an hour or more was spent observing the one at Salt Creek. No evidence of breeding, such as a mate, nest, nest building or young was discerned.

If you have time for only one stop during while birding the sea's northeast shore, Park Headquarters and Varner Harbor are recommended as the most productive for all categories of birds.

Sonny Bono National Wildlife Refuge Headquarters —Rock Hill

Fieldwork: Barbara Massey, Pete Sorenson,
Richard Zembal
Table of Occurrence: Barbara Massey
Text: Barbara Massey, Pete Sorenson

There are several units in the NWR; the headquarters at Rock Hill, Unit 1, and the Hazard Unit. The headquarters unit (NWRHq) is the subject of this chapter. It lies on the southeast shore of the sea, bounded on the north by Red Hill and on the south by Obsidian Butte. It was established in 1930 and originally encompassed more than 37,000 acres, most of which are now under water. The steadily rising level of the sea has reduced the land mass to less than 2,000 acres.

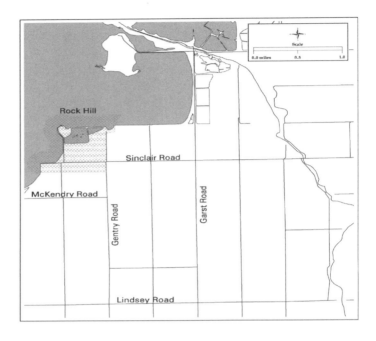

Several different habitats provide diversity at NWRHq. Around the parking lot at the entrance there is a very nice, if small, area that has been planted with native species such as mesquite, palo verde, box thorn and cottonwood. It provides habitat for resident birds and attracts passerine migrants in season. Agricultural fields on both sides of the buildings are planted with crops that attract geese. There is a series of diked ponds northwest of the buildings; one of them has several islands that were created to provide nesting sites for gulls, terns and skimmers. Several ponds have dense cattails growing in shallow water. Rock Hill, a mound that rises about 100 feet above the sea, is a landmark along the south shore like Red Hill and Obsidian Butte.

If one is limited for time and can visit only 1 or 2 sites at the sea, the refuge is strongly recommended as a starting place. Because it has more habitat diversity than many other sites there is greater species diversity. Informative brochures are available at a small visitors' center. A shaded picnic site at the parking area is a good lunch stop.

Driving Directions

From the town of Westmorland take Forrester Road north, jog right at Walker to Gentry and continue north to the end, where Gentry joins Sinclair Road. Turn left into the refuge. Total distance approximately 10 miles. From the east side, turn off Highway 111 at Sinclair and drive west about 5.5 miles to the refuge entrance.

Trail description and vegetation

Native vegetation planted around the parking lot is worth examining for resident passerines all year round, and for migrants in season. Beyond the picnic area a trail out to Rock Hill is bordered by a row of screwbean mesquite that separates it from a field sown with a grain crop. This hedgerow provides good habitat for several resident birds. Where the trail meets the causeway out to Rock Hill, cattail marshes on the west side provide habitat for herons, egrets and rails. The causeway separates open water on the west side from ponds on the east. Nesting islands were created in the first pond, and are heavily used in the breeding season. From approximately April through July the trail is off-limits to visitors from the first pond on; thus a spotting scope is very helpful. In the non-breeding season one can walk out to and up Rock Hill for a good view of the open sea. East of Rock Hill and the nesting pond there are more diked and cattail-filled ponds; but these are often closed to the public.

Birds

Counts were done February through December 1998; January, May, July, and November 1999; and January 2000. On these 16 counts 128 species were seen (see table on page 271). The number of species per count ranged from 37 to 53 with August the month of highest species diversity.

The diversity of habitat on the refuge attracted many species not easily seen elsewhere. Around the parking lot one could often see such upland residents as Common Ground-Dove, Verdin, Northern Mockingbird, and Abert's Towhee at any season. Ruby-crowned Kinglet, Yellow-rumped Warbler and White-crowned Sparrow were present in winter. The thickets of native plants attracted migrating passerines in spring and fall. Rare birds are seen here occasionally, such as the Virginia's Warbler seen during the count period.

The agricultural fields along the trail were often visited by geese (Snow, Ross's, Canada), egrets (Great, Snowy, Cattle), and White-faced Ibis. In the freshwater marshes at the end of the west-heading trail, Black-crowned Night Heron, both adult and immature, were almost always present in fair numbers, along with an occasional Green Heron. Yuma Clapper Rail, Sora, Marsh Wren, Common Yellowthroat, Red-winged and Yellow-headed Blackbird were also freshwater marsh denizens. All of these species except Sora were known (or presumed) nesters.

The shore on the west side of the diked ponds was favored by Ring-billed, California and Herring Gulls, and occasionally by flocks of Bonaparte's Gulls. Hundreds of Eared Grebes, White Pelicans, Double-crested Cormorants and Ruddy Ducks rafted on the open water.

Ducks of many species used the first pond, but particularly Cinnamon Teal and Northern Shoveler. Shorebirds also found the pond good foraging habitat. Black-necked Stilt and American Avocet were almost always present; Greater Yellowlegs, Willet, Western and Least Sandpiper were there in season. It was a good place to set up a spotting scope and do some leisurely observation of the many waterbirds regularly present.

One of the stellar attractions of this site was the larid nesting colonies. The artificial islands in the largest pond offered safe and appropriate habitat for gulls, terns and skimmers. Gull-billed Tern have nested at the sea since at least 1927 (Pemberton 1927); Black Skimmer nesting was initiated in 1972 (McCaskie et. al. 1974), and Caspian Tern colonization began in 1992 (McCaskie 1992). All these species have had continuous nesting records. In 1999 there were 44 pairs of Gull-billed Tern, 377 Black Skimmer, 211 Caspian Tern, and one Laughing Gull nesting on the islands (Shuford et. al. 2000).

Unusual sightings

Gull-billed Tern and Black Skimmer could be seen at other sites but since they nested at NWRHq they were always present during the breeding season; Gull-billed Tern in May and June, Black Skimmer May through September. Thayer's Gull, rarely identified at the sea, was seen once in April 1998. Costa's Hummingbird and Virginia's Warbler were also rare, each seen at only one other site.

SONNY BONO NATIONAL WILDLIFE REFUGE—UNIT 1 (AND POE ROAD)

Fieldwork: John Konecny with
assistance from Richard Zembal
Text and Table of Occurrence: Barbara Massey

Driving Directions

One of 3 units of the NWR, Unit 1 is on the southwest shore just west of the New River Delta. From Highway 86 take the Bannister Road turnoff approximately 3.5 miles west of the town of Westmorland. Go east on Bannister for about 0.25 mile and turn left on Vendel Road. Follow this dirt road 1 mile to the refuge; close to shore there is a parking lot and an observation deck.

The Poe Road shoreline is reached by turning off Highway 86 at Poe Road approximately 3 miles west of Bannister. A dirt road leads to the sea, a mile to the north.

Trail description and vegetation

The count site started with the agricultural fields along Vendel, where Snow Geese flocked. Shallow water inlets and sand bars lie along the shore and diked ponds a little farther inland. Some of the ponds have open water and are favored by waders and waterfowl; others are dense with cattails, providing good habitat for coots and rails. Arrowweed and iodine bush grow along the dikes. The fields along the entry road are planted with forage grains for geese. There is a 2-story viewing platform from which the ponds and their occupants can be seen. At dusk it serves as a vantage point for watching incoming flocks that come to roost at the New River Delta. A spotting scope is handy.

There is a rough track along an irrigation ditch perpendicular to Vendel and just inland from the ponds which leads east to the tree-lined dike that borders the New River. The delta can be seen partially from the dike. All of the area described was included in the counts.

The shoreline from Poe Road to the New River Delta was also part of the counts. From Poe Road and from Vendel we could see the intervening shoreline and its birds with the aid of a spotting scope. From Vendel we could scope the shoreline east to the delta.

Poe Road leads straight to the sea. Birds roost along the shoreline and raft on the open water. These are the only usable habitat as there are no ponds and the vegetation is scant.

Birds

Counts were done January through December 1998; January, March, and May 1999. On these 15 counts, 103 species were seen (see table on page 277). The number of species per count ranged from 36 to 71 with March and April the months of highest species diversity.

Present on all counts were American White Pelican, Double-crested Cormorant, Great Blue Heron, Great Egret, Snowy Egret, Black-crowned Night-Heron, Mallard, Killdeer, Black-necked Stilt, American Avocet, Western Sandpiper, and Ring-billed Gull. On almost every count there were Pied-billed Grebe, Eared Grebe, Cattle Egret, Cinnamon Teal, Northern Shoveler, Northern Pintail, Black-bellied Plover, California Gull, Forster's Tern, Mourning Dove and Marsh Wren.

The open ponds near the shore were a favored site for flocks of White Pelican, White-faced Ibis, Ring-billed Gull, and ducks of many species. Clapper Rail, Sora, Common Moorhen and American Coot were frequently seen or heard in ponds with marsh vegetation.

In fall and winter Snow Geese flocked in large numbers in the fields and a Northern Harrier often coursed over the marshes.

The ponds along the road that had open water were sometimes so crowded in winter months with ducks of several species—American Wigeon, Cinnamon Teal, Northern Shoveler, Northern Pintail, Green-winged Teal—that they could scarcely be counted, and it was quite a spectacle when they took off in unison.

The New River Delta was a major rookery for Great Blue Heron with 484 pairs nesting in 1999 (Shuford *et. al.* 2000). A small number of Double-crested Cormorant and Great Egret also nested.

Poe Road was a favorite site for flocks of American White Pelican and

Ring-billed Gull. No species were recorded there that did not also occur at Unit 1. A few pairs of Double-crested Cormorant and Great Blue Heron nested in snags offshore.

The New River Delta was the site of a nocturnal roost, and the observation tower at Unit 1 was a good spot for observing the evening arrival. The fields between Vendel Road and the tower usually attracted large flocks of Snow Geese. American White Pelicans, White-faced Ibis and Cattle Egrets arrived by the hundreds before dusk and settled in the shallow waters of the river and in the surrounding trees.

Unusual sightings

Infrequently seen waterbirds included Common Goldeneye, Red Knot, Sanderling, and Common Snipe. A Horned Grebe was present on an April count in 1998; this bird is rare on inland waters and was seen elsewhere only at Obsidian Butte. Four Mountain Plovers were seen once in the fields in November 1998, one of just two sightings on the counts. Mountain Plover was a regular winter presence in the Imperial Valley, but most often seen foraging in agricultural fields farther inland.

In courtship display the male Red-winged Blackbird fluffs out his brilliant wing patches. This species nests in large colonies in marshes at Finney Lake, Wister Unit, and other sites, as well as in tall grasses in agricultural fields. (Photo by Peter L. Knapp)

Yellow-headed Blackbirds often nest in the same marshes with the Red-winged Blackbird, although always outnumbered by their more common cousins. (Photo by Peter L. Knapp)

The Marsh Wren is associated with marshes throughout the year; this bird is seldom seen away from the cattails. (Photo by Peter L. Knapp)

A rare sighting of a Mountain Bluebird (above) was captured on film near the Salton Sea.

Large flocks of Tree Swallows (right) roost and forage at Ramer and Finney Lakes in the winter months.
(Both photos by Peter L. Knapp)

The American Avocet (above) nests in many shallow ponds and marshes around the shore; its long-legged chicks are identifiable at an early age.

The Greater Roadrunner (left) just can't help behaving like a cartoon character. Its appearance is unpredictable and always a delight to the observer. (Both photos by Peter L. Knapp)

Black-necked Stilts nest in the same shallow marshes and ponds favored by the American Avocet. No, this bird's legs are not bent the wrong way. (Photo by Peter L. Knapp)

The Mountain Plover is listed as a species of concern by both state and federal agencies; a small population winters regularly in the Imperial Valley, foraging opportunistically in newly plowed agricultural fields. (Photo by Peter L. Knapp)

Small flocks of Sandhill Cranes (above) are regular wintor visitors in the Imperial Valley. They can best be seen at nocturnal roosts; during the day they forage widely in the agricultural fields of the valley.

The Wood Stork (right) is a rare post-breeding summer visitor to the southeast shore of the Salton Sea. It is best seen at the Alamo River Delta and Wister Unit. (Both photos by Peter L. Knapp)

The Barn Owl (above) is a resident bird, but not often encountered. This one found a comfortable niche in a stack of hay bales.

Gull-billed Terns (left top) have nested at the Salton Sea for decades. In recent years, nesting colonies have been located at Sonny Bono National Wildlife Refuge on the south shore, and off Johnson Street at the north end.

An American Bittern (left) stalks its prey through low marsh grass. (All photos by Peter L. Knapp)

The Imperial Valley is well populated by Burrowing Owls. They find good roosts and nest sites in holes in berms along the numerous drainage ditches. The holes are usually excavated by ground squirrels, then taken over and enlarged by owls. This individual found a home in a culvert. (Photo by Peter L. Knapp)

A Least Bittern skulks through marsh vegetation.
(Photo by Peter L. Knapp)

A Yellow-footed Gull displays its handsome feet at Sonny Bono National Wildlife Refuge. This gull can be seen year-round at the Salton Sea, but does not nest.

Caspian Terns (above) nest at Sonny Bono National Wildlilfe Refuge.

Cattle Egrets (left) have nested in the Imperial Valley since 1970. Finney Lake, where this photo was taken in 1979, was a preferred nesting site for many years, but has now been abandoned for a similar site at adjacent Ramer Lake. (All photos by Peter L. Knapp)

Brown Pelicans have made sporadic attempts to nest at Obsidian Butte in recent years, but have not yet become established breeders. This individual is in breeding plumage. (Photo by Peter L. Knapp)

The Black Skimmer forages in unique fashion, flying just above the water with its lower mandible used as a spoon to catch small fish. (Photo by Peter L. Knapp)

A mixed flock of Black-necked Stilts, White-faced Ibis and *Dowitcher* spp. forage in an agricultural field. The watering regime in the valley is in constant flux, and wading birds of many species move around to find newly-flooded fields.
(Photo by Peter L. Knapp)

The partially submerged snags that line the shores of the sea are favored sites for roosting and nesting waterbirds. Here, Double-crested Cormorants festoon a drowned snag against a brilliant sunset. (Photo by Peter L. Knapp)

A few White-faced Ibis and Ring-billed Gulls are in company with a flock of Cattle Egrets. (Photo by Peter L. Knapp)

Looking up at the sky is a must around the Salton Sea. A flock of White Pelicans in flight is one of many satisfying rewards for doing so. (Photo by Peter L. Knapp)

This communal roost (above) hosts Great Blue Herons, Cattle Egrets, and Double-crested Cormorants.

The Chocolate Mountains (left) provide an elegant backdrop for a densely packed flock of Snow Geese.
(Both photos by Peter L. Knapp)

Great Blue Herons (above) nest in a snag.

Shorebirds against a darkening sky (right).
(Both photos by Peter L. Knapp)

The pilings of an old pier at the Naval Test Base on the western shore make an excellent roost for White Pelicans.
(Photo by Peter L. Knapp)

Flock of Snow Geese come in to roost at dusk.
(Photo by Peter L. Knapp)

The air is filled with Snow Geese. (Photo by Peter L. Knapp)

White-faced Ibis in V formation as they arrive to roost for the night. (Photo by Peter L. Knapp)

Sunset over the Salton Sea. (Photo by Peter L. Knapp)

WEST SIDE

Fieldwork: Carol Roberts, Pete Sorenson
Text: Barbara Massey, Carol Roberts, Pete Sorenson
Table of Occurrence: Barbara Massey

Three sites along the west shore between the Avenues and Unit 1 were censused for 1 year (1998). From north to south they were Desert Shores, Salton Sea Beach, and Salton City. They are towns with permanent residents who live mostly in mobile homes. The towns all have marinas and the quiet presence of retirement communities. Bird use was not impressive compared with other sites, and we decided not to visit them in the second year. The data have been combined in the table on page 282, using the same format as for the Avenues and SSSRA, with occurrence for the 3 sites tabulated separately.

Marca

Eighty-two species were seen at the 3 sites. The usual assemblage of waterbirds and shorebirds found all around the sea were here as well, particularly in winter: Eared Grebe, Western Grebe, White Pelican, Brown Pelican, Double-crested Cormorant, Great Blue Heron, Great Egret, Snowy Egret, Black-bellied Plover, Snowy Plover, Killdeer, Black-necked Stilt, American Avocet, Greater Yellowlegs, Willet, Spotted Sandpiper, Western and Least Sandpiper, Dowitcher spp. Ring-billed Gull, California Gull, Herring Gull, and Caspian Tern. Resident birds associated with human disturbance were present at all sites: Rock Dove, European Starling, and Great-tailed Grackle.

There were several unusual sightings that are listed below under the individual sites.

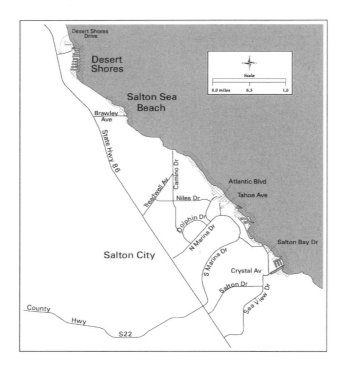

Desert Shores

Driving Directions: Turn off Highway 86 at the community of Desert Shores approximately 2 miles south of 84th Avenue and 2 miles north of Salton Sea Beach. Drive east to the shore.

Site Description and Vegetation: The town is comprised of mobile homes. The shoreline has been transformed into a series of embayments that were intended to be marinas, and which attract mostly gulls. Vegetation was very sparse and of little importance to birds.

Birds

Thirteen counts were done: January through December 1998, and January 1999; 45 species were seen (see table on page 282). No unique species were seen.

Although this site was not a particularly interesting area for birds, the small barnacle lagoon and the salt flats along the shoreline at the south edge of the dredged marina supported small breeding populations of Snowy Plover and Black-necked Stilt.

Salton Sea Beach

Driving Directions: Turn off Highway 86 at the town of Salton Sea Beach, 5.7 miles north of Salton City, 2.0 miles south of Desert Shores. Drive east to the shore.

Site Description and Vegetation: There is no natural vegetation of importance to birds along the shoreline.

Birds

Thirteen counts were done: January through December 1998, and January 1999; 53 species were seen (see table on page 282).

Species observed were typical of shore and water birds found elsewhere. Though habitats were not unique or of high intrinsic value, the shoreline beach in the center of town, and two small shoreline lagoons along the north side of town (accessed by secondary residential streets) were of most interest. Derelict, flooded structures on former residential lots within the lagoons added cultural and historical curiosity to the bird mix, which was highlighted by breeding Snowy Plover and Black-necked Stilt, Wilson's and Red-necked Phalarope during migration, and roosting herons and egrets in flooded, dead trees.

Unusual bird sightings were 7 Red Knots in May 1998, and a Large-billed Savannah Sparrow in March 1998.

Salton City

Driving Directions

To reach the south end of the town, take the well-marked turnoff at South Marina Drive, 12.5 miles north of the junction of Highways 86 and 78. If coming from the north the turnoff is about 6.5 miles south of

Salton Sea Beach. Head east on South Marina Drive toward the sea and take a right onto Riviera Circle, then left on Salton Drive to Seaview and left again to Crystal. Ahead you will see a lagoon that usually has many water birds.

To cruise the shoreline, turn north on Salton Bay Drive from Crystal and then right on Marina Drive. All right turns off Marina go to the shore. This town was once a thriving resort with a lakefront yacht club and other amenities. The rise in water level in the 1970s partially drowned many of the buildings, leaving a photogenic trail of disintegration that has attracted several famous photographers. Unfortunately the yacht club was demolished in 2000, leaving only photographs as a visual reminder of a boom gone bust. The last right turn, Tahoe, leads to Palm Beach RV Park which has a nature trail, a natural shoreline, and many birds.

Site Description and Vegetation

The lagoon at the south end is an arm of the sea, probably constructed with a marina in mind. It provides quiet water for ducks and shore birds. The town shoreline has been modified with U-shaped, cement-walled embayments for boats and hosts mostly gulls. The RV park at the north end is a good birding site. A tiny city park off South Marina Drive has a few resident birds and attracts a few migrant passerines.

Vegetation is of little importance to the birds that are seen here because they are almost all water-associated. At the south end lagoon there is tamarisk and cattail in the drainage ditch and quail bush on the dikes. In the RV park the native scrub includes iodine bush, quail bush, desert goldenbush and an occasional tamarisk. Some planting of cacti and succulents has also been done.

Birds

Twelve counts were done: January through November 1998, and January 1999. Sixty-three species were seen (see table on page 282). This site had more species than the other westside towns. Large flocks of Black-necked Stilt, Ring-billed Gull, California Gull, and Herring Gull were present on most counts. Western and Least Sandpiper flocks were also seen regularly.

In addition to the usual species there were several sightings of birds rare to the sea. Three Ruddy Turnstones were seen in April 1998, and two Black Scoters were spotted in May 1998.

WHITEWATER RIVER DELTA

Fieldwork: Richard Zembal with assistance
from Barbara Massey
Table of Occurrence: Barbara Massey
Text: Barbara Massey, Richard Zembal

The Whitewater River once flowed freely from Mt. San Gorgonio in the San Bernardinos through the Coachella Valley to the Salton Sink, providing a riparian corridor through the desert that must have been a boon to birds and mammals as well as humans. Today its final few miles are a sad reminder of how California has abused its rivers; it is channeled and lined, and serves mainly as a drainage ditch for the valley's agricultural fields. Even so, its vegetation harbors native birds and migrants in season, and is considered the best riparian habitat at the Salton Sea.

Driving Directions

From Highway 111 on the northwest side, turn off onto Highway 195 at Mecca. The first street across the railroad tracks is Lincoln, which goes south only. Drive approximately 3 miles on Lincoln to where the paved road ends and a dirt road continues south. Just a few yards farther the dirt road splits and the left fork goes up onto a dike, for which 4-wheel drive is usually not necessary. The counts began there and continued along the dike approximately 2 miles farther to its terminus at the sea.

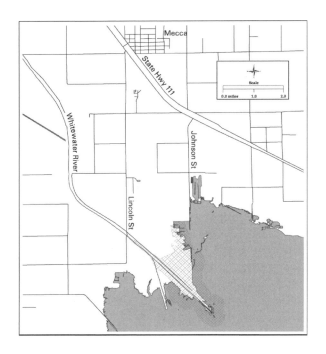

Site Description and Vegetation

The Whitewater River (drainage ditch) flows on the west side of the dike. It is still a riparian corridor, although the native vegetation has been heavily invaded by salt cedar. Willows and cottonwoods occur in scattered small stands and attract migrants. Cattails grow densely all along the ditch. Desert scrub lies between the ditch and the dike, dominated by saltbush and intermixed with bush seepweed.

At the end of the road the shore curves into bays on both sides of a spit. The shallow waters have sand bars, many drowned snags and a soft-mud shoreline, providing multiple habitats for roosting, foraging and nesting water birds. A spotting scope is an important adjunct to binoculars here. The east side can be viewed easily from the road; the west side usually by walking out to the end of the spit, unless the water is too high. The beach is thickly encrusted with barnacles and the water's edge often lined with dead fish. It is wise to be careful about walking on wet patches, you can easily break through the crust and become mired.

Walking the road is preferable to driving it, as desert and riparian birds can be seen and heard all along the way. The best route is to walk to the sea on the dike, which provides an overview of the desert scrub on the east side and the riparian corridor on the west; then return via the track along the river channel, where you are closer to the riparian birds.

Birds

Counts were done May through December 1998; January, March, April, May, July, and November 1999; and January 2000. On these 15 counts 127 species were seen (see table on page 287). The number of species per count ranged from 44 to 69 with April the month of the highest species diversity. A varied waterfront (snags, sand bars, mud flats, shallow waters) augmented by a 2-mile riparian corridor plus the surrounding desert scrub, created a diversity of habitat that attracted many species.

The shoreline with its snags and sand bars attracted a host of water birds. Throughout the year Double-crested Cormorant, Great Blue Heron, Great Egret and Black-crowned Night-Heron perched in the snags. Osprey were regularly seen fishing and then perched high in a snag eating a fish. In spring the snags became nest sites; in 1998 75 Great Blue Heron nests were counted in May.

Flocks of ducks, including Northern Pintail, Northern Shoveler, and Lesser Scaup dabbled in the shallow waters. Small flocks of Brant were seen in May and June. The sand bars, mud flats and shallow waters were favored foraging areas for shore birds, including Black-necked Stilt, American Avocet, Willet, Marbled Godwit, Western Sandpiper, Least Sandpiper and Dowitcher spp. Killdeer and Snowy Plover nested on the sandbars. The cattail stands at the sea's edge harbored American Coot, Common Moorhen, Yuma Clapper Rail and Sora.

Rafts of American White Pelicans were ever-present in the shallow-water embayments around the delta along with large congregations of Eared Grebes, Ruddy Ducks and several gull species. From the shore one could see birds rafted on the water as far as the eye could reach.

The riparian corridor provided some of the best habitat for upland birds around the sea. Residents included American Kestrel, Gambel's Quail, Mourning Dove, Common Ground-Dove, Greater Roadrunner, and Ladder-backed Woodpecker, all seen regularly. Passerines in residence in the cattails and in vegetation on the edges of the ditch included Black Phoebe, Marsh Wren, Common Yellowthroat and Song Sparrow. The desert scrub between the ditch and the dike and on the east side of the road was home to Loggerhead Shrike, Verdin, Bewick's Wren, Cactus Wren, Black-tailed Gnatcatcher and Abert's Towhee. Breeding was documented for all of them.

Migrants used the delta on their spring and fall passages. Some species remained to nest, such as Lesser Nighthawk, White-winged Dove, Ash-throated Flycatcher, Western Kingbird, and Bullock's Oriole. Several migrants were also winter visitors—Yellow-rumped Warbler and White-crowned Sparrow.

Unusual sightings

A Black Rail was heard twice in the cattails in January and March 1999. Crissal Thrasher was an uncommon bird around the sea, occurring at only two other sites (Finney and Ramer Lakes) and seen most often here.

WISTER UNIT—STATE IMPERIAL WILDLIFE AREA

Fieldwork: Kathy Keane, Mark Wimer with
assistance from Bob Miller, Carolyn Shaputnic,
Paul Jorgensen, Barbara Massey, Richard Zembal
Table of Occurrence: Barbara Massey
Text: Kathy Keane, Mark Wimer

Wister Unit's large size and diverse habitats render it a wonderful birding spot. It was acquired by the state in 1956 and is managed by CDFG. Located near the town of Niland, it is bounded by Highway 111 on the east, the sea on the west, Mallard Road on the north and Sinclair Road on the south. It covers approximately 5,900 acres and consists primarily of diked ponds managed for waterfowl and other types of hunting, with approximately 36 miles of crisscrossing roads to access the ponds.

Driving Directions

From the north take Highway 111 south toward the town of Niland. Approximately 10.5 miles south of Bombay Beach there is a sign for the Wister Waterfowl Area at Davis Road. A right turn leads to the CDFG headquarters building. You can get information from CDFG wardens here during hunting season; at other times of the year, maps may be avail-

Narca

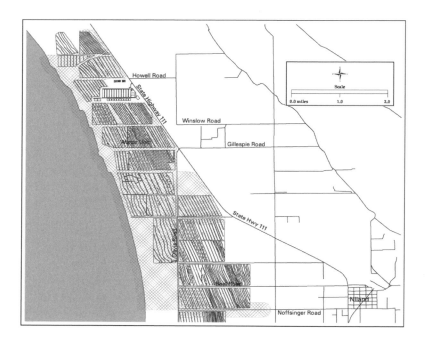

able at kiosks here and at the junction of Mallard Road and Highway 111. From Davis Road you can turn right onto one of many dirt roads, some of which lead to the sea, or continue south to other parts of the unit. During the winter months there are usually large flocks of Snow Geese in an agricultural field managed for them just past the headquarters building on the left.

Coming from the south on Highway 111 the Davis Road turnoff is approximately 6 miles north of Niland.

Trail description and vegetation

The Wister Unit is divided into numbered and lettered management units by CDFG, separated by primary diked roads trending east to west, many of them bestowed with bird names (Mallard, Honker, Ibis, Willet). Signs identifying many of the units, corresponding to the map available at the kiosks, are present during hunting season but absent the remainder of the year. Most of the roads are lined with tamarisk, saltbush, or both. They provide some value for upland birds, at least from a structural standpoint, for lack of native tall trees in the area. Some units, particularly those closest to Highway 111 near Niland, support upland habitat dominated by weedy vegetation including western sunflower, nonnative grasses and tamarisk. Others support primarily cattails, or are shallow ponds with emergent freshwater vegetation, and some are deep and primarily open water. The units closest to the sea are either dense with mesquite or freshwater marsh vegetation, or are characterized by very shallow water and unvegetated salt flats. The units vary in size, although most are more than 0.5 mile in length, trending northwest to southeast, and are separated widthwise into smaller sections by narrow diked roads and trails. Access to the sea is available along Honker, Beach and McDonald Roads. However, after rains the roads may be very muddy, especially close to the sea, so caution should be exercised. Park and walk where it gets muddy, rather than risk becoming mired. Birding during hunting season (November through January) is not recommended, even though hunting is not allowed during some weekdays and in some sections. It is best to call 760-359-0577 to inquire about a non-hunting day for birding.

The Wister Unit was too large for one person to census and was divided into 2 sections. The northern section—Beach Road north to Mallard Road—was done almost exclusively by Kathy Keane. It took 5-8 hours and was generally censused on consecutive days; part of it late in the afternoon of the first day, the rest the following morning. Periodically, assistance was available from other censusers. The southern section (Beach Road south to Noffsinger Road) was done by Mark Wimer until he left for the east coast in August 1999 and Bob Miller took over. This section was smaller and took 4 to 5 hours. It was done in the early morning, when lighting was generally best for using a spotting scope to scan the large, partially inundated areas at the edge of the sea.Carolyn Shaputnic did several counts of the area from Beach Road to CDFG headquarters; and Paul Jorgensen, Barbara Massey and Dick Zembal each did several counts as pinch-hitters. Although survey coverage focused on areas west of Davis Road where the flooded cells provided habitat for water birds, the uplands were hospitable to migrants and summer nesting birds, and thus also worth visiting. This was particularly true of the fields and hedgerows north of Beach and close to Highway 111.

Because of the very large acreage, surveys were conducted by driving diked roads as much as possible to view all of the sections, using a window-mounted spotting scope. The sea itself was not visible from most access roads as dense stands of tamarisk trees lines the shore. A short trek through mud and then tamarisk was necessary to reach the beach. But it was worth doing in order to see Mullet Island with its thousands of breeding cormorants, the dead snags that lie offshore and host herons and cormorants, and the beach with its gulls, pelicans and shore birds.

Birds

Counts were done every month in 1998; January, March, May, July, September, and November 1999; and January 2000. A total of 163 species was seen on these 19 counts (see table on page 293). The number of species per count ranged from 64 to 89 with January the month of highest species diversity, followed closely by June (85), September (82) and April (79).

The Wister Unit had the highest species diversity of all the sites. It also had the largest number of individuals of any site; the peak was 21,600 birds on the count in January 1998.

Shorebirds were most abundant during post-breeding migration from late July to early November, with notable exceptions such as Red-necked Phalarope (a flock of 429 in April 1998). Killdeer, Black-necked Stilt, American Avocet, Greater Yellowlegs, Willet and Dowitcher spp. were observed year-round. Stilt Sandpiper was an unusual visitor seen on 4 occasions.

Larids were more numerous in the winter months. Generally the most abundant gull was Ring-billed, followed by California, Herring and Bonaparte's Gull. Dense flocks too far away to speciate were also noted during most surveys. Less common were Laughing and Yellow-footed Gull, which arrived at Wister in July and August as post-breeders. Caspian and Forster's Tern were observed during most surveys but were more numerous in summer. Black Tern, Gull-billed Tern and Black Skimmer were summer visitors. Aerial fish foragers other than terns included Belted Kingfisher (seen 6 times) and Brown Pelican, seen regularly but more abundant in late summer.

Wading birds observed regularly and in high numbers were Great Blue Heron, Great Egret, Snowy Egret, Black-crowned Night-Heron and White-Faced Ibis. The Wister Unit was a prime site for marsh birds, including American Bittern, Green Heron, Yuma Clapper Rail, and Sora. Virginia Rails were seen on 6 counts. Common Moorhens were often-seen residents, and American Coots were abundant. The endangered Yuma Clapper Rail was more numerous here than anywhere else at the sea, and is managed with care by CDFG.

Waterfowl numbers usually exceeded those for other bird groups and were higher during the winter months, although small numbers of most species were also present in spring and summer. Northern Shoveler and Ruddy Duck were generally most abundant, along with Snow Geese from November through January. Green-winged Teal, Cinnamon Teal, Northern Pintail, Gadwall, Redhead, and American Wigeon were present in smaller (but substantial) numbers. Eared and Western Grebe were more common in winter, while Pied-billed Grebe were observed year-round.

Several birds of prey frequented Wister Unit; Northern Harrier was the most common, particularly during the fall and winter. Red-tailed Hawk and American Kestrel, although common elsewhere, were each recorded only 4 times, while Peregrine Falcon were seen 8 times. A Bald Eagle was seen in January 1998, and there were 3 sightings of a Merlin.

Many upland birds were present throughout the year, including Mourning Dove, Verdin, Black Phoebe, Black-tailed Gnatcatcher, American Pipit, Loggerhead Shrike, Meadowlark, Abert's Towhee, Great-tailed Grackle, Brown-headed Cowbird and House Finch. Less frequent in occurrence were Common Ground-Dove, Gambel's Quail, Greater Roadrunner, Northern Mockingbird, and Phainopepla. White-Winged Dove and Lesser Nighthawk came for the summer to nest. Common winter visitors were White-crowned Sparrow, Ruby-crowned Kinglet, Blue-Gray Gnatcatcher and Yellow-rumped Warbler

Infrequently seen landbirds included Vaux's Swift, Ladder-backed Woodpecker, Northern Flicker, Bewick's Wren, Ash-throated Flycatcher, Cassin's Kingbird, Cactus Wren, Bewick's Wren, Lincoln's Sparrow and Blue Grosbeak, seen 2 times each. Ring-Necked Pheasant, Pacific Slope Flycatcher, Plumbeous Vireo, Warbling Vireo, Horned Lark, House Wren, Yellow Warbler, Townsend's Warbler, Yellow-breasted Chat,

Western Tanager, Black-headed Grosbeak, Brewer's Sparrow, Lark Sparrow, Sage Sparrow, Dark-eyed Junco and Tricolored Blackbird were seen once each.

Passerines associated with freshwater marsh habitats were Marsh Wren, Common Yellowthroat, Song Sparrow and Red-Winged Blackbird, all residents. Yellow-headed Blackbird came to nest from March through September.

Breeding was confirmed for many species. The most prominent breeders were the Great Blue Heron and Double-crested Cormorant with nests built on dead snags offshore. The major cormorant nesting site at the sea was on Mullet Island not far offshore and birds could be seen carrying nest material over Wister Unit to the island. Nests or young of Killdeer and Black-necked Stilt were spotted frequently during early June surveys, and the more secretive Snowy Plover was also seen courting and giving distraction displays. (Wister Unit was second only to Alamo for breeding Snowy Plover.) Downy young Cinnamon Teal, Gadwall and Redhead were spotted on the impoundments during the early June surveys. Recently fledged Gull-billed, Caspian, and Forster's Tern appeared in July, begging from adults, but were not observed nesting at Wister Unit. The presence and/or territorial singing during the breeding season by the following species suggested probable nesting: Pied-Billed Grebe, American Bittern, Green Heron, Yuma Clapper Rail, American Coot, Common Moorhen, Sora, Ruddy Duck, American Avocet, Mourning Dove, Black Phoebe, Loggerhead Shrike, Verdin, Marsh Wren, Black-tailed Gnatcatcher, Common Yellowthroat, Song Sparrow, Abert's Towhee, Red-winged Blackbird, Meadowlark, Great-tailed Grackle, Brown-headed Cowbird and House Finch.

Unusual sightings

Uncommon species included Wood Stork (seen on 4 summer counts), Little Blue Heron and Least Bittern on 2 counts, and four Chilean Flamingos in July 1999. Flamingos are nonnatives that have long been resident at the Salton Sea (see "Species Accounts - Nonnative Species").

A Eurasian Wigeon was present in November 1998; an American Golden Plover was on the mud flats in October 1998; a Parasitic Jaeger was seen in August 1998; 3 Franklin's Gulls were seen in May 1998; and a Little Gull was observed in May 1999.

Unusual upland birds included a Plumbeous Vireo in May 1998, Sprague's Pipit in February 1998, and American Redstart in September 1999.

ADDITIONAL SITES

Two sites were visited fairly regularly in 1998 but did not generate data that justified continuing coverage in 1999. They were Hayes Street and Naval Test Base. A 3rd site, a Eucalyptus grove in Westmorland, was a major nesting site in 1999.

Hayes Street

Driving Directions

This site is on the northwest shore. Turn off Highway 111 approximately 2 miles east of Johnson Street and follow a paved road south 2.5 miles to the end.

Site Description and Vegetation

The road is lined with agricultural fields and orchards almost to the shore. Tamarisk and iodine bush grow along the shore. There are inlets with sand bars frequented by shore birds. A barnacled beach strings along the shore.

Birds

We visited Hayes Street 9 times in 1998, and most of the 79 species seen were also seen at Johnson Street. The exceptions were Gambel's Quail, Red-necked Phalarope, Heermann's Gull, Barn Owl, Blue-gray Gnatcatcher and Crissal Thrasher, each seen 1 to 2 times at Hayes Street. Killdeer, Black-necked Stilt, and Ring-billed Gull were always present, and Verdin, Marsh Wren and Northern Mockingbird were in residence.

Naval Test Base

Driving Directions

Heading north on Highway 86, turn east 4.1 miles north of the junction of Highways 78 and 86 onto an unmarked but paved road. If driving south the turnoff is 8.2 miles south of Salton City. Drive 3.3 miles to the gates of the old Naval Test Base. The area is under the jurisdiction of two federal agencies, BLM and BR. In 2001 it became the site of a restoration project and public access was sometimes restricted. The project will continue through 2003, after which the site will be open at all times to the public.

Site Description and Vegetation

The entry area is a rather desolate clearing with a few stands of tamarisk but no native vegetation. One can look out over the sea from a berm built along the shore. The remains of an old pier provide a roosting site for cormorants and pelicans. Snags also provide perches. A line of utility poles out in the water and parallel to shore provides roosting and nesting sites.

The shore can be walked both north and south. Our census was along the north shore and covered approximately 1 mile of shoreline. Desert scrub lines the shore. Towards the end of the count area, salt flats with several salt encrusted ponds provide nesting habitat for Snowy Plover.

Birds

On 8 visits in 1998, we saw 56 species. Double-crested Cormorant, White and Brown Pelican, Great Blue Heron and Ring-billed Gull were the most common water birds. Snow Plovers nested on the saltflats to the north, 7 to 10 pairs were there in the spring of 1998.

There were several sightings of birds rare to the sea. A Prairie Falcon was present in June 1998, one of 4 sightings during the counts. A Black-throated Sparrow was seen in May 1998, one of two sightings for this desert species for which there is little suitable habitat around the sea.

Westmorland Eucalyptus Grove

Driving Directions

To get to the grove, go south out of Westmorland on State Highway 30 (named Forrester Road on the road maps, but Center Road in the town itself) for approximately 1.5 miles. The road makes a rather sharp S curve at that point and crosses a major canal. Do not cross the canal but turn west on the road on the north bank. Go approximately 1 mile to a good sized grove of eucalyptus trees.

Birds

In 1999 this grove was the major nesting site at the sea for Cattle Egret. The birds deserted their usual nesting site at Ramer Lake early in the season and renested in the eucalyptus grove. It is not known whether this site has been used as a backup in other years, nor whether it will be used again. But in 1999 there were 4000 pairs nesting here along with a few pairs of Snowy Egret and Black-crowned Night-Heron.

Summation of Species Seen on Counts at All Sites

	Wister Unit	Whitewater	West Side***	State Recreation Area**	Red Hill County Park	Ramer Lake	Obsidian Butte	NWR - Unit 1	NWR - Rock Hill	Johnson Street	Finney Lake	Fig Lagoon	Bombay Beach	The Avenues*	Alamo River Delta
Common Loon												•			•
Pied-billed Grebe	•	•		•	•	•	•	•	•	•	•	•		•	
Horned Grebe							•	•							
Eared Grebe	•	•	•	•	•	•	•	•	•	•	•	•	•	•	•
Western Grebe	•	•	•	•	•	•	•	•	•	•	•	•	•	•	•
Clark's Grebe	•	•	•	•	•	•	•	•	•	•	•	•	•	•	•
American White Pelican	•	•	•	•	•		•	•	•	•	•	•	•	•	•
Brown Pelican	•	•	•	•	•		•	•	•		•	•	•	•	•
Double-crested Cormorant	•	•	•	•	•										•
Magnificent Frigatebird									•		•			•	
American Bittern									•			•			
Least Bittern		•				•				•	•			•	
Great Blue Heron	•	•	•	•	•	•	•	•	•	•	•			•	•
Great Egret	•	•	•	•	•	•	•	•	•	•	•			•	•
Snowy Egret	•	•	•	•	•	•	•	•	•	•	•	•	•	•	•

	AL	AV	BB	FI	FIN	JO	Hq	U1	OB	RA	RED	SSS	WE	WH	WI
Little Blue Heron	•														•
Cattle Egret	•	•		•	•	•	•	•	•	•	•	•	•	•	•
Green Heron	•	•	•	•	•	•	•	•	•	•	•	•	•	•	•
Black-crowned Night-Heron	•	•	•	•	•	•	•	•	•	•	•	•	•	•	•
White-faced Ibis	•	•		•	•	•	•	•	•	•	•	•	•	•	•
Wood Stork	•														
Turkey Vulture	•	•	•	•	•	•	•	•	•	•	•	•	•	•	•
Lesser Flamingo											•				
Chilean Flamingo		•												•	
Flamingo spp.	•														
Fulvous Whistling-Duck					•					•				•	
Greater White-fronted Goose										•					
Snow Goose		•				•	•	•	•	•	•	•		•	•
Ross' Goose		•					•	•			•				•
Canada Goose		•					•			•	•	•		•	
Brant		•	•		•	•	•		•				•	•	•
Mute Swan	•														
Gadwall		•				•	•	•	•	•	•	•		•	•
Eurasian Wigeon		•												•	
American Wigeon		•		•	•	•	•		•	•	•	•		•	•
Mallard	•	•	•		•	•	•	•	•	•	•	•		•	•
Blue-winged Teal	•				•	•									•

	AL	AV	BB	FI	FIN	JO	Hq	UI	OB	RA	RED	SSS	WE	WH	WI
Cinnamon Teal	•	•	•	•	•	•	•	•	•	•	•	•	•	•	•
Northern Shoveler	•	•	•	•	•	•	•	•	•	•	•	•	•	•	•
Northern Pintail	•	•	•	•	•	•	•	•	•	•	•	•	•	•	•
Green-winged Teal	•	•	•	•	•	•	•	•	•	•	•	•	•	•	•
Canvasback	•	•				•	•	•	•	•	•		•		•
Redhead	•	•	•	•		•	•	•	•	•	•	•	•	•	•
Ring-necked Duck		•		•		•									
Greater Scaup		•													
Lesser Scaup	•	•	•	•	•	•	•	•	•	•	•	•	•	•	•
Surf Scoter	•	•	•		•	•		•				•	•		
Black Scoter	•	•										•			
Bufflehead	•	•	•	•	•	•	•	•	•	•	•	•	•	•	•
Common Goldeneye	•	•	•			•	•	•	•	•	•	•			
Red-breasted Merganser		•			•	•	•	•	•	•	•	•	•		
Ruddy Duck	•	•	•	•	•	•	•	•	•	•	•	•	•	•	•
Osprey	•	•	•	•	•	•	•	•	•	•	•	•	•	•	•
White-tailed Kite	•														
Bald Eagle															•
Northern Harrier	•	•	•	•	•	•	•	•	•	•	•	•	•	•	•
Sharp-shinned Hawk	•	•	•	•	•	•	•	•	•	•		•		•	•
Cooper's Hawk	•	•	•	•	•	•	•	•		•		•			•
Red-shouldered Hawk		•			•										

	AL	AV	BB	FI	FIN	JO	Hq	U1	OB	RA	RED	SSS	WE	WH	WI
Red-tailed Hawk	•	•	•		•	•	•	•	•	•	•	•		•	•
American Kestrel	•	•	•	•	•	•	•	•	•	•	•	•	•	•	•
Merlin	•			•	•	•	•		•	•			•	•	•
Peregrine Falcon	•	•							•	•					•
Prairie Falcon						•				•					•
Ring-necked Pheasant								•	•						
Gambel's Quail		•		•	•	•	•		•	•				•	•
Black Rail														•	
Clapper Rail	•				•	•	•	•	•	•	•	•		•	•
Virginia Rail		•			•	•	•		•	•				•	
Sora	•	•			•	•	•	•	•	•	•	•		•	•
Common Moorhen	•	•	•	•	•	•	•	•	•	•	•	•	•	•	•
American Coot	•	•	•	•	•	•	•	•	•	•	•	•	•	•	•
Black-bellied Plover	•	•	•	•	•	•	•	•	•	•	•	•	•	•	•
American Golden-Plover															
Snowy Plover	•	•	•		•	•	•	•		•	•	•	•	•	•
Semipalmated Plover	•	•	•		•	•	•	•		•	•	•	•	•	•
Killdeer	•	•	•	•	•	•	•	•	•	•	•	•	•	•	•
Mountain Plover								•			•				
Black-necked Stilt	•	•	•	•	•	•	•	•	•	•	•	•	•	•	•
American Avocet	•	•	•	•	•	•	•	•	•	•	•	•	•	•	•
Greater Yellowlegs	•	•			•	•	•	•	•	•	•	•	•	•	•

97

	AL	AV	BB	FI	FIN	JO	Hq	UI	OB	RA	RED	SSS	WE	WH	WI
Lesser Yellowlegs		•				•	•	•	•	•	•	•	•	•	•
Willet	•	•	•		•	•	•	•	•	•	•	•	•	•	•
Spotted Sandpiper		•	•		•	•	•	•	•	•	•	•	•	•	•
Whimbrel	•	•	•		•	•	•	•	•	•	•	•	•	•	•
Long-billed Curlew	•	•		•	•	•	•	•	•	•	•	•	•		•
Marbled Godwit	•	•	•		•	•	•	•	•	•	•	•	•	•	•
Ruddy Turnstone								•					•		
Red Knot			•					•				•	•		
Sanderling	•											•	•		
Western Sandpiper	•	•	•	•	•	•	•	•	•	•	•	•	•	•	•
Least Sandpiper	•	•	•	•	•	•	•	•	•	•	•	•	•	•	•
Baird's Sandpiper	•								•						
Dunlin	•	•	•		•	•	•	•	•	•	•	•	•	•	•
Stilt Sandpiper	•						•								
Peep (*Calidris* spp.)	•		•		•	•	•	•	•	•	•	•	•	•	•
Dowitcher spp.	•	•	•	•	•	•	•	•	•	•	•	•	•		•
Common Snipe		•			•			•	•						
Wilson's Phalarope	•	•	•		•		•	•	•	•	•	•	•		•
Red-necked Phalarope	•	•	•		•		•	•	•	•	•	•	•	•	•
Parasitic Jaeger			•												
Laughing Gull	•	•								•	•			•	•
Franklin's Gull												•			•

	AL	AV	BB	FI	FIN	JO	Hq	U1	OB	RA	RED	SSS	WE	WH	WI
Little Gull															•
Bonaparte's Gull	•	•				•	•	•	•	•	•	•	•	•	•
Heermann's Gull			•					•	•						
Ring-billed Gull	•	•	•	•	•	•	•	•	•	•	•	•	•	•	•
California Gull	•	•	•			•	•	•	•	•	•	•	•	•	•
Herring Gull	•	•	•	•		•	•	•	•	•	•	•	•	•	•
Thayer's Gull	•	•				•	•					•			
Lesser Black-backed Gull											•				
Yellow-footed Gull	•	•			•	•		•	•	•	•	•	•	•	•
Western Gull	•					•	•			•	•				•
Glaucous-winged Gull	•	•									•	•			
Sabine's Gull									•						
Gull spp.	•	•	•	•	•	•	•	•	•	•	•	•	•	•	•
Gull-billed Tern	•	•	•	•	•	•	•	•	•	•	•	•	•	•	•
Caspian Tern	•	•	•	•	•	•	•	•	•	•	•	•	•	•	•
Common Tern		•				•						•			
Forster's Tern	•	•	•	•	•	•	•	•	•	•	•	•	•	•	•
Least Tern		•													
Black Tern	•	•			•	•		•	•	•	•	•	•	•	•
Black Skimmer	•	•	•	•	•	•		•		•	•	•	•	•	•
Rock Dove		•	•			•	•		•			•	•		•
Spotted Dove		•													

	AL	AV	BB	FI	FIN	JO	Hq	U1	OB	RA	RED	SSS	WE	WH	WI
White-winged Dove	•	•		•	•	•	•	•	•	•	•	•	•	•	•
Mourning Dove	•	•		•	•	•	•	•	•	•	•	•	•	•	•
Inca Dove				•						•					
Common Ground-Dove	•			•	•	•	•	•	•	•	•	•	•	•	•
Greater Roadrunner		•		•	•	•	•	•	•	•	•	•	•	•	•
Barn Owl				•	•				•	•					
Great Horned Owl				•					•	•	•		•		•
Burrowing Owl	•			•	•	•	•	•	•	•	•	•	•	•	•
Lesser Nighthawk	•		•	•	•	•	•	•	•		•	•	•	•	•
Vaux's Swift					•	•	•								•
White-throated Swift						•		•	•			•		•	
Costa's Hummingbird		•					•					•		•	
Anna's Hummingbird		•										•			
Belted Kingfisher	•			•	•	•	•	•	•	•	•		•	•	•
Red-naped Sapsucker					•										
Ladder-backed Woodpecker	•				•		•			•			•	•	•
Northern Flicker				•	•		•			•			•	•	•
Western Wood-Pewee					•	•	•			•		•			•
Willow Flycatcher				•	•					•		•			
Pacific-slope Flycatcher				•	•	•				•				•	•
Empidonax spp.		•			•									•	•
Black Phoebe	•	•	•	•	•	•	•	•	•	•	•		•		•

	AL	AV	BB	FI	FIN	JO	Hq	U1	OB	RA	RED	SSS	WE	WH	WI
Eastern Phoebe		•													
Say's Phoebe		•	•	•	•	•	•	•	•	•	•	•	•	•	•
Vermilion Flycatcher										•					
Ash-throated Flycatcher		•	•	•	•	•	•	•	•	•	•		•	•	•
Cassin's Kingbird			•		•	•	•							•	•
Western Kingbird		•	•	•	•	•	•	•	•	•	•	•	•	•	•
Loggerhead Shrike		•	•	•	•	•	•	•	•	•	•	•	•	•	•
Plumbeous Vireo															•
Cassin's Vireo							•								
Warbling Vireo				•	•					•					•
American Crow						•									
Common Raven		•	•	•	•	•		•					•	•	•
Horned Lark		•										•			
Tree Swallow		•	•	•	•	•	•	•	•	•	•	•	•	•	•
Violet-green Swallow		•	•				•					•			
No. Rough-winged Swallow		•	•	•	•	•	•	•	•	•	•	•	•	•	•
Bank Swallow			•							•					
Cliff Swallow		•	•	•	•	•	•	•	•	•	•	•	•	•	•
Barn Swallow		•	•	•	•	•	•	•	•	•	•	•	•	•	•
Verdin		•	•	•	•				•					•	•
Bushtit									•						
Cactus Wren		•		•			•			•		•		•	•

	AL	AV	BB	FI	FIN	JO	Hq	U1	OB	RA	RED	SSS	WE	WH	WI
Bewick's Wren		•												•	•
House Wren		•		•		•								•	•
Marsh Wren	•	•	•	•	•	•			•	•		•		•	•
Ruby-crowned Kinglet	•	•		•	•	•	•	•	•	•		•	•	•	•
Blue-gray Gnatcatcher		•		•	•	•	•		•	•			•	•	•
Black-tailed Gnatcatcher		•	•	•	•	•	•		•	•		•		•	•
Western Bluebird											•				
Mountain Bluebird				•											
Northern Mockingbird		•	•	•	•	•	•		•	•		•	•	•	•
Sage Thrasher		•			•										
California Thrasher					•										
Crissal Thrasher				•	•	•	•		•	•			•	•	
European Starling		•	•	•	•	•	•		•	•		•	•	•	•
American Pipit	•	•	•	•	•	•	•		•	•		•	•	•	•
Sprague's Pipit									•			•			
Cedar Waxwing												•			
Phainopepla		•		•	•	•	•			•		•	•	•	•
Orange-crowned Warbler	•	•	•	•	•	•	•		•	•		•	•	•	•
Nashville Warbler					•	•				•					
Virginia's Warbler								•							
Lucy's Warbler				•			•								
Yellow Warbler		•	•	•		•	•	•		•				•	•

	AL	AV	BB	FI	FIN	JO	Hq	U1	OB	RA	RED	SSS	WE	WH	WI
Yellow-rumped Warbler	•	•	•	•	•	•	•	•	•	•	•	•	•	•	•
Black-throated Gray Warbler		•			•					•				•	•
Townsend's Warbler					•					•					•
Hermit Warbler					•										
American Redstart															•
MacGillivray's Warbler										•					
Common Yellowthroat	•	•	•		•	•	•	•	•	•	•	•	•	•	•
Wilson's Warbler		•		•	•	•	•		•	•		•		•	•
Yellow-breasted Chat			•		•					•		•		•	•
Summer Tanager												•			
Western Tanager	•				•					•					•
Spotted Towhee														•	
Abert's Towhee	•	•	•	•	•	•	•		•	•	•	•		•	•
Chipping Sparrow									•						
Brewer's Sparrow				•										•	•
Lark Sparrow		•												•	•
Black-throated Sparrow	•														
Sage Sparrow		•	•											•	•
Savannah Sparrow	•	•	•		•	•	•		•	•		•		•	•
Savannah Sparrow (Large-billed)	•								•				•		
Song Sparrow	•	•	•		•	•	•	•	•	•	•	•		•	•
Lincoln's Sparrow	•	•			•		•								

	AL	AV	BB	FI	FIN	JO	Hq	U1	OB	RA	RED	SSS	WE	WH	W1
White-crowned Sparrow	•	•	•	•	•	•	•	•	•	•	•	•	•	•	•
Golden-crowned Sparrow									•			•			
Dark-eyed Junco					•					•					•
Black-headed Grosbeak					•										•
Blue Grosbeak							•		•					•	•
Lazuli Bunting					•										
Red-winged Blackbird	•	•	•	•	•	•	•	•	•	•	•	•	•	•	•
Tricolored Blackbird		•			•	•			•			•		•	•
Western Meadowlark		•	•	•	•	•	•		•	•	•	•	•	•	•
Yellow-headed Blackbird	•	•		•	•	•	•	•	•	•	•	•	•	•	•
Brewer's Blackbird		•			•	•	•			•	•	•	•	•	
Great-tailed Grackle	•	•	•	•	•	•	•	•	•	•	•	•	•	•	•
Brown-headed Cowbird	•	•	•	•	•	•	•	•	•	•	•	•	•	•	•
Hooded Oriole	•	•		•	•	•	•		•	•		•	•		
Bullock's Oriole	•	•			•			•	•	•				•	•
Scott's Oriole		•													
House Finch	•	•		•	•	•	•	•	•	•	•	•	•	•	•
Lesser Goldfinch	•	•		•	•	•	•	•		•					
Lawrence's Goldfinch		•							•						
American Goldfinch												•	•		
House Sparrow	•	•	•	•	•	•	•	•	•	•	•	•	•	•	•

Key
*   Data pooled for 76, 89, 81, 84 Avenue
**   Data pooled for Desert Beach, State Park Headquarters, Salt Creek
*** Data pooled for Desert Shores, Salton Sea Beach, Salton City
• = present

Monthly Occurrence of Species on Counts

Species	Jan	Feb	Mar	Apr	May	Jun	Jul	Aug	Sep	Oct	Nov	Dec
Common Loon	•		•							•	•	•
Pied-billed Grebe	•	•	•	•	•	•	•	•	•	•	•	•
Horned Grebe	•	•	•	•					•			•
Eared Grebe	•	•	•	•	•	•	•	•	•	•	•	•
Western Grebe	•	•	•	•	•	•	•	•	•	•	•	•
Clark's Grebe	•	•	•	•	•	•	•	•	•	•	•	•
American White Pelican	•	•	•	•	•	•	•	•	•	•	•	•
Brown Pelican	•	•	•	•	•	•	•	•	•	•	•	•
Double-crested Cormorant	•	•	•	•	•	•	•	•	•	•	•	•
Magnificent Frigatebird					•	•						
American Bittern	•	•	•	•	•	•	•	•	•	•	•	•
Least Bittern					•	•	•	•	•	•	•	
Great Blue Heron	•	•	•	•	•	•	•	•	•	•	•	•
Great Egret	•	•	•	•	•	•	•	•	•	•	•	•
Snowy Egret	•	•	•	•	•	•	•	•	•	•	•	•
Little Blue Heron						•	•	•	•			
Cattle Egret	•	•	•	•	•	•	•	•	•	•	•	•
Green Heron	•	•	•	•	•	•	•	•	•	•	•	•
Black-crowned Night-Heron	•	•	•	•	•	•	•	•	•	•	•	•
White-faced Ibis	•	•	•	•	•	•	•	•	•	•	•	•

Species	Jan	Feb	Mar	Apr	May	Jun	Jul	Aug	Sep	Oct	Nov	Dec
Wood Stork									•			
Turkey Vulture	•	•	•	•	•	•	•	•	•	•	•	•
Lesser Flamingo	•											
Chilean Flamingo			•				•					
Flamingo spp.								•		•		
Fulvous Whistling-Duck				•	•	•	•	•				
Greater White-fronted Goose	•								•			
Snow Goose	•	•	•	•	•	•				•	•	•
Ross's Goose	•	•				•					•	•
Canada Goose	•	•	•							•	•	•
Brant	•	•	•	•	•	•	•	•	•			
Mute Swan							•					
Gadwall	•	•	•	•	•	•	•	•	•	•	•	•
Eurasian Wigeon		•									•	
American Wigeon	•	•	•	•	•	•	•	•	•	•	•	•
Mallard	•	•	•	•	•	•	•	•	•	•	•	•
Blue-winged Teal	•	•	•	•	•	•	•	•	•	•	•	•
Cinnamon Teal	•	•	•	•	•	•	•	•	•	•	•	•
Northern Shoveler	•	•	•	•	•	•	•	•	•	•	•	•
Northern Pintail	•	•	•	•	•	•	•	•	•	•	•	•
Green-winged Teal	•	•	•	•	•	•	•	•	•	•	•	•
nvasback	•	•	•	•	•	•				•	•	•

	Jan	Feb	Mar	Apr	May	Jun	Jul	Aug	Sep	Oct	Nov	Dec
Redhead	•	•	•	•	•	•	•	•	•	•	•	•
Ring-necked Duck	•	•								•	•	
Greater Scaup	•										•	
Lesser Scaup	•	•	•	•	•	•	•	•	•	•	•	•
Surf Scoter			•	•	•	•	•	•			•	
Black Scoter				•	•	•	•					
Bufflehead	•	•	•	•	•		•				•	•
Common Goldeneye	•						•			•	•	•
Red-breasted Merganser	•	•	•	•	•	•	•			•	•	•
Ruddy Duck	•	•	•	•	•	•	•	•	•	•	•	•
Osprey	•	•	•	•	•	•		•	•	•	•	•
White-tailed Kite	•											
Bald Eagle	•											•
Northern Harrier	•	•	•	•	•	•	•	•	•	•	•	•
Sharp-shinned Hawk	•	•	•	•						•		•
Cooper's Hawk	•	•	•	•	•	•				•	•	•
Red-shouldered Hawk	•	•	•	•			•			•	•	•
Red-tailed Hawk	•	•	•	•	•	•	•	•	•	•	•	•
American Kestrel	•	•		•	•	•	•	•	•	•	•	•
Merlin	•	•							•	•	•	•
Peregrine Falcon	•	•				•		•	•	•	•	•
Prairie Falcon						•			•		•	

Species	Jan	Feb	Mar	Apr	May	Jun	Jul	Aug	Sep	Oct	Nov	Dec
Ring-necked Pheasant										•		
Gambel's Quail	•	•	•	•	•	•	•	•	•	•	•	•
Black Rail	•		•									
Clapper Rail	•	•	•	•	•	•	•	•	•	•	•	•
Virginia Rail	•	•	•	•		•	•	•	•	•	•	•
Sora	•	•	•	•	•	•	•	•	•	•	•	•
Common Moorhen	•	•	•	•	•	•	•	•	•	•	•	•
American Coot	•	•	•	•	•	•	•	•	•	•	•	•
Black-bellied Plover	•	•	•	•	•	•	•	•	•	•	•	•
American Golden-Plover									•			
Snowy Plover	•	•	•	•	•	•	•	•	•	•	•	•
Semipalmated Plover	•	•	•	•	•	•	•	•	•	•	•	•
Killdeer	•	•	•	•	•	•	•	•	•	•	•	•
Mountain Plover			•								•	•
Black-necked Stilt	•	•	•	•	•	•	•	•	•	•	•	•
American Avocet	•	•	•	•	•	•	•	•	•	•	•	•
Greater Yellowlegs	•	•	•	•	•	•	•	•	•	•	•	•
Lesser Yellowlegs	•	•	•	•	•	•	•	•	•	•	•	•
Willet	•	•	•	•	•		•	•	•	•	•	•
Spotted Sandpiper	•	•	•	•	•	•	•	•	•	•	•	•
Whimbrel		•	•	•	•	•	•	•	•			
Long-billed Curlew	•	•	•	•	•	•	•	•	•	•		•

	Jan	Feb	Mar	Apr	May	Jun	Jul	Aug	Sep	Oct	Nov	Dec
Marbled Godwit	•	•	•	•	•	•	•	•	•	•	•	•
Ruddy Turnstone		•	•	•				•	•	•	•	
Red Knot				•					•			
Sanderling				•	•			•		•		
Western Sandpiper	•	•	•	•	•	•	•	•	•	•	•	•
Least Sandpiper	•	•	•	•			•	•	•	•	•	•
Baird's Sandpiper								•				
Dunlin	•	•	•	•	•	•	•	•	•	•	•	•
Stilt Sandpiper	•	•		•	•	•	•	•	•	•	•	•
Peep (*Calidris* spp.)	•	•	•	•	•	•	•	•	•	•	•	•
Dowitcher spp.	•	•	•	•	•	•	•	•	•	•	•	•
Common Snipe	•	•	•	•						•	•	•
Wilson's Phalarope	•	•		•	•	•	•	•	•	•	•	•
Red-necked Phalarope	•	•		•	•	•	•	•	•	•	•	•
Parasitic Jaeger								•				
Laughing Gull	•			•	•	•	•	•	•	•		
Franklin's Gull				•	•	•		•	•			
Little Gull					•							
Bonaparte's Gull	•	•	•	•	•	•	•	•	•	•	•	•
Heermann's Gull	•	•	•	•	•	•	•	•	•	•	•	•
Ring-billed Gull	•	•	•	•	•	•	•	•	•	•	•	•
California Gull	•	•	•	•	•	•	•	•	•	•	•	•

	Jan	Feb	Mar	Apr	May	Jun	Jul	Aug	Sep	Oct	Nov	Dec
Herring Gull	•	•	•	•	•	•	•	•	•	•	•	•
Thayer's Gull		•		•							•	
Lesser Black-backed Gull	•											
Western Gull	•	•	•	•	•							
Yellow-footed Gull	•	•	•	•	•	•	•	•	•	•	•	•
Glaucous-winged Gull			•	•	•				•			•
Sabine's Gull										•	•	
Gull spp.	•	•	•	•	•	•	•	•	•	•	•	•
Gull-billed Tern		•	•	•	•	•	•	•	•			
Caspian Tern	•	•	•	•	•	•	•	•	•	•	•	•
Common Tern							•	•	•			
Forster's Tern	•	•	•	•	•	•	•	•	•	•	•	•
Least Tern						•						
Black Tern				•	•	•	•	•	•	•		
Black Skimmer				•	•	•	•	•	•	•		
Rock Dove	•	•	•	•	•	•	•	•	•	•	•	•
Spotted Dove			•									
White-winged Dove				•	•	•	•	•	•	•		
Mourning Dove	•	•	•	•	•	•	•	•	•	•	•	
Inca Dove					•				•			
Common Ground-Dove	•	•	•	•	•	•	•	•	•	•	•	•
Greater Roadrunner	•	•	•	•	•	•	•	•	•	•	•	•

	Jan	Feb	Mar	Apr	May	Jun	Jul	Aug	Sep	Oct	Nov	Dec
Barn Owl					•	•	•	•				
Great Horned Owl		•	•	•	•	•	•	•	•	•	•	
Burrowing Owl	•	•	•	•	•	•	•	•	•	•	•	
Lesser Nighthawk	•	•		•	•	•	•	•	•	•	•	
Vaux's Swift				•					•			
White-throated Swift				•	•							
Costa's Hummingbird					•							•
Anna's Hummingbird	•	•		•						•	•	•
Belted Kingfisher	•	•		•				•	•	•	•	•
Red-naped Sapsucker				•								
Ladder-backed Woodpecker	•		•	•	•	•	•	•	•	•	•	•
Northern Flicker	•									•	•	•
Western Wood-Pewee					•	•	•	•	•			
Willow Flycatcher					•	•		•	•			
Pacific-slope Flycatcher					•				•			
Empidonax spp.					•			•				
Black Phoebe	•	•	•	•	•	•	•	•	•	•	•	•
Eastern Phoebe	•										•	•
Say's Phoebe	•	•	•	•	•	•	•	•	•	•	•	•
Vermilion Flycatcher	•			•				•	•	•	•	
Ash-throated Flycatcher			•	•	•	•	•	•	•			
Cassin's Kingbird				•	•	•	•	•				

Species	Jan	Feb	Mar	Apr	May	Jun	Jul	Aug	Sep	Oct	Nov	Dec
Western Kingbird				•	•	•	•	•	•			
Loggerhead Shrike	•	•	•	•	•	•	•	•	•	•	•	•
Plumbeous Vireo				•								
Cassin's Vireo									•			
Warbling Vireo				•	•				•			
American Crow					•							
Common Raven	•	•	•	•	•	•	•	•	•	•	•	•
Horned Lark	•											•
Tree Swallow	•	•	•	•	•	•	•	•	•	•	•	•
Violet-green Swallow	•	•	•	•		•	•				•	
No. Rough-winged Swallow	•	•	•	•	•	•	•	•	•	•	•	
Bank Swallow						•	•					
Cliff Swallow		•	•	•	•	•	•	•	•	•		
Barn Swallow		•	•	•	•	•	•	•	•	•	•	•
Verdin	•	•	•	•	•	•	•	•	•	•	•	•
Bushtit						•						
Cactus Wren	•	•	•	•	•	•	•	•	•	•	•	•
Bewick's Wren	•	•	•	•	•	•	•		•	•	•	•
House Wren	•	•	•	•					•	•	•	•
Marsh Wren	•	•	•	•	•	•	•	•	•	•	•	•
Ruby-crowned Kinglet	•	•	•							•	•	•
Blue-gray Gnatcatcher	•	•	•	•	•	•			•	•	•	•

	Jan	Feb	Mar	Apr	May	Jun	Jul	Aug	Sep	Oct	Nov	Dec
Black-tailed Gnatcatcher	•	•	•	•	•	•	•	•	•	•	•	•
Western Bluebird			•									
Mountain Bluebird				•								
Northern Mockingbird	•	•	•	•	•	•	•	•	•	•	•	•
Sage Thrasher	•	•										
California Thrasher					•							
Crissal Thrasher	•	•	•	•	•	•	•	•	•	•	•	•
European Starling	•	•	•	•	•	•	•	•	•			•
American Pipit	•	•	•	•	•					•	•	
Sprague's Pipit		•										
Cedar Waxwing	•											
Phainopepla	•	•	•	•	•	•		•	•	•	•	•
Orange-crowned Warbler	•	•	•	•	•	•		•	•	•	•	•
Nashville Warbler				•	•				•			
Virginia's Warbler				•								
Lucy's Warbler							•					
Yellow Warbler				•	•			•	•	•	•	
Yellow-rumped Warbler	•	•	•	•	•	•		•	•	•	•	•
Black-throated Gray Warbler				•	•				•			
Townsend's Warbler			•	•	•							
Hermit Warbler					•							
American Redstart									•			

	Jan	Feb	Mar	Apr	May	Jun	Jul	Aug	Sep	Oct	Nov	Dec
MacGillivray's Warbler					•							
Common Yellowthroat	•	•	•	•	•	•	•	•	•	•	•	•
Wilson's Warbler			•	•	•				•		•	
Yellow-breasted Chat				•	•	•	•					
Summer Tanager							•					
Western Tanager			•		•		•		•			
Spotted Towhee			•									•
Abert's Towhee	•	•	•	•	•	•	•	•	•	•	•	•
Chipping Sparrow				•								
Brewer's Sparrow			•						•			
Lark Sparrow	•				•	•				•		
Black-throated Sparrow					•			•				
Sage Sparrow	•					•	•		•	•	•	•
Savannah Sparrow	•	•	•				•	•	•	•	•	•
Savannah Sparrow (Large-billed)			•						•	•	•	•
Song Sparrow	•	•	•	•	•	•	•	•	•	•	•	•
Lincoln's Sparrow	•	•	•	•	•				•	•	•	•
White-crowned Sparrow	•	•	•	•	•				•	•	•	•
Golden-crowned Sparrow										•	•	
Dark-eyed Junco	•	•								•		•
Black-headed Grosbeak				•				•				
Blue Grosbeak				•	•	•	•					

	Jan	Feb	Mar	Apr	May	Jun	Jul	Aug	Sep	Oct	Nov	Dec
Lazuli Bunting					•							
Red-winged Blackbird	•	•	•	•	•	•	•	•	•	•	•	•
Tricolored Blackbird			•									
Western Meadowlark	•	•	•	•	•	•	•	•	•	•	•	•
Yellow-headed Blackbird		•	•	•	•	•	•	•	•	•		
Brewer's Blackbird	•	•	•	•	•	•	•	•	•	•	•	•
Great-tailed Grackle	•	•	•	•	•	•	•	•	•	•	•	•
Brown-headed Cowbird			•	•	•	•	•	•	•	•		
Hooded Oriole			•	•	•	•	•	•				
Bullock's Oriole				•	•	•						
Scott's Oriole	•											
House Finch	•	•	•	•	•	•	•	•	•	•	•	•
Lesser Goldfinch	•	•	•	•	•	•	•	•	•	•	•	
Lawrence's Goldfinch	•											
American Goldfinch						•						
House Sparrow	•	•	•	•	•	•	•	•	•	•	•	•

Key
• = present

116

NOCTURNAL ROOSTING

Nocturnal roosting of colonial waterbirds in the Imperial Valley was a nightly occurrence during the count period, and was one of the most spectacular birding experiences we were privileged to enjoy there. Roosting species were American White Pelican, Double-crested Cormorant, Cattle Egret, White-faced Ibis, Snow Goose, Sandhill Crane and Gull spp. Small aggregations of Great and Snowy Egret were also observed, particularly at Fig Lagoon and Sunbeam Lake. White-faced Ibis and Cattle Egret dominated the scene; both species were present in the valley in the thousands throughout the year and returned to their preferred roosts nightly after foraging all day. Other species such as Sandhill Crane and Snow Goose were present only in winter and the cranes, in particular, tended to move around among roosting sites.

Roosting requirements differed as to species. American White Pelicans roosted on the sea or in ponds and on sand bars close to shore, they were not seen inland. Snow Geese usually roosted on dry land but close to the sea. Egrets and White-faced Ibis generally perched in trees and snags over water while Sandhill Cranes stood in shallow wetlands. Cattle Egrets, White-faced Ibis and Sandhill Cranes found roost sites in the valley miles from the sea. Many sites in the Imperial Valley have been used as roosts (see map on page 118) and there are long-used sites that have been abandoned

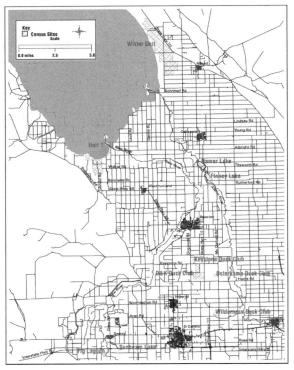

Night roosts used in 1998, 1999

for unknown reasons (see Finney Lake below). Directions for finding the sites are included below.

Counts

In 1998 we did monthly counts at Ramer and Finney Lakes, Fig Lagoon and Sunbeam Lake, all of which had permanent water and were reputed to be in regular use. The duck Clubs (D & K, Osterkamp, Wilderness and "Keystone") had water in their ponds only during the hunting season; as the ponds dried the birds relocated. The other sites listed below (Unit 1, Wister) were visited infrequently.

Ramer Lake provided a dramatic experience at every visit. We were in place about one-half hour before sunset to watch the birds as they arrived, coming in continuous waves across the sky. We usually spent the night, and found that the birds were settled by dusk and all was quiet until daylight, even though thousands of birds were present a few yards from our campsite. Soon after daylight they would begin to leave for foraging sites in the valley, again in waves. Results of the counts at Ramer Lake are shown in the table below. Two species were dominant, Cattle Egret and White-faced Ibis; both were present every month. Cattle Egret numbers peaked in September and October, augmented by large numbers of juveniles after the breeding season. White-faced Ibis numbers were substantial (more than 1,500) July through March, but dropped

Nocturnal roosting data - Ramer Lake 1998

	Jan	Feb	Mar	Apr	May	Jun	Jul	Aug	Sep	Oct	Nov	Dec
Double-crested Cormorant	5	0	0	604	23	322	199	347	2000	561	420	50
Great Egret	59	19	22	50	50	0	0	0	0	0	0	
Cattle Egret	1800	1400	1100	5000	5000	2700	9550	14850	17150	16900	4200	2050
Black-crowned Night Heron	62	29	0	6	7	0	0	0	0	0	0	0
White-faced Ibis	3400	1550	4100	1900	111	132	2450	5250	3200	8250	3800	3250
Red-winged Blackbird	0	0	0	0	0	0	4075	1312	670	875	500	0

to fewer than 150 in May and June when breeding was underway elsewhere.

To get an estimate of the number of individuals going to roost in the valley, we organized a simultaneous roost count on 27 January 1999 at 9 sites (see table on next page). Ten species were tabulated; White-faced Ibis far outnumbered all others with a total of approximately 16,800.

In 1999 roost counts were done January through March and August through December by PRBO personnel at 7 sites: Ramer Lake, Osterkamp Duck Club and Unit 1 regularly; Finney Lake when it was active; and D & K, "Keystone" and Wilderness Duck Clubs when they

Simultaneous count of night roosts in Imperial Valley 1/27/99

Participants: Ken Corey, Paul Jorgenson, Doug Julian, John Konecny, Barbara Massey, Bob Miller, Kathy Molina, Dave Shuford, the Wagoner brothers, Dick Zembal

	White-faced Ibis	Cattle Egret	Double-crested Cormorant	Sandhill Crane	White Pelican	Snow Goose	Great Blue Heron	Black-crowned Night-Heron	Great Egret	Snow Egret
Ramer Lake	1150	3000	40	0	0	0	0	40	0	0
Finney Lake	0	0	0	0	0	0	0	0	0	0
Osterkamp*	1990	0	0	7	0	0	0	0	0	0
D&K 0	0	0	0	0	0	0	0	0	0	
Keystone	8390	227	0	248	0	0	0	0	0	0
Wilderness	4630	0	0	0	0	0	0	0	0	0
Unit 1**	680	6000	0	0	850	8800	0	0	0	0
New River Delta***	0	0	250	0	1370	0	117	85	10	18
Fig Lagoon	0	195	12	0	0	0	0	0	2	0
Sunset Lake	0	450	21	0	0	0	0	0	6	0
TOTAL	16840	9872	323	255	2220	8800	117	125	18	18

*   Osterkamp, D&K, Keystone and Wilderness are duck clubs. For locations see page 118
**   Unit 1 of Salton Sea National Wildlife Refuge
*** eastside embankment

had water. Only Cattle Egret and White-faced Ibis numbers were tallied, both species approached 40,000 in the autumn (Shuford *et. al.* 2000).

Roosts

D & K Duck Club

This site is located between Dogwood Road and State Highway 111, and between Harris and Keystone Roads just north of Harris. During the counts, viewing was good from the verge on the north side of Harris Road about half way between Dogwood and Highway 111. The duck club consisted of a series of diked ponds that were created for hunters. There was open water, marsh vegetation and some upland shrubbery around the dikes. It was well used in January and February 1998 by White-faced Ibis, and in November and December by Cattle Egret and White-faced Ibis. In the other months it was inactive.

Fig Lagoon

Located southwest of El Centro between Derrick and Drew Roads, Fig Lagoon is just south of Interstate 8. For directions see chapter on Fig Lagoon. There were reeds and cane at the water's edge and trees and shrubs in the upland area. Viewing was good from the dike around the lagoon. This roost was minor in terms of numbers of birds, but was used regularly by Cattle Egret in 1998 (49 -770 per count) and intermittently by White-faced Ibis (2 - 129 per count).

Finney Lake

This site is located between Albright and Rutherford Roads just east of Kershaw Road. For directions see chapter on Finney Lake. The large pond at the north end of the lake was the site of the roost. Emergent snags similar to those at Ramer Lake provided perches for the birds. Viewing was very good from the dike on the west side of the pond.

Formerly a major roost for White-faced Ibis, Finney Lake was used only occasionally during the count period. In 1998 birds could be seen flying over Finney Lake to Ramer Lake. However, in September and October several thousand ibis and a few hundred Cattle Egret arrived and stayed, although far more were counted the same evening at Ramer Lake.

"Keystone" Duck Club

This site is located between Dogwood Road and State Highway 111 on the north side of Keystone Road. Turn off State Highway 111 at Keystone and drive west approximately 1 mile. The shallow water ponds on the north side of the road served as a roost site and were well viewed from Keystone Road. They were flooded only January - March and in those months Sandhill Crane (approximately 200) and many gulls of undetermined species used this roost.

Osterkamp Duck Club

Located just north of Harris Road on the west side of McConnell Road, this site was best viewed from the edge of McConnell Road. The ponds were dry except in winter and not regularly used as a roost. But on a count in December 1998, 2250 White-faced Ibis and 300 Sandhill Crane were present.

Ramer Lake

This site is located between Albright and Rutherford Roads just west of Kershaw Road. For directions see chapter on Ramer Lake. The roost site was in the south pond where emergent snags formed a thick tangle and provided perches for thousands of birds. The dike that separates the two ponds provided good viewing. Use of Ramer Lake as a roost is described above (see "Counts"). The site was also used for nesting in 1998 (see Nesting).

Sunbeam Lake

Located southwest of El Centro just east of Drew Road, Sunbeam Lake is between Ross Road and Interstate 8. Take the Drew Road exit off

Interstate 8 and go north about 0.5 mile. This tamarisk-edged lake was used by Cattle Egrets in winter; 2,200 were seen there in February. A small number of Double-crested Cormorant, Great Egret, and Snowy Egret came to roost intermittently.

Unit 1

This site is located along the south shore of the sea at the north end of Vendel Road. For directions see chapter on Unit 1. A viewing platform adjacent to the parking lot offered excellent oversight of the area, which included ponds with marsh vegetation, large agricultural fields, and in the distance the New River Delta, lined with large tamarisk.

Unit 1 was not monitored regularly but on a few occasions in winter when it was visited there were hundreds of American White Pelican on the edge of the sea, White-faced Ibis in the tamarisk, and thousands of Snow Geese in the agricultural fields.

Wister Unit

This site is located on the southeastern shore of the sea on the west side of State Highway 111. For directions see chapter on Wister Unit. The northernmost ponds were a favored roost for Snow Geese.

Wilderness Duck Club

This site is located east of State Highway 111 between Worthington and Aten Roads. Viewing was good from the dirt road on the south side. The site had shrubs and ponds but no tall trees. In 1998 it was a major roosting site for Cattle Egret, White-faced Ibis, and Gull spp. from January - March, but was deserted for the rest of the year.

NESTING

Documentation of breeding was sporadic except for colonially nesting waterbirds. Resident species in habitat where breeding could be expected were all too easily overlooked during counts, as they were both secretive and quiet. Thus, our records are conservative; and many more species nested at some of the sites than were found.

During the count period breeding was documented for 50 species; for 17 additional species nesting was presumed but not confirmed (see table on next page). For information on where breeding occurred, refer to the individual species in Species Accounts.

Information for 1998 is from our counts. For 1999, information from the counts was supplemented by data on colonial waterbirds from the PRBO report on Salton Sea birds for that year (Shuford *et. al.* 2000). The report did not cover breeding by upland birds.

Generally speaking, the breeding scene at the Salton Sea was dominated by colonially nesting waterbirds and water-associated birds like Marsh Wren, Common Yellowthroat and Red-winged Blackbird. In addition there were a few uncommon breeders like Fulvous Whistling-Duck, Lesser Nighthawk and Crissal Thrasher.

BREEDING STATUS (1998-1999)

Refer to Species Accounts for information on where breeding occurred

Breeding confirmed		Breeding probable
Pied-billed Grebe	California Gull	Least Bittern
Western Grebe	Gull-billed Tern	Mallard
Clark's Grebe	Caspian Tern	American Kestrel
Double-crested Cormorant	Black Skimmer	Yuma Clapper Rail
Great Blue Heron	Burrowing Owl	Sora
Great Egret	Lesser Nighthawk	White-winged Dove
Snowy Egret	Black Phoebe	Mourning Dove
Cattle Egret	Western Kingbird	Common Ground-Dove
Green Heron	Loggerhead Shrike	Greater Roadrunner
Black-crowned Night-Heron	Cliff Swallow	Bewick's Wren
Fulvous Whistling-Duck	Verdin	Say's Phoebe
Gadwall	Cactus Wren	Ash-throated Flycatcher
Cinnamon Teal	Marsh Wren	Crissal Thrasher
Redhead	Black-tailed Gnatcatcher	Yellow-breasted Chat
Bufflehead	Northern Mockingbird	Abert's Towhee
Ruddy Duck	European Starling	Blue Grosbeak
Ring-necked Pheasant	Common Yellowthroat	Western Meadowlark
Gambel's Quail	Song Sparrow	
Common Moorhen	Red-winged Blackbird	
American Coot	Yellow-headed Blackbird	
Snowy Plover	Great-tailed Grackle	
Killdeer	Brown-headed Cowbird	
Black-necked Stilt	Bullock's Oriole	
American Avocet	House Finch	
Laughing Gull	House Sparrow	

Waterbirds

The most impressive breeding sights at the Salton Sea were the large rookeries of colonial waterbirds. The term 'waterbirds" includes the following families: Pelicanidae (pelicans) Phalacrocoracidae (cormorants), Ardeidae (herons, bitterns, egrets, night-herons) and Laridae (gulls, terns, skimmers).] Rookeries were sited all around the sea, but concentrated along the southeastern shore; locations are shown on the map below.

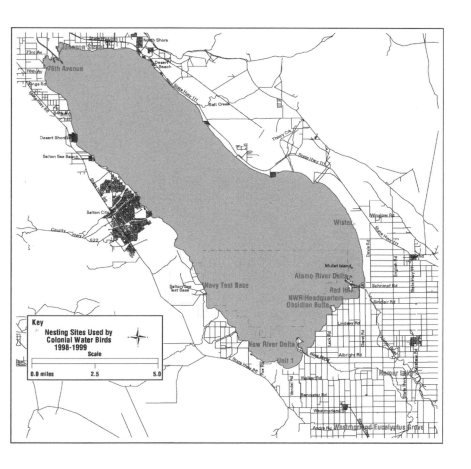

Most nesting sites had multiple species, depending on the diversity of habitat available. Alamo River Delta, for example, had sizeable numbers of Double-crested Cormorant, Great Blue Heron, Great Egret, Snowy Egret and Cattle Egret.

The following species bred colonially in 1998-1999:

Double-crested Cormorant - nested primarily on Mullet Island, a barren outcrop in the sea off the Alamo River Delta, where 5,425 nests were counted in 1999 (Shuford *et. al.* 2000).

Great Blue Heron - sites with more than 100 pairs were located at Johnson St, Alamo River Delta, New River Delta and 76 Ave.

Great and Snowy Egret - nested in smaller numbers at widely scattered locales; colonies with more than 25 nests were at Johnson St, Alamo River Delta, 76th Ave, and Ramer Lake.

Cattle Egret - Ramer Lake hosted the largest colony in 1998 with approximately 10,000 nests; in 1999 the birds abandoned this site early in the season and nested at Westmorland Eucalyptus Grove. The 2nd largest colony was at Alamo River Delta.

Black-crowned Night-Heron - nested only at Johnson St, 76th Ave, and Westmorland Eucalyptus Grove, with the largest group (77 nests) at Johnson St.

Gull-billed Tern - nested at NWRHq and Johnson St.

Caspian Tern - nested only at National Wildlife Refuge HQ (Rock Hill)

Black Skimmer - nested at Johnson St and nearby Colfax Ave on the north shore and NWRHq; in 1999 both north shore locations were abandoned before any chicks were fledged.

The following were the major sites used by colonial waterbirds in 1998-1999:

Ramer Lake, Johnson St, an island off Colfax St, Wister Unit, Mullet Island, Alamo River Delta, Red Hill, NWRHq, Obsidian Butte, New River Delta, NWR Unit 1, Naval Test Base, 76th Ave, and Westmorland Eucalyptus Grove. Locations are shown on the map. Most of these sites can be observed, and directions for finding them are in the chapter texts or in the section on Additional Sites (Naval Test Base, Westmorland Eucalyptus Grove). Two islands were used as nest sites, both are off-limits to all except USFWS personnel: a partially submerged man-made island off Colfax St. served as a nest site for Black Skimmer, and Mullet Island has annually hosted thousands of Double-crested Cormorant nests.

Ducks

Ducks nested individually in ponds at many sites. Fulvous Whistling-Duck, Gadwall, Mallard, Cinnamon Teal, Redhead and Ruddy Duck were documented as nesters. A Bufflehead family was observed at the north end during the count period. For detailed information see Species Accounts.

Others

Large Cliff Swallow nesting colonies were found at Finney and Ramer Lakes. Red-winged and Yellow-headed Blackbirds formed large mixed colonies in the cattail stands at Finney and Ramer Lakes, NWRHq and other sites.

Marsh Wren and Common Yellowthroat were numerous at both Finney and Ramer Lakes, nesting densely but individually; Marsh Wrens nested in the reed beds and cattails, Common Yellowthroats in the scrub vegetation around the lake edges.

Migrants that arrived in spring and bred around the Salton Sea were White-winged Dove, Lesser Nighthawk, Western Kingbird, Ash-throated Flycatcher, Yellow-breasted Chat, Blue Grosbeak, and Bullock's Oriole. These species were present in small numbers; the paucity of appropriate habitat was a limiting factor for most upland birds.

Species Accounts

The species seen during the counts are listed according to the American Ornithologists' Union Check-list of North American Birds, 1998. The information is organized as follows:

1. The common and scientific names are given on the first line of each entry.

2. The status of the species at the Salton Sea is given on the second line. Terms used for status are:

Resident: birds that are present all year whose nesting has been documented. Species that have a migratory component to their population are designated as both resident and migrant.

Migrant: birds that are en route to breeding or wintering grounds in spring or fall or both. For some migrants the sea is the end point of migration and part of the population stays for a season (usually winter or summer). These species are designated as both migrant and visitor.

Visitor: birds of seasonal occurrence, for example those that winter at the sea, come in summer to breed, or visit occasionally to rarely but are not out of range. Species that are present year-round but do not breed are also considered visitors.

Modifiers give the frequency of occurrence. The terms used are:

Common: Occurring in large numbers and/or being widespread in the region; seen more than 50 times at various sites during the count period.

Fairly common: Occurring in middle-range numbers; seen 26 - 50 times during the count period.

Uncommon: Occurring usually in small numbers in proper season and habitat; seen 11 - 25 times during the count period.

Rare: Occurring irregularly even in proper habitat; seen 1 - 10 times during the count period.

Accidental: Occurring outside their normal range or rarely seen vagrants. Most were seen only 1 time.

3. Counts For species seen at any of the sites on any of the counts during the census period from January 1998 through January 2000, a brief account of its appearance is given with the following information: the range in number of individuals on the counts followed in parentheses by the month in which the smallest and largest number occurred, the species' occurrence during the year, the sites at which it was seen, and the sites where it occurred most frequently or in greatest concentrations.

4. Comments Breeding status, range, history of occurrence at the sea and other pertinent information is given, if available.

Key to abbreviations:

Alamo	Alamo River Delta
The Avenues	76, 79, 81, 84 Avenues
NWRHq	Sonny Bono National Wildlife Refuge Headquarters, Rock Hill
Obsidian Butte	Kornbloom Road to Sonny Bono NWR
Red Hill	Red Hill County Park and ponds of the Hazard Unit of Sonny Bono NWR adjacent to Garst
SSSRA	3 sites in the Salton Sea State Recreation Area: Desert Beach, State Park Headquarters, and Salt Creek

Unit 1	Unit 1 of Sonny Bono NWR plus Poe Road
West Side	3 sites on the west shore: Salton City, Salton Sea Beach, Desert Shores
Whitewater	Whitewater River Delta
Wister Unit	Wister Unit of the State Imperial Wildlife Area

Common Loon *Gavia immer*
Status: Accidental visitor
Counts: Single bird seen once; in March 1998 at Fig Lagoon.
Comments: The first ornithologist to visit the Salton Sea saw a dozen Common Loons in full breeding plumage in April 1908 (Grinnell 1908). Now the species is a rare winter visitor (Shuford *et. al.* 1999).

Pied-billed Grebe *Podilymbus podiceps*
Status: Common resident
Counts: 17 (May) - 83 (November). Present on all counts and at all sites except Bombay Beach. Most numerous at Unit 1, Finney Lake, Ramer Lake, and Wister Unit.
Comments: Nesting was documented at Finney Lake, Obsidian Butte, Ramer Lake and Whitewater.

Horned Grebe *Podiceps auritus*
Status: Rare visitor
Counts: 1 - 2 birds seen 3 times; in February and September at Obsidian Butte and in April at Unit 1.
Comments: Unlike its close relative the Eared Grebe, this species is rare at the sea.

Eared Grebe *Podiceps nigricollis*
Status: Common year-round visitor
Counts: 43 (August) - 39,150 (December). Present on all counts and at all sites, with huge numbers in winter when thousands rafted on the sea; a small, non-breeding population remained through the summer. Large assemblages off Unit 1, Salt Creek, and Desert Beach (SSSRA), among

others. Numbers mu¡ch reduced May - September, when most left to nest elsewhere. Smallest numbers at the brackish lakes such as Fig Lagoon, Finney Lake, Ramer Lake.

Comments: The Salton Sea and the Gulf of California are major wintering areas for this species; the sea is also a major stopover during migration (Jehl 1988). In 1988, two winter counts estimated the population as 1 - 1.75 million in January and 3.5 million in March (Jehl 1988). Recent counts show a decline in numbers; the latest estimate was 321,575 in December 1999 (Shuford *et. al.* 2000). Major die-offs from unknown causes occurred at the sea in 1992 and 1994; an estimated 150,000 grebes died in 1992 (Shuford *et. al.* 1999). Nesting has occurred infrequently.

Western Grebe *Aechmophorus occidentalis*
Status: Common resident
Counts: 27 (August) - 171 (April). Present on all counts and all sites except Bombay Beach; most numerous at Finney Lake, SSSRA, and Alamo.
Comments: Breeding documented at Finney and Ramer Lakes with juveniles seen in June and July. Both Western and Clark's Grebes were seen at most sites, but the ratio was approximately 10 to 1. Mixed-species courtship was observed at Ramer Lake, where it was possible to see the birds at close range. Intermediate birds (presumably hybrids) are present in most populations that have been studied; although mixed-species pairs reportedly make up less than 5% of the population (Storer and Neuchterlein 1992).

Clark's Grebe *Aechmophorus clarkii*
Status: Common resident
Counts: 1 (December) - 38 (June). Seen in all months and at most sites (not Bombay Beach, NWRHq, or Unit 1); seen most easily at Finney and Ramer Lakes where they could be observed close-up, and at Alamo and Whitewater.
Comments: Breeding documented at Finney and Ramer Lakes with juveniles seen in June and July. See comments under Western Grebe.

American White Pelican *Pelecanus erythrorhynchos*
Status: Common year-round visitor, migrant
Counts: 713 (August) - 8,500 (January). Present on all counts and at all sites except Finney Lake. Very large flocks in fall and winter, especially off Alamo, Unit 1 and Wister Unit; numbers lowest in July and August.
Comments: Soon after the sea was formed White Pelicans nested on an island at the south end. Joseph Grinnell found 980 active nests and more under construction in the spring of 1908 (Grinnell 1908). In recent years the birds have not bred, but the sea continues to be of major importance both as a stopover during migration and as a major wintering ground. A count in March 1998 estimated 26,500 birds (McCaskie 1998) and 24,974 were counted in December 1999 (Shuford *et. al.* 2000).

Brown Pelican *Pelecanus occidentalis*
Status: Common resident, migrant
Counts: 16 (May) - 1,360 (September). Present on all counts and at all sites except Johnson Street. Largest numbers February - October. Most numerous at Alamo and Obsidian Butte.
Comments: This species was first documented as a breeding bird in 1996 (McCaskie 1996) and has since nested sporadically at Obsidian Butte. No successful nesting occurred during the count period. The population is concentrated at south end of sea.

Double-crested Cormorant *Phalacrocorax auritus*
Status: Common resident, migrant
Counts: 1,800 (April) - 12,260 (November). Present on all counts and at all sites. Large flocks in winter at the Avenues, Whitewater and Johnson Street at the north end, and Alamo at the south end. Numbers greatest in November and December.
Comments: The population is generally larger in winter, but many remain and breed during the spring and summer. In 1999 approximately 5,400 pairs nested around the sea. The largest nesting colony was on Mullet Island off the southeast shore; other small, scattered colonies were at Johnson Street, Alamo, Unit 1, Ramer Lake, and Wister Unit (Shuford *et. al.* 2000). Die-offs have occurred in recent years: in 1997, 1600 birds, mostly nestlings, succumbed to Newcastle's Disease; in 1998 a large-scale failure of nesting on Mullet Island was also attributed to Newcastle's Disease (Shuford *et. al.* 1999).

Magnificent Frigatebird *Fregata magnificens*
Status: Accidental Visitor
   Counts: Single bird seen 2 times high overhead in June 1998 at the Avenues and in July 1998 at Finney Lake.

American Bittern *Botaurus lentiginosus*
Status: Uncommon visitor
Counts: 1 - 3 in most months (not August or November), but 8 in February; in freshwater marshes at Fig Lagoon, NWRHq and Whitewater, but most often at Wister Unit.
Comments: A secretive marsh bird that is probably undercounted; it is considered a wintering species in southern California but very possibly breeds at Wister Unit.

Least Bittern *Ixobrychus exilis*
Status: Fairly common visitor, probable breeder
Counts: 1 - 5 per count. Present in all seasons, but mostly in summer; not seen December - April. One to two at a time at Johnson Street, Whitewater, Wister Unit; 4 to 5 at a time in June and July at Finney and Ramer Lakes.
Comments: This species winters mainly in Mexico (particularly in Baja California) and moves north to breed; breeding and winter ranges over-lap at the Salton Sea. Because of its secretive nature it can be difficult to see, but there were 29 sightings during the counts, making it a fairly common visitor and reasonably easy to find.

Great Blue Heron *Ardea herodias*
Status: Common resident
Counts: 195 (March) - 640 (June). Present on all counts and all sites; numbers doubled June - October. Largest numbers at the Avenues, Johnson Street, Alamo, Unit 1, all of which were major nesting sites.
Comments: This species resides all around the sea. Nesting was docu-mented at the Avenues, Alamo, Johnson Street, Mullet Island, New River Delta, Unit 1, West Side, Whitewater and Wister Unit (Shuford *et. al.* 2000). A few pairs also nested at Bombay Beach, Red Hill, and SSSRA.

Great Egret *Ardea alba*
Status: Common resident
Counts: 90 (January) - 577 (September). Seen on all counts and at all sites; most regularly and in largest numbers at the Avenues, Alamo, Unit 1 and West Side.
Comments: Nested at Alamo, the Avenues, Johnson Street, Ramer Lake, Whitewater, Wister Unit (Shuford *et. al.* 2000).

Snowy Egret *Egretta thula*
Status: Common resident
Counts: 28 (January) - 833 (July). Seen on all counts and at all sites; largest numbers June - September at Alamo, Wister Unit.
Comments: The major concentration of the population was at Alamo, with lesser numbers at Wister Unit and the Avenues. Nesting was documented at the Avenues, Alamo, Johnson Street, Ramer Lake and Wister Unit.

Little Blue Heron *Egretta caerulea*
Status: Accidental visitor
Counts: Single birds seen 2 times in November 1998 and December 1998 at Wister Unit.
Comments: This heron resides in Mexico and farther south, but has been seen throughout the United States as a rare transient.

Cattle Egret *Bubulcus ibis*
Status: Common resident
Counts: 77 (November) - 17,300 (September). Seen on all counts and at all sites except Bombay Beach.
Comments: This species first nested at the Salton Sea in 1970 (Garrett and Dunn 1981). Its numbers have increased hugely and today's nesting and roosting colonies number in the thousands. The birds forage in the agricultural fields throughout the Imperial Valley during the day and roost communally at night, with the major night roost at Ramer Lake (see "Nocturnal Roosting"). A very large nesting colony at Ramer Lake in summer 1998 had an estimated 10,000 pairs; and about 40 pairs nested at the north end off Johnson Street. In 1999 the birds deserted

Ramer Lake and the major colonies were at Alamo and a new site - a eucalyptus grove south of the town of Westmorland (see "Additional Sites").

Green Heron *Butorides virescens*
Status: Common resident
Counts: 8 (January) - 56 (July). Seen on all counts and at all sites except Bombay Beach.
Comments: Although it occurs in small numbers, this species is seen regularly all around the sea. Nesting was documented at NWRHq, Finney Lake, SSSRA and presumed at Ramer Lake, Wister Unit and other sites; largest numbers were found from May - August .

Black-crowned Night-Heron *Nycticorax nycticorax*
Status: Common resident
Counts: 39 (January) - 336 (June). Seen on all counts and at all sites except Red Hill; most frequent and numerous at Johnson Street, Whitewater, and Unit 1.
Comments: Night-Herons were a constant presence around the sea; numbers were highest April - July. In 1999 the major nesting colonies were at the Avenues and Johnson Street with most nests (77) at Johnson Street (Shuford *et. al.* 2000). Nesting was also documented at SSSRA.

White-faced Ibis *Plegadis chihi*
Status: Common resident, migrant
Counts: 45 (March) - 8,450 (October). Seen on all counts and at most sites (not Bombay Beach or West Side). Largest numbers at Ramer Lake where they roosted at night and were still present in the early morning when the counts took place.
Comments: This species has been wintering in the Imperial Valley since the early 1940s (Shuford *et. al.* 1996). In 1998 - 1999 the birds were present all year but in reduced numbers in June and July when many left to nest. They roosted communally at night at Ramer Lake and other sites (see "Nocturnal Roosting") and foraged widely in flooded agricultural fields and shallow ponds during the day. After a steep decline in numbers in the 1970s, the California wintering population increased dramatically in the 1980s and 1990s. The Imperial Valley has become a major win-

tering area for this species; a statewide survey in 1994 - 1995 tallied approximately 16,000 ibis in the valley, about 57% of the total population (Shuford *et. al.* 1996).Winter and breeding ranges overlap at the Salton Sea. Breeding was once a regular occurrence; in 1992 and 1993 approximately320 pairs nested at Finney Lake (K. Sturm in Earnst *et. al.* 1998). In recent years it has become a rare event; in 1999 a few pairs nested at Ramer Lake. Banding data indicate that many wintering ibis return to western Nevada to breed (E. Kelchin in Shuford *et. al.* 1996).

Wood Stork *Mycteria americana*
Status: Rare summer visitor
Counts: 1 - 17 seen on 5 counts June - September at Alamo and Wister Unit.
Comments: This species breeds in Mexico and Florida and wanders widely in the United States post-season. The south end of the sea is the only post-breeding site in California where it is a regular visitor. Through the 1970s it was common during the summer months. In September 1964 an estimated 1000 birds were seen, and a July 1977 count tallied 650 birds (Garrett and Dunn 1981). A dramatic, but undocumented decline has since occurred. On our counts Wood Storks were seen only 11 times in two summers, and at only two sites. There were 17 birds on the August 1998 count, and 19 in July 1999. A one-day summer count is long overdue.

Turkey Vulture *Cathartes aura*
Status: Common year-round visitor
Counts: 1 (January) - 46 (July). Seen overhead at all sites, in all seasons; larger numbers July and September during migration.
Comments: With so many dead fish constantly available along the shoreline, it was surprising that vultures were not more abundant.

Fulvous Whistling-Duck *Dendrocygna bicolor*
Status: Rare summer (breeding) visitor
Counts: 1 - 8 adults seen April - July at Finney and Ramer Lakes (and once overhead at Johnson Street and Whitewater).
Comments: This species has been present at the sea since at least 1927 (Pemberton 1927), and was reported as a fairly common but declining

summer resident at the south end of the Salton Sea through the 1970s (Garrett and Dunn 1981). It is now rare, although still regular. In 1998 - 1999, individuals or small groups were seen on 10 counts May - September. Breeding was documented only at Finney Lake where a brood of 10 chicks was seen with parents in July 1999. Nesting probably occurred also at Ramer Lake, but was not documented. This duck is resident in south Florida and is a summer breeding bird along the Texas coast; in Mexico it is resident along both coasts. The small migratory population at the Salton Sea seems most likely to have come north from Mexico.

Greater White-fronted Goose *Anser albifrons*
Status: Accidental visitor
Counts: 1 sighting of 27 birds in January 2000 at Ramer Lake

Snow Goose *Chen caerulescens*
Status: Common winter visitor
Counts: 2 (June) - 14,100 (November). Present on many counts and at most sites (not Bombay Beach, Fig Lagoon, Finney Lake, West Side); in greatest numbers November - January at NWRHq, Wister Unit (northern section) and Unit 1.
Comments: Thousands wintered at the south end of the sea, feeding in the agricultural fields and roosting at night, mostly at Unit 1 and Wister Unit; infrequent at the north end.

Ross's Goose *Chen rossii*
Status: Common winter visitor
Counts: 1 (June) - 346 (November). Present and identifiable at Alamo, NWRHq, Unit 1, and Wister Unit. Greatest numbers November - January at Wister Unit (northern part), NWRHq, Unit 1.
Comments: In the midst of flocks of Snow Geese, the smaller Ross's Goose could sometimes be detected. It was difficult to determine numbers in a flock of thousands, so they were probably underestimated.

Canada Goose *Branta canadensis*
Status: Fall and winter visitor
Counts: 1 (October) - 486 (December). Seen infrequently on counts

October - February; seen at the Avenues, Alamo, Finney Lake, Johnson Street, NRWHQ, Ramer Lake, SSSRA, and Unit 1.

Comments: This species was common in the agricultural fields of the Imperial Valley in winter, but was an uncommon visitor at the count sites.

Brant *Branta bernicla*
Status: Fairly common migrant
Counts: 1 - 109 (May). Seen January - September, but largest numbers May - July. Mostly at Whitewater and Wister Unit, but also at Alamo, Bombay Beach, Johnson Street, Obsidian Butte, West Side and the Avenues.
Comments: This migrant winters principally in the lagoons of Baja California and migrates along the coast. Although May is late for water-fowl to be heading north, that is when most Brant were seen at the Salton Sea.

Gadwall *Anas strepera*
Status: Common resident
Counts: 11 (May) - 1,080 (August). Present on all counts and at most sites (not Fig Lagoon, SSSRA, West Side); largest numbers and most frequent sightings at Wister Unit.
Comments: Nesting documented at Johnson Street and Wister Unit .

Eurasian Wigeon *Anas penelope*
Status: Accidental visitor
Counts: Single bird seen once in November 1998 at Wister Unit.
Comments: This species is a rare but regular out-of-range winter visitor on the west coast and at the Salton Sea.

American Wigeon *Anas americana*
Status: Common year-round visitor
Counts: 3 (May) - 3400 (December, January). Present on all counts and at most sites (not Bombay Beach, Fig Lagoon, Red Hill, West Side); very few May - July; largest flocks in December and January at the south end of the sea at NWRHq and Unit 1.
Comments: Although a few individuals remain at the Salton Sea in summer, there is no record of nesting.

Mallard *Anas platyrhynchos*
Status: Common resident
Counts: 16 (April) - 166 (December). On all counts and at all sites except West Side. A few flocks of about 100 seen, but most sightings were of fewer than 5 birds.
Comments: Mallards breed throughout the Imperial Valley, but mostly in irrigation ditches and small bodies of water not included in the counts.

Blue-winged Teal *Anas discors*
Status: Uncommon visitor
Counts: 2 (October) - 18 (May). Usually 1 - 2 pairs. Seen in all seasons; at Alamo, Finney Lake, Johnson Street, Obsidian Butte, Ramer Lake, Red Hill, SSSRA, Whitewater, and Wister Unit.
Comments: This species was seen more frequently than expected; it has reportedly been a rare migrant at the sea (Shuford *et. al.* 2000).

Cinnamon Teal *Anas cyanoptera*
Status: Common resident, migrant
Counts: 12 (November) - 1,270 (August). On all counts and at all sites except West Side. Most frequently seen and in largest numbers at Fig Lagoon, Finney Lake, Johnson Street, NWRHq, Ramer Lake, and Wister Unit. Small numbers in summer.
Comments: Most of the population breeds elsewhere but a small population remains through the summer; nesting was documented at Finney Lake, Wister Unit, and Obsidian Butte.

Northern Shoveler *Anas clypeata*
Status: Common year-round visitor
Counts: 7 (June) - 14,000 (February). Present on all counts and at all sites; abundant except May-July when there were very few; largest numbers in January, February, and September at Wister Unit, followed by NWRHq, Alamo, and Unit 1.
Comments: One of the most numerous and widespread waterfowl at the sea for most of the year, this species virtually disappeared during the breeding season.

Northern Pintail *Anas acuta*
Status: Common year-round visitor
Counts: 5 (June) - 2,250 (November). Present in all months and at all sites except Fig Lagoon. Few seen April - September; largest numbers at Wister Unit, Unit 1, NWRHq.
Comments: This species was common in winter, but very small numbers stayed during the breeding season April - July.

Green-winged Teal *Anas crecca*
Status: Common year-round visitor
Counts: 4 (May) - 3,000 (January). Seen on all counts and at all sites; most numerous and frequent at Alamo, Unit 1, AND Wister Unit.
Comments: This species was common except in June and July when numbers were much reduced.

Canvasback *Aythya valisineria*
Status: Uncommon visitor
Counts: 1 (June) - 120 (February) but usually fewer than 40. A few seen in all months except July and October; mostly at Johnson Street and Unit 1, a few also at Alamo, NWRHQ, Red Hill and Wister Unit.
Comments: Highest numbers were present in February and November.

Redhead *Aythya americana*
Status: Common resident, migrant
Counts: 9 (November) - 401 (January). Present in every month but small numbers August - November. Seen at all sites, most frequently at Johnson Street and Wister Unit. Flocks of more than 100 seen at Bombay Beach, Johnson Street, NWRHq, Wister Unit.
Comments: Nesting was documented at Wister Unit, NWRHq and Johnson Street.

Ring-necked Duck *Aythya collaris*
Status: Rare winter visitor
Counts: 1 - 124 (January). Seen on 5 counts, October - February; at Bombay Beach, Johnson Street, and Wister Unit. Usually only a few birds; one large flock at Johnson Street in January 1998.
Comments: This species was considered an uncommon visitor to the

Salton Sea prior to 1980 (Garrett and Dunn 1981), and its status has not changed.

Greater Scaup *Aythya marila*
Status: Accidental visitor
Counts: 2 sightings of 2 and 3 birds; in November and January at the Avenues.
Comments: Considered an uncommon winter visitor to southern California except for fairly regular appearances at the Salton Sea (Garrett and Dunn 1981), this species was seen less often than was expected on the counts. However, the difficulty in separating it from the far more common Lesser Scaup may have resulted in underreporting.

Lesser Scaup *Aythya affinis*
Status: Common year-round visitor
Counts: 1 (June) - 1,980 (November). Present in all seasons and all months except August; at all sites except Finney and Ramer Lakes; largest numbers November - February, very few in summer. Most frequent and in greatest numbers at Unit 1, Johnson Street, and Red Hill.

Surf Scoter *Melanitta perspicillata*
Status: Uncommon visitor
Counts: 1 (November) - 15 (March). Seen on 7 counts March - November; usually 1 or 2 individuals, but 15 in March 1998 at Fig Lagoon. Also at the Avenues, Bombay Beach, Johnson Street, SSSRA, Unit 1 and West Side.

Black Scoter *Melanitta nigra*
Status: Accidental visitor
Counts: 2 sightings: 2 birds in May 1998 at West Side, 2 in July 1998 at the Avenues Comments: This species was a casual visitor to the Salton Sea prior to 1980 (Garrett and Dunn 1981); its occurrence has not increased.

Bufflehead *Bucephala albeola*
Status: Fairly common visitor
Counts: 2 (May) - 84 (December). Present on 12 counts and at most sites (not Bombay Beach, Finney Lake, SSSRA); greatest numbers

November - January at Unit 1, but also seen regularly in small numbers at Johnson Street and Wister Unit.

Comments: A female with two half-grown ducklings was seen at the north end of the Salton Sea on 1 May 1999, the southernmost nesting record for this species (McCaskie 1999b).

Common Goldeneye *Bucephela clangula*
Status: Uncommon visitor
Counts: 1 - 12 seen on 5 counts at 7 sites. One summer sighting at Alamo, all others in December and January at the Avenues, Bombay Beach, Johnson Street, NWRHq, SSSRA and Unit 1.
Comments: The status of this species has not changed since 1980 when it was an uncommon to fairly common visitor (Garrett and Dunn 1981).

Red-breasted Merganser *Mergus serrator*
Status: Fairly common visitor, migrant
Counts: 2 (November) - 42 (September). Seen on most counts and in most months (not August, October); usually not more than 6 birds but 42 at Obsidian Butte in September. Seen at the Avenues, Johnson Street, NWRHq, Obsidian Butte, Red Hill, SSSRA, Unit 1 and West Side.

Ruddy Duck *Oxyura jamaicensis*
Status: Common resident, migrant
Counts: 254 (August) - 15,300 (February). Present on all counts and at all sites; huge flocks in winter; small numbers May - September; greatest numbers at Unit 1 and Wister Unit.
Comments: The sea is a major wintering area for this species, its numbers are surpassed only by Eared Grebe. Most of the population goes elsewhere to breed, but during the count period small numbers nested in marsh habitat at Finney Lake, NWRHq, Johnson Street and probably Ramer Lake and Wister Unit.

Osprey *Pandion haliaetus*
Status: Common year-round visitor
Counts: 4 - 23 per count, 23 in October. Present on all counts and at most sites (not Ramer Lake, SSSRA, West Side). Most frequently seen at the Avenues, Obsidian Butte, Unit 1, Whitewater and Wister Unit.

Comments: Although this species was present all year, there was no evidence of nesting.

White-tailed Kite *Elanus leucurus*
Status: Rare visitor
Counts: 2 sightings of single birds in January 1999 at the Avenues.
Comments: This species' range has expanded inland in the past 40 years. It has bred sporadically near NWRHq.

Bald Eagle *Haliaeetus leucocephalus*
Status: Rare winter visitor
Counts: Single bird seen once in January 1998 at Wister Unit
Comments: The presence of this species is spotty in southern California.

Northern Harrier *Circus cyaneus*
Status: Common year-round visitor
   Counts: 1 (April, May, June) - 35 (November, January). Present on most counts and in all months except August; at all sites except West Side. Most frequent at Wister Unit where numbers were also largest. Also frequented Ramer and Finney Lakes. Greatest numbers November - January.
   Comments: Although this species was present all year, there was no evidence of nesting. Its preferred nesting habitat, tall reeds and grasses, is plentiful at Wister Unit.

Sharp-shinned Hawk *Accipiter striatus*
Status: Rare fall and winter visitor
Counts: 1 - 2 seen on 5 counts October - February at Finney Lake, NWRHQ, Ramer Lake and Wister Unit.
Comments: Minimum habitat is available for this woodland hawk.

Cooper's Hawk *Accipiter cooperii*
Status: Uncommon fall and winter visitor
Counts: 1 - 5 seen on 9 counts October - March. Seen at Alamo, the Avenues, Fig Lagoon, Finney Lake, Johnson Street, NWRHq, Ramer Lake, and Wister Unit but mostly at Ramer and Finney Lakes and the Avenues.

Comments: Minimum habitat is available for this woodland hawk.

Red-shouldered Hawk *Buteo lineatus*
Status: Rare winter visitor
Counts: 1 - 4 per count, 4 in January. Seen on 9 counts, in all seasons; 1 bird seen at Finney Lake, all others at the Avenues.

Red-tailed Hawk *Buteo jamaicensis*
Status: Uncommon fall and winter visitor
Counts: 1 - 9 (January). Seen on 10 counts September - March at most sites (not Bombay Beach, Red Hill, or West Side); most often at Finney Lake.
Comments: A resident species in most of the United States, this hawk is not as plentiful around the sea as might be expected.

American Kestrel *Falco sparverius*
Status: Common resident
Counts: 2 - 25 (December). Present on all counts and at all sites. Seen most often at Unit 1, followed by Whitewater, the Avenues and Alamo.
Comments: Nesting was not documented at the count sites, but presumably occurred locally.

Merlin *Falco columbarius*
Status: Uncommon fall and winter visitor
Counts: 1 - 2 birds seen on 8 counts September - February. Seen at Alamo, Fig Lagoon, Ramer Lake, Red Hill, West Side and Wister Unit.
Comments: This species winters widely in the United States and Mexico.

Peregrine Falcon *Falco peregrinus*
Status: Fairly common year-round visitor
Counts: 1 - 4 birds seen on 14 counts in all seasons; mostly at the south end of the sea at Alamo, Obsidian Butte, Red Hill and Wister Unit, but also at the Avenues at the north end.

Prairie Falcon *Falco mexicanus*
Status: Rare visitor
Counts: Single birds seen on 4 counts in June, September, November; at

Johnson Street, Red Hill and Wister Unit.
Comments: A year-round resident of California, this falcon needs tall cliffs for nesting.

Ring-necked Pheasant *Phasianus colchicus*
Status: Rare resident
Counts: 1 - 2 birds seen 3 times in May and October at Finney Lake, Obsidian Butte and Wister Unit.
Comments: This introduced grassland species was stocked as a game bird and is well established in southern California. There is minimal proper habitat for it along the sea shore and it is more readily encountered in the agricultural fields.

Gambel's Quail *Callipepla gambelii*
Status: Common resident
Counts: 1 - 52 (May). Present on every count; most common at the Avenues, Whitewater and Wister Unit; seen also at Fig Lagoon, Finney Lake, NWRHq, Ramer Lake and Red Hill.
Comments: Nesting was documented at Whitewater and presumably occurred at several other sites.

Black Rail *Laterallus jamaicensis*
Status: Rare visitor
Counts: Single bird heard 2 times in January and March 1999 at Whitewater. Comments: This reclusive marsh bird is reported to be non-migratory in California. It has bred around the sea (Evens *et. al.* 1991) but was not detected during the breeding season. There is little information about its life history.

Yuma Clapper Rail *Rallus longirostris yumanensis*
Status: Fairly common resident
Counts: 1 (November) - 32 (June). Heard in all months except February and on most counts; most common at Wister Unit, but also present at Alamo, Finney Lake, Johnson Street, NWRHQ, Ramer Lake, SSSRA, Unit 1, Whitewater.
Comments: This subspecies was listed as endangered in 1970, along with the other two subspecies in California. In North America it occurs pri-

marily along the lower Colorado River. Formerly a summer (breeding) visitor to the freshwater marshes around the south end of the sea, the bird now is apparently in residence, breeding in cattail and reed marshes.

Virginia Rail *Rallus limicola*
Status: Uncommon year-round visitor
Counts: 1 - 7 per count, usually 1 - 2 but 7 in December. Single birds heard on 9 counts and in all seasons; at the Avenues, Finney Lake, Johnson Street, Ramer Lake, and Wister Unit.
Comments: This secretive bird of the cattail marshes is heard more than seen. Formerly a common resident at the Salton Sea (Garrett and Dunn 1981) it is now mostly a winter visitor.

Sora *Porzana carolina*
Status: Common (breeding?) resident
Counts: 1 - 8 per count, usually 1 - 2 but 8 in December. Heard on every count at sites all around the sea, predominantly at Wister Unit but also at Alamo, the Avenues, Finney Lake, Obsidian Butte, NWRHq, Ramer Lake, SSSRA, Unit 1 and Whitewater.
Comments: This species was formerly considered a winter visitor in southern California (Garrett and Dunn 1981) but its status may be changing. It was present throughout the year during the count period, although in greater numbers from late summer through winter than during the breeding season. Breeding was not documented but was considered probable at Wister Unit and other sites.

Common Moorhen *Gallinula chloropus*
Status: Common resident
Counts: 7 (April) - 97 (August). Seen on all counts and at all sites except West Side. Most common at Ramer and Finney Lakes where juveniles were seen in June.
Comments: Nesting documented at Finney Lake, Obsidian Butte, SSSRA and Whitewater.

American Coot *Fulica americana*
Status: Common resident
Counts: 417 (July) - 5,800 (February). Seen on all counts and at all sites;

most abundant at Wister Unit.

Comments: One of the most common residents, although numbers were reduced in June and July. Nesting was documented at Finney Lake, Obsidian Butte, Ramer Lake,SSSRA and Whitewater.

Sandhill Crane *Grus canadensis*
Status: Winter visitor
Counts: Not seen on counts.
Comments: Like the Mountain Plover, this species winters in the Imperial Valley, with flocks feeding and roosting in the agricultural fields. It neither fed nor roosted at the count sites but was observed on roost counts (see "Nocturnal Roosting"). The birds usually arrive in December and leave for their northern breeding grounds in February. A flock of 200 - 350 wintered in 1998; and there was a similar number in 1999 (Shuford *et. al.* 2000).

Black-bellied Plover *Pluvialus squatarola*
Status: Common year-round visitor, migrant
Counts: 24(July) - 326 (February). Present on every count and at most sites (not at Fig Lagoon, Finney Lake, or Ramer Lake). Largest numbers October - February; as many as 103 non-breeding birds present May - July.
Comments: In summer many of the wintering birds go north to breed, but a non-breeding population stays on; large numbers in February and March suggest a migratory component to the population.

American Golden-Plover *Pluvialus dominica*
Status: Accidental
Counts: Single bird seen once in October 1998 at Wister Unit.

Snowy Plover *Charadrius alexandrinus*
Status: Common resident, migrant
Counts: 2 (January) - 99 (July). Present in all months except October and on most counts; seen at Alamo, the Avenues, Bombay Beach, Johnson Street, SSSRA, Unit 1, West Side, Whitewater, and Wister Unit.
Comments: The Salton Sea is one of the main inland breeding areas for this species with nesting concentrated on the salt flats edging the sea

(Shuford *et. al.* 1995). In 1999 the largest concentrations were on the West Side during the nesting season and at Wister Unit and Alamo in winter (Shuford *et. al.* 2000).

Semipalmated Plover *Charadrius semipalmatus*
Status: Common winter visitor, migrant
Counts: 1 (August, September) - 100 (April). Seen in all seasons and all months except December; greatest numbers in April and July indicating a large migratory component. Seen at most sites (not Fig Lagoon, Finney Lake, or Red Hill) but predominantly at Alamo. Fair numbers at Bombay Beach, Unit 1, and Wister Unit.
Comments: Although this species was present all year, there were very few in winter.

Killdeer *Charadrius vociferus*
Status: Common resident
Counts: 61 (November) - 160 (May). Present on all counts and at all sites; nested at many sites. Numbers much increased May - October. Largest numbers at the south end of the sea at Wister Unit, Alamo, and NWRHq.
Comments: This ubiquitous and vocal shorebird is well adapted to the harsh Salton Sea environment; it nested on beaches and salt flats all around the shoreline.

Mountain Plover *Charadrius montanus*
Status: Winter visitor
Counts: 2 sightings: 4 birds in November at Unit 1, 1 bird at Red Hill in March.
Comments: Like the Sandhill Crane, this species winters in the Imperial Valley, with flocks feeding and roosting in the agricultural fields. It did not habitually feed or roost at the count sites. The birds arrive in mid-October and head north again in mid-February. In 1999 there were 3 surveys in the agricultural areas and the peak number seen was 3,758 in December (Shuford *et. al.* 2000)

Black-necked Stilt *Himantopus mexicanus*
Status: Common resident, migrant

Counts: 667 (January) - 6,220 (July). Present on all counts and at all sites. Numbers swelled in summer as juveniles appeared. Largest numbers at Alamo and Wister Unit. Many also at Unit 1, Obsidian Butte, Red Hill. Juveniles in June and July at these sites and at others with ponds.

Comments: The sea is a major year-round residence for this species. The shallow ponds just inland from the sea at Unit 1, Obsidian Butte, Alamo and Red Hill provide nest sites for hundreds of pairs. Nesting was documented at Finney Lake, Johnson Street, Obsidian Butte, Ramer Lake, SSSRA, West Side, Whitewater and Wister Unit.

American Avocet *Recurvirostra americana*
Status: Common resident, migrant
Counts: 1,005 (May) - 8,820 (September). Present on all counts and at all sites. Numbers highest June - November. Concentrated at south end of sea, especially at Wister Unit and Alamo; large numbers also at Red Hill and Unit 1.

Comments: The sea is a major year-round residence for this species. The shallow ponds just inland from the sea provide nest sites for hundreds of pairs. Nesting was documented at Alamo, Obsidian Butte, Red Hill, Unit 1 and Wister Unit.

Greater Yellowlegs *Tringa melanoleuca*
Status: Common year-round visitor
Counts: 5 (May) - 84 (October). Present on all counts and at all sites except Bombay Beach and Fig Lagoon; more than 20 per count except May and June, when there were very few. Seen most often and in largest numbers at Unit 1, Wister Unit.

Comments: This species was a regular presence on most counts throughout the year.

Lesser Yellowlegs *Tringa flavipes*
Status: Fairly common winter visitor
Counts: 1 (July) - 32 (December). Present in all months except in May and June; 26 - 32 birds seen December - March, 1 - 2 in other months. Seen at the Avenues, Finney Lake, Johnson Street, Obsidian Butte, Red Hill, West Side, Whitewater and Wister Unit. Most common at

Obsidian Butte (in ponds), smaller numbers on West Side, Johnson Street..
Comments: This species was a lesser presence than its congener, and was infrequent except in winter months.

Willet *Catoptrophorus semipalmatus*
Status: Common year-round visitor, migrant
Counts: 39 (May) - 740 (November). Present on all counts and at all sites except Fig Lagoon; largest numbers October - January at Alamo, Obsidian Butte, Unit 1, West Side, and Whitewater.
Comments: Occurrence of this species was similar to that of the Black-bellied Plover, with the population falling off in summer, but a non-breeding population that stayed on.

Spotted Sandpiper *Actitis macularia*
Status: Common visitor
Counts: 1 (May) - 13 (April). A few present on most counts and at all sites except Fig Lagoon. Most frequent at Finney and Ramer Lakes, Johnson Street and Obsidian Butte.
Comments: This species was present in all months with small peaks in April and August when they were in migration. Breeding was suspected but not confirmed.

Whimbrel *Numenius phaeopus*
Status: Fairly common migrant
Counts: 1 (July) - 31 (August). Seen February - September, usually fewer than 8 per count; seen at most sites (not Bombay Beach, Fig Lagoon, SSSRA, or West Side), most commonly at the Avenues, then Alamo, Ramer Lake, Red Hill, and Unit 1.
Comments: Both number of individuals and frequency of occurrence of this species during migration were less than expected.

Long-billed Curlew *Numenius americanus*
Status: Common year-round visitor, migrant
Counts: 1 (March) - 836 (November). Seen every month, but highest numbers September - February. Seen at most sites (not Bombay Beach, Ramer Lake, Whitewater), most commonly at Alamo and Red Hill.

Comments: This species was primarily a fall migrant and winter visitor, but a small number stayed on through the breeding season.

Marbled Godwit *Limosa fedoa*
Status: Common year-round visitor
Counts: 18 (April) - 583 (January). Seen on all counts and at many sites (not Fig Lagoon, Finney Lake, or Ramer Lake); largest numbers at Red Hill and Alamo.
Comments: The pattern of use by this species was difficult to determine. There were very few birds in April during spring migration; peak counts were in January and February, July and October, encompassing winter and fall migration. But there were respectable numbers in the other months. Thus, it was not primarily a winter visitor nor a migrant, but more like a nonbreeding resident.

Ruddy Turnstone *Arenaria interpres*
Status: Rare migrant
Counts: 1 - 8 birds seen 6 times in April, August, September - November; once at West Side, all other times at Obsidian Butte.
Comments: Mainly a coastal bird, but seen at scattered inland sites during migration.

Red Knot *Calidris canutus*
Status: Rare migrant
Counts: 1-5 birds seen 5 times; 4 times in April and once in September. Seen at Bombay Beach, Unit 1 and West Side.

Sanderling *Calidris alba*
Status: Rare migrant
Counts: 1 - 20 seen 6 times in April, May and August at the Avenues, Obsidian Butte, SSSRA, Unit 1 and West Side.

Western Sandpiper *Calidris mauri*
Status: Common year-round visitor, migrant
Counts: 4 (May) - 19,000 (July). Seen on all counts and at all sites. Numbers at Alamo were very large, lesser sites were Unit 1, Whitewater and Wister Unit.

Comments: Although present all year, this species was primarily a migrant, with peak numbers in March, July and August.

Least Sandpiper *Calidris minutilla*
Status: Common visitor
Counts: 40 (July) - 932 (February). Seen in all months except May and June but largest numbers December - February. Seen at all sites except Fig Lagoon; largest numbers at the southeast end of the sea at Wister Unit, Alamo and NWRHq.
Comments: This species was primarily a wintering bird; during the migratory months numbers were half what they were December - February.

Baird's Sandpiper *Calidris bairdii*
Status: Accidental visitor
Counts: Single bird seen once in August 1998 at Obsidian Butte.

Dunlin *Calidris alpina*
Status: Fairly common visitor, migrant
Counts: 3 (August) - 72 (January and February). Present on most counts and in every month except May and June; at all sites except Fig Lagoon and Ramer Lake. Largest numbers at Wister Unit and Alamo.
Comments: Although present almost all year, its occurrence was mostly as a winter visitor and spring migrant.

Stilt Sandpiper *Calidris himantopus*
Status: Uncommon winter visitor, migrant
Counts: 1 (October) - 73 (November). Seen on 9 counts July - February but mostly November - January and during the southward migration in July. Seen at Alamo, NWRHq, and Wister Unit; most sightings and most birds at Alamo. Usually in small flocks.
Comments: This species has long been a transient at the south end of the sea during migration (Garrett and Dunn 1981). During the count period it still preferred the south end but was more a winter visitor than a migrant in transit.

"Peeps" *Calidris* spp.
Status: Common visitor, Migrant
Counts: 80 (May) - 2,380 (September). Seen on all counts; seen at the Avenues, Alamo, Bombay Beach, Finney Lake, Ramer Lake, Red Hill, West Side and Wister Unit.
Comments: When speciating Western and Least Sandpipers at a distance could not be done with certainty they were lumped together as Peeps. The category was used on almost every count, and 17,900 small sandpipers were designated as Peeps. Most could be assumed to be Western Sandpipers, since the ratio of Western to Least was 12 to 1 where the flocks were close enough to discern species, and other small sandpipers were infrequently seen.

Dowitcher spp. *Limnodromus* spp.
Status: Common year-round visitor
Counts: 10 (May) - 6,000 (March). Seen on all counts at all sites. Largest numbers October - April at Wister Unit and Alamo.
Comments: It was often difficult to speciate Long-billed (*L. scolopaceus*) from Short-billed Dowitcher (*L. griseus*). In fact, more were classed as Dowitcher spp. (23,900) on the counts than as Long-Billed Dowitcher (19,150). Because the censusers were very experienced at bird identification and were not comfortable speciating large flocks of dowitchers from a distance, we have used the category Dowitcher spp. The category was used on every count, with as many as 3,100 observed in July. The vast majority could be assumed to be Long-billed, because the Short-billed Dowitcher is known to be rare at the sea, and only 103 birds were identified as such.

Common Snipe *Gallinago gallinago*
Status: Uncommon fall and winter visitor
Counts: 1 - 8 per count, 8 in December and January. Seen on 11 counts September - February at the Avenues, Finney Lake, Ramer Lake, Unit 1 and Wister Unit. Most common at Wister Unit where as many as 7 per count were observed in December and January.
Comments: This species was often flushed from marshy edges of ponds.

Wilson's Phalarope *Phalaropus tricolor*
Counts: Fairly common visitor, migrant
Counts: 1 (May) - 690 (July). Large numbers seen during fall migration July - September, but a few seen in all months except January and March. One flock of 120 seen during spring migration in April at NWRHq. Observed at the Avenues, Alamo, Bombay Beach, NWRHq, Obsidian Butte and West Side; most common at Alamo, NWRHq.

Red-necked Phalarope *Phalaropus lobatus*
Status: Fairly common visitor, migrant
Counts: 1 (January) - 650 (July). Largest numbers during migration but a few seen in all months except March and December. Seen at Alamo, the Avenues, Bombay Beach, Finney Lake, NWRHq, Obsidian Butte, Unit 1, West Side, Whitewater, and Wister Unit; most common at Wister Unit, fair numbers at the Avenues.

Parasitic Jaeger *Stercorarius parasiticus*
Status: Accidental visitor
Counts: A juvenile was seen at 2 sites in late summer 1998; at Wister Unit on 28 August and Bombay Beach on 30 August; very possibly the same individual.

Laughing Gull *Larus atricilla*
Status: Fairly common visitor
Counts: 1 (January and August) - 80 (July). Seen in all seasons but mostly post-breeding June - August. Seen at most sites (not Bombay Beach, Fig Lagoon, Johnson Street, NWRHq, or West Side); most common at Alamo, Obsidian Butte and Wister Unit.
Comments: There is a long but sporadic history of nesting by this species at the sea; in 1999 there was one unsuccessful attempt at NWRHq (Shuford *et. al.* 2000).

Franklin's Gull *Larus pipixcan*
Status: Rare visitor
Counts: 3 sightings of 1 - 2 birds; in April and June 1998 at SSSRA, in May 1998 at Wister Unit.

Little Gull *Larus minutus*
Status: Accidental
Counts: Single bird seen once in May 1999 at Wister Unit
Comments: This species brought many rare-bird enthusiasts to the sea; its occurrence in southern California is very rare.

Bonaparte's Gull *Larus philadelphia*
Status: Common winter visitor
Counts: 12 (August) - 1,310 (April). Seen every month and on most counts, but mostly November - April. Seen at all sites except Fig Lagoon and Finney Lake; most numerous and frequent at Wister Unit, followed by West Side and Obsidian Butte.

Heermann's Gull *Larus heermanni*
Status: Rare visitor
Counts: 7 sightings; single birds seen February - September at Fig Lagoon, Obsidian Butte, NWRHq and Wister Unit; a small flock of 13 seen once in June at Fig Lagoon.

Ring-billed Gull *Larus delawarensis*
Status: Common year-round visitor
Counts: 1,070 (March) - 16,500 (November). Seen on all counts and at all sites. Mostnumerous at the Avenues and Unit 1.
Comments: The most numerous and widespread gull at the Salton Sea; rarely fewer than 1000 per count. Many stayed throughout the breeding season; the species could be considered a non-breeding resident.

California Gull *Larus californicus*
Status: Common resident
Counts: 219 (June) - 8,200 (November). Seen on all counts and at most sites (not at Fig Lagoon, Finney Lake, or Ramer Lake). Most numerous at the Avenues, lesser numbers but still many at SSSRA and Unit 1.
Comments: This species is an established breeder at the south end of the sea, although in small numbers. In 1999 there were 40 pairs nesting at NWRHq (Shuford *et. al.* 2000).

Herring Gull *Larus argentatus*
Status: Common year-round visitor
Counts: 12 (June) - 2,250 (November). Seen on all counts, most abundant November - February, fewer than 200 per count in other months; seen at all sites except Finney Lake, most numerous at the Avenues, Red Hill and SSSRA.
Comments: Although present year-round, this species was seen mostly in winter. There are no breeding records.

Thayer's Gull *Larus thayeri*
Status: Rare visitor
Counts: 3 sightings of 1 - 2 birds in February at SSSRA, in April at NWR, and in November at the Avenues.

Lesser Black-backed Gull *Larus fuscus*
Status: Rare visitor
Counts: 1 sighting of 1 bird; in January 2000 at SSSRA.
Comments: A European gull that is a regular winter visitor to the east coast, this species is rare in the west.

Yellow-footed Gull *Larus livens*
Status: Common visitor
Counts: 3 (November) - 323 (July). Seen on most counts, in all months, but numbers much larger June - September. Seen at most sites (not at Fig Lagoon, Finney Lake, Ramer Lake, or West Side); most numerous at Obsidian Butte, Wister Unit, Unit 1 and NWRHq.
Comments: Long considered a subspecies of the Western Gull which it closely resembles, this bird is resident in Mexico and breeds on islands in the Gulf of California. It was first noted at the Salton Sea in August 1965, and its numbers have increased until now there are hundreds every year. It is mainly a post-breeding wanderer, but a few can be seen in all months. There have been scattered sightings in California and Arizona but only at the Salton Sea is it seen regularly.

Western Gull *Larus occidentalis*
Status: Rare visitor
Counts: 1 - 4 seen on 5 counts January - May at Alamo, NWRHq, and

Red Hill.
Comments: This species is abundant along the coast, but rarely strays inland as far as the Salton Sea.

Glaucous-winged Gull *Larus glaucescens*
Status: Rare visitor
Counts: 5 sightings of single birds at the Avenues, SSSRA, Red Hill, and Unit 1.

Sabine's Gull *Xema sabini*
Status: Accidental visitor
Counts: Single bird seen once in November at Obsidian Butte.

Gull spp. *Larus* spp.
Status: Common year-round visitor
Counts: 930 (March) - 7,300 (January). Present on all counts and at most sites (not Fig Lagoon, Obsidian Butte or SSSRA).
Comments: Gulls at a distance were plentiful. Because the censusers were very experienced at bird identification and were not comfortable speciating large flocks of gulls from a distance, we have used the category Gull sp. The category was used on every count and 38,500 gulls were thus designated.

Gull-billed Tern *Sterna nilotica*
Status: Fairly common summer (breeding) visitor
Counts: 5 (March) - 172 (June). Seen May - August at most sites (not Bombay Beach, Fig Lagoon, or SSSRA); most common and frequent at NWRHq where they nested.
Comments: This species has bred at the Salton Sea since at least 1927 when 450 nests were found on 3 islands (Pemberton 1927). It winters along the coast of Mexico. In 1999, 101 pairs nested at the sea, with 44 pairs at NWRHq and 57 pairs at Johnson Street (Shuford *et. al.* 2000).

Caspian Tern *Sterna caspia*
Status: Common resident
Counts: 3 (January) - 2,019 (August). Seen on all counts and at every site; most common and frequent at NWRHq.

Comments: There is a long history of nesting by this species at the Salton Sea; in 1999, 211 pairs bred at NWRHq (Shuford *et. al.* 2000).

Common Tern *Sterna hirundo*
Status: Rare visitor
Counts: 1 - 29 seen on 4 counts from July - September at the Avenues, Johnson Street, and SSSRA.
Comments: This species was formerly noted as a "common fall transient" (Garrett and Dunn 1981); it was far less frequently encountered during the 2-year count period reported here.

Forster's Tern *Sterna forsteri*
Status: Common resident
Counts: 1 (January) - 687 (August). Seen on all counts, a few in winter and early spring but large numbers May - November. Seen at all sites but concentrated at the southeast end of the sea; largest numbers at Alamo, Red Hill, NWRHq, and Obsidian Butte.
Comments: There has been sporadic nesting by this species since 1970 (Garrett and Dunn 1981); nesting was not documented during the count period.

Least Tern *Sterna antillarum*
Status: Accidental visitor
Counts: Single bird seen once in June at the Avenues.
Comments: This species nests coastally in southern and central California; vagrants visit inland lakes.

Black Tern *Chlidonias niger*
Status: Fairly common (post breeding) summer visitor
Counts: 1 (April and October) - 650 (July and August). Seen April - October but mostly June - September. At all sites except Fig Lagoon; largest numbers at Alamo, Red Hill, and Johnson Street.
Comments: This species is regular summer and autumn visitor to the Salton Sea after breeding farther north; it is rarely seen in spring.

Black Skimmer *Rynchops niger*
Status: Common summer (breeding) visitor

Counts: 1 (November) - 511 (July). Seen April - September (plus 1 out-of-season visitor in November) at all sites except Bombay Beach and Fig Lagoon; largest numbers at NWRHq.

Comments: This species has been breeding at the Salton Sea since 1972 (Molina 1996) and has been monitored annually since 1991. In1999 there were 457 pairs at 3 nesting sites: NWRHq, Johnson Street and Colfax Street (located between Johnson and Hayes Streets). NWRHq was the major site with 377 nests (Shuford *et. al.* 2000).

Rock Dove *Columba livia*
Status: Common resident
Counts: 4 - 125 (Feb). Seen on all counts; seen at the Avenues, Bombay Beach, Finney Lake, NWRHq, Obsidian Butte, SSSRA (where nesting was documented), Unit 1, West Side and Wister Unit. Most numerous at West Side.

Spotted Dove *Streptopelia chinensis*
Status: Accidental visitor
Counts: Single bird seen once at the Avenues in March .
Comments: This introduced species is well established along the southern California coast; although its numbers are decreasing. A small population is resident at the north end of the sea.

White-winged Dove *Zenaida asiatica*
Status: Common summer (breeding) visitor
Counts: 1 (April) - 108 (July). Seen April - September at most sites (not Bombay Beach, Obsidian Butte, Red Hill, or West Side). Largest numbers at Finney Lake, then Ramer Lake and the Avenues.
Comments: This species comes to the southern California deserts (including the Salton Sea area) to nest, then mostly returns south to winter. Nesting was presumed but not documented.

Mourning Dove *Zenaida macroura*
Status: Common resident
Counts: 13 (January) - 346 (May). Seen on all counts, more numerous April - August. Seen at all sites except Bombay Beach. Most common at Wister Unit, Unit 1, Finney Lake, and Ramer Lake.

Comments: Nested at Finney Lake, SSSRA and presumably at other sites.

Inca Dove *Columbina inca*
Status: Rare visitor
Counts: 2 sightings: 2 birds in May 1999 at Ramer Lake, 1 in December 1999 at Finney Lake.
Comments: Southeastern California is the western limit of this species.

Common Ground-Dove *Columbina passerina*
Status: Common resident
Counts: 3 (April and November) - 38 (July). Seen on all counts and at all sites except Bombay Beach. Most common at Ramer Lake, Finney Lake, and NWRHq.
Comments: Nests locally.

Greater Roadrunner *Geococcyx californianus*
Status: Common resident
Counts: 1 - 6 seen on all counts and at most sites (not Alamo, Bombay Beach, Red Hill, SSSRA, or West Side).
Comments: Nests locally.

Barn Owl *Tyto alba*
Status: Rarely seen resident
Counts: 1 - 2 seen on 5 counts May - August at Finney and Ramer Lakes.
Comments: A common, if infrequently seen resident of the lowlands of California, this species is apparently rare in the Salton Sea area.

Great Horned Owl *Bubo virginianus*
Status: Rarely seen resident
Counts: 3 sightings of 1 - 2 birds in May, July, and November at Ramer Lake and Wister Unit.
Comments: This species occurs in small numbers in the Salton Sea area.

Burrowing Owl *Athene cunicularia*
Status: Resident
Counts: 1 - 9 (June). Seen mostly at Unit 1. Present also at Fig Lagoon,

Finney Lake, Johnson Street, NWRHq, Obsidian Butte, Ramer Lake, Red Hill, and Wister Unit.
Comments: The Imperial Valley has provided good habitat for Burrowing Owls for decades. The berms that line the dikes in the valley's agricultural fields make ideal sites for their burrows (Garrett and Dunn 1981). The birds were uncommon at the count sites where such berms were not abundant. Nesting was documented near Finney Lake.

Lesser Nighthawk *Chordeiles acutipennis*
Status: Common summer (breeding) visitor
Counts: 1 - 58 (June). Seen mostly April - August, but 1 - 2 birds in all seasons. Seen at most sites (not NWRHq, Red Hill, or Unit 1). Most common at Wister Unit, Finney Lake, and Bombay Beach.
Comments: This species winters mostly south of the United States border and comes to southeastern California to breed. The environs of the Salton Sea are a major breeding area, particularly the scrub along the eastern shore. Nesting documented at Bombay Beach, Obsidian Butte, Ramer Lake and Whitewater.

Vaux's Swift *Chaetura vauxi*
Status: Rare migrant
Counts: Migrating groups of 4 - 25 seen overhead 4 times in April at Johnson Street, NWRHq, Whitewater, and Wister Unit; 1 bird seen in September over Wister Unit.
Comments: This species was seen only in flight during migration.

White-throated Swift *Aeronautes saxatalis*
Status: Rare spring visitor
Counts: 3 - 18 birds seen overhead 4 times in April and May at Johnson Street, SSSRA, Unit 1 and Whitewater.
Comments: The rocky cliffs that are habitat for this resident California species are in short supply in the immediate vicinity of the Salton Sea; the birds seen were probably foraging from home bases in the Chocolate Mountains and other ranges in the vicinity.

Anna's Hummingbird *Calypte anna*
Status: Rarely seen resident

Counts: Single birds seen 4 times in January, February and October at the Avenues.

Comments: This species is resident in the Imperial Valley but was rarely seen at the count sites; residential areas provide more suitable habitat.

Costa's Hummingbird *Calypte costae*
Status: Rare visitor

Counts: Single birds seen 2 times in May and December at NWRHq and SSSRA.

Comments: Lack of suitable habitat has kept this species from becoming a more common visitor to the Salton Sea area (Garrett and Dunn 1981).

Belted Kingfisher *Ceryle alcyon*
Status: Common fall and winter visitor

Counts: 1 (August) - 14 (October). Seen on most counts and in all months except May - July. Seen at most sites (not Bombay Beach, SSSRA, or Unit 1), most frequently at Finney Lake, Obsidian Butte, Johnson Street, and Ramer Lake.

Comments: No breeding records in the area.

Red-naped Sapsucker *Sphyrapicus nuchalis*
Status: Accidental visitor

Counts: Single bird seen once in April at Finney Lake.

Ladder-backed Woodpecker *Picoides scalaris*
Status: Uncommon resident

Counts: 1 - 5 seen on many counts and in most months. Seen at the Avenues, Finney Lake, NWRHq, Ramer Lake, Whitewater and Wister Unit; most frequently at Whitewater.

Comments: This species is closely associated with desert woodlands, and is found at a few sites around the sea where there is remnant native riparian vegetation.

Northern Flicker *Colaptes auratus*
Status: Uncommon winter visitor

Counts: 1 - 7 seen on 7 counts October - January at the Avenues, Finney Lake, NWRHq, Ramer Lake, Whitewater and Wister Unit; most at

NWRHq.
Comments: Although there seems to be suitable habitat (open country with large trees), this widespread species was seen less often in winter than expected.

Western Wood-Pewee *Contopus sordidulus*
Status: Rare migrant
Counts: 1 - 10 seen on 5 counts May - September but mostly May; at Fig Lagoon, Finney Lake, Johnson Street, NWRHq, Ramer Lake, Salt Creek, and Wister Unit.

Willow Flycatcher *Empidonax traillii*
Status: Rare migrant
Counts: 1 - 6 seen on 3 counts in May, June, and September; at Fig Lagoon, Finney Lake, Ramer Lake, and SSSRA.

Pacific-slope Flycatcher *Empidonax difficilis*
Status: Rare migrant
Counts: Seen on 2 counts: 5 in May, 4 in September; at Finney Lake, Ramer Lake, and Wister Unit.

Empidonax spp. *Empidonax* spp.
Status: Rare migrant
Counts: 1 - 3 unidentifiable small flycatchers seen on 3 counts in May, September at Finney Lake, NWRHq, Ramer Lake, Whitewater, and Wister Unit.

Black Phoebe *Sayornis nigricans*
Status: Common resident
Counts: 15 (March) - 77 (October). Seen on all counts and at all sites. Most common at Wister Unit, followed by Ramer and Finney Lakes.
Comments: Nesting was documented at NWRHq, Obsidian Butte and presumably occurred elsewhere. Nests often built under bridges that cross irrigation canals in the valley (K. Sturm, pers. comm.). Numbers were somewhat larger October - December.

Eastern Phoebe *Sayornis phoebe*
Status: Accidental visitor
Counts: Single birds seen 2 times in December and January at the Avenues.
Comments: This phoebe has been reported several times around the sea (see "Rare Species seen during the Count Period").

Say's Phoebe *Sayornis saya*
Status: Common resident
Counts: 1 - 46 (December). Fewer than 10 per count February - August; sharp increase to 21 - 46 per count September - January. Seen in every month, on most counts. Seen at every site, most numerous at Wister Unit.
Comments: The increase in numbers per count September - January indicated some in-migration for the winter. Nesting was documented at SSSRA, presumed at other sites.

Vermilion Flycatcher *Pyrocephalus rubinus*
Status: Rare winter visitor
Counts: 4 sightings: 1 bird present October, December, and January at Ramer Lake in the winter of 1998 - 1999; a pair seen at Ramer Lake in January 2000.
Comments: This species has long been a rare winter visitor to the Salton Sea (Garrett and Dunn 1981).

Ash-throated Flycatcher *Myiarchus cinerascens*
Status: Uncommon summer visitor, migrant
Counts: 1 - 4 seen April - August at Finney Lake, Johnson Street, NWRHq, Ramer Lake, Unit 1, Whitewater and Wister Unit.
Comments: The presence of 2 - 4 birds through the spring and summer indicated probable breeding at Whitewater, although it was not documented.

Cassin's Kingbird *Tyrannus vociferans*
Status: Rare migrant
Counts: 1 - 7 per count, 7 in June. Seen on 5 counts April - August at Johnson Street, NWRHq, West Side, Whitewater, and Wister Unit.

Western Kingbird *Tyrannus verticalis*
Status: Common summer (breeding) visitor
Counts: 3 (March) - 69 (June). Seen March - August at all sites except Bombay Beach. Most common at Obsidian Butte, Unit 1, and Wister Unit.
Comments: Nesting was documented at Ramer Lake, Obsidian Butte, Red Hill, Whitewater, and Wister Unit.

Loggerhead Shrike *Lanius ludovicianus*
Status: Common resident
Counts: 1 - 39 (September). On all counts and at all sites except Bombay Beach. Most common and frequent at Wister Unit.
Comments: Nesting was documented at Whitewater and deemed probable at Wister Unit.

Plumbeous Vireo *Vireo plumbeus*
Status: Accidental visitor
Counts: Single bird seen once in April at Wister Unit.

Cassin's Vireo *Vireo cassinii*
Status: Rare migrant
Counts: Single bird seen once in September at NWRHq.

Warbling Vireo *Vireo gilvus*
Status: Rare migrant
Counts: 1 - 13 seen on 3 counts in April, May, and September. Seen at Finney and Ramer Lakes in May, at Wister Unit in September.

American Crow *Corvus brachyrhynchos*
Status: Rare visitor
Counts: 2 sightings: flock of 50 in May at Johnson Street, 2 at Wister Unit in January.
Comments: This species is widespread in the United States except in the southwestern deserts.

Common Raven *Corvus corax*
Status: Fairly common visitor

Counts: 2 - 18 (October). Seen on all counts and at many sites: the Avenues, Bombay Beach, Fig Lagoon, Johnson Street, SSSRA, Unit 1, West Side, Whitewater, and Wister Unit. Most common at Desert Beach (SSSRA) and Unit 1.
Comments: This species is widespread throughout the southwestern deserts. It is resident in the area, but there is no suitable nesting habitat (cliffs and tall conifers) near the sea.

Horned Lark *Eremophila alpestris*
Status: Rare fall and winter visitor
Counts: 1 - 62 seen on 4 counts September - January; usually single birds (at Wister Unit and SSSRA) but 2 flocks of 27 and 35 birds in December on the western side of the sea (the Avenues and West Side)
Comments: While this species is considered common in the Imperial Valley, it was rare at the count sites, where appropriate dry and open habitat was limited.

Tree Swallow *Tachycineta bicolor*
Status: Common year-round visitor, migrant
Counts: 3 - 1,275 seen on all counts and at all sites except West Side. Most abundant at Ramer and Finney Lakes in August.
Comments: This species was present all year, but not as a breeding bird. Finney and Ramer Lakes appeared to provide wintering habitat.

Violet-green Swallow *Tachycineta thalassina*
Status: Rare visitor
Counts: 1 - 30 seen on 4 counts in January, March, August; at the Avenues, NWRHq, and SSSRA. A flock of 10 seen in January at NWRHq.

Northern Rough-winged Swallow *Stelgidopteryx serripennis*
Status: Common spring migrant, winter visitor
Counts: 2 (January) - 255 (March). Seen on many counts from November - July at all sites except Bombay Beach. Most abundant at Finney Lake and Wister Unit.

Bank Swallow *Riparia riparia*
Status: Rare migrant
Counts: 3 sightings: 10 birds in April at Finney Lake, 1 in July at Bombay Beach, 20 in September at Ramer Lake.
Comments: This swallow was seen infrequently on the counts, although it is a regular migrant through the area.

Cliff Swallow *Petrochelidon pyrrhonota*
Status: Common resident, migrant
Counts: 2 (January) - 3,050 (July). Seen on most counts (not in November or December) and at all sites except the Avenues. Most common at Ramer and Finney Lakes.
Comments: This was the most abundant swallow at the Salton Sea; two large nesting colonies were observed at Finney and Ramer Lakes.

Barn Swallow *Hirundo rustica*
Status: Fairly common visitor, migrant
Counts: 2 (June) - 272 (September). Seen in all months except February and July but mostly as a fall migrant. Seen at all sites except Red Hill and West Side; most common at Wister Unit and Obsidian Butte (ponds).
Comments: Nesting was not documented, although there has been local nesting in the past (Garrett and Dunn 1981).

Verdin *Auriparus flaviceps*
Status: Common resident
Counts: 27 (September) - 150 (July). Seen on all counts and at all sites. Largest numbers at Whitewater and Finney Lake.
Comments: This desert species has adapted well to the disturbed tamarisk and scrub habitat around the Salton Sea. Nesting was documented at Finney Lake, Obsidian Butte, SSSRA, Whitewater and presumed at other sites.

Bushtit *Psaltriparus minimus*
Status: Rare visitor
Counts: Single bird seen once in June at Obsidian Butte.

Cactus Wren *Campylorhynchus brunneicapillus*
Status: Fairly common resident
Counts: 1 - 13 (May). Seen on most counts, in every month except August; seen at the Avenues, Finney Lake, Johnson Street, NWRHq, Ramer Lake, SSSRA, Whitewater, and Wister Unit.
Comments: This species has adapted well to the disturbed tamarisk and scrub habitat around the Salton Sea. Nesting was documented at Whitewater.

Bewick's Wren *Thyromanes bewickii*
Status: Uncommon resident
Counts: 1 - 8 birds seen on 9 counts; 8 in January but all other sightings were of 1 - 2 birds. Seenat the Avenues, Finney Lake, Whitewater, and Wister Unit.
Comments: Breeding was probable at Whitewater, where there is an abundance of scrub habitat that is less disturbed than at most other sites.

House Wren *Troglodytes aedon*
Status: Rare fall and winter visitor
Counts: Seen on 3 counts; 5 in February at Johnson Street and Wister Unit, 2 in September at Finney Lake, 1 in December at Whitewater.

Marsh Wren *Cistothorus palustris*
Status: Common resident
Counts: 18 (September) - 311 (April). Seen on all counts and at all sites except Red Hill and West Side. Most common at Wister Unit and Finney Lake; also healthy populations at Ramer Lake and Whitewater.
Comments: This species nested densely in emergent vegetation in the ponds at Finney Lake; 200 singing males were counted in January 1998. Many also nested at Ramer Lake, Unit 1, Whitewater and Wister Unit.

Ruby-crowned Kinglet *Regulus calendula*
Status: Fairly common fall and winter visitor
Counts: 1 (March) - 15 (October). Seen October - March at the Avenues, Alamo, Finney Lake, NWRHq, Ramer Lake, SSSRA, Whitewater and Wister Unit; most common at Wister Unit and Ramer Lake.

Blue-Gray Gnatcatcher *Polioptila caerulea*
Status: Fairly common visitor
Counts: 1 - 8 (January). Seen in all months except July and August but mostly November - January; at the Avenues, Fig Lagoon, Finney Lake, NWRHq, Ramer Lake, Whitewater and Wister Unit. Seen most frequently at Wister Unit, Ramer Lake, and Finney Lake.
Comments: Nesting was not expected or documented.

Black-tailed Gnatcatcher *Polioptila melanura*
Status: Common resident
Counts: 1 - 35 (July). Seen on all counts at the Avenues, Fig Lagoon, Finney Lake, Johnson Street, NWRHq, Ramer Lake, SSSRA, Whitewater and Wister Unit; largest numbers were at Whitewater.
Comments: Nested at Whitewater and presumably at Wister Unit and other sites.

Western Bluebird *Sialia mexicana*
Status: Rare visitor
Counts: Single bird seen once in March at Red Hill .

Mountain Bluebird *Sialia currucoides*
Status: Rare visitor
Counts: Single bird seen once in April at Fig Lagoon.

Northern Mockingbird *Mimus polyglottos*
Status: Common resident
Counts: 1 - 18 (December), usually fewer than 10. Seen on all counts and at most sites (not Alamo, Bombay Beach, Obsidian Butte, or Red Hill). Nesting documented at SSSRA.

Sage Thrasher *Oreoscoptes montanus*
Status: Rare visitor
Counts: Single bird seen once in January at the Avenues.

California Thrasher *Toxostoma redivivum*
Status: Rare visitor
Counts: Single bird seen once in May at Finney Lake.

Comments: This species is endemic to California's coastal chaparral and has rarely been found elsewhere. (There is one report from Medford, Oregon [Cody 1998].) It was surprising to find one singing from the top of a tamarisk at Finney Lake on 25 May 1998. The song was typical for the species - rich, harsh, and repetitive - unlike the softer and sweeter tones of the Crissal Thrasher, which is similar in appearance.

Crissal Thrasher *Toxostoma crissale*
Status: Uncommon resident
Counts: 1 - 6 (April). Seen on 8 counts throughout the year at Finney Lake, Ramer Lake and Whitewater; most often at Whitewater.
Comments: This species is at the western limit of its range in the Salton Sink and the Anza-Borrego Desert. Singing males in spring at Ramer Lake and Whitewater indicated nesting.

European Starling *Sturnus vulgaris*
Status: Common resident
Counts: 18 (July) - 443(January). Seen on all counts and at many sites (not at Alamo, Bombay Beach, Johnson Street, Red Hill, or Unit 1). Largest flocks at the Avenues, SSSRA, Finney and Ramer Lakes.
Comments: Nested wherever cavities (natural or man-made) were available.

American Pipit *Anthus rubescens*
Status: Common visitor
Counts: 3 (March) - 248 (November). Seen October - May at most sites (not at Fig Lagoon, Red Hill, or Unit 1). Often in flocks up to 150. Most often seen and largest flocks at Wister Unit.
Comments: This species has traditionally wintered in the lowlands of southern California, flocking in agricultural fields and desert flats (Garrett and Dunn 1981).

Sprague's Pipit *Anthus spragueii*
Status: Rare visitor
Counts: 3 birds seen once in February at Wister Unit.

Cedar Waxwing *Bombycilla cedrorum*
Status: Rare visitor
Counts: Flock of 30 seen once in January at SSSRA.
Comments: This species winters throughout southern California but is irruptive in occurrence, following food sources (e.g. berries).

Phainopepla *Phainopepla nitens*
Status: Fairly common fall and winter visitor
Counts: 2 - 15 seen on 10 counts October - June, but mostly October - January. Seen at the Avenues, Finney Lake, Johnson Street, NWRHq, Ramer Lake, SSSRA, Whitewater, and Wister Unit; most often at Finney and Ramer Lakes.
Comments: This species spends most of the year in the desert, but moves to the coast in late spring to stay for the summer; it nests in both areas. Nesting was not observed on the counts.

Orange-crowned Warbler *Vermivora celata*
Status: Fairly common visitor, migrant
Counts: 1 - 52 (May). Seen in all seasons and all months except July. Usually not more than 8 birds per count but migrant flocks of as many as 30 were seen in May. Seen at most sites (not Red Hill, Unit 1, or West Side); most frequently at Alamo and Wister Unit.
Comments: This species was primarily a spring migrant, but a few were present on most counts throughout the year.

Nashville Warbler *Vermivora ruficapilla*
Status: Rare migrant
Counts: 3 sightings of 1 - 2 birds in April, May, and September at Finney and Ramer Lakes.
Comments: This species is a regular spring migrant in the area but was rarely seen on the counts.

Virginia's Warbler *Vermivora virginiae*
Status: Rare migrant
Counts: 2 sighting of single birds in April 1998 at NWRHq and Obsidian Butte.
Comments: This species is west of its breeding range at the sea, but has been seen in migration in fall and winter (Shuford *et. al.* 1999) .

Lucy's Warbler *Vermivora luciae*
Status: Rare visitor
Counts: Single bird seen once in July at Finney Lake.
Comments: This species nests mostly east of California, although a small breeding population was formerly present intermittently at the north end of the Salton Sea (Garrett and Dunn 1981) and there is one currently in the Borrego Valley (Massey 1998).

Yellow Warbler *Dendroica petechia*
Status: Uncommon migrant
Counts: 1 - 30 (May). Seen during migration only, in April and May and August - November. Seen at Fig Lagoon, Finney Lake, Johnson Street, NWRHq, Ramer Lake, Unit 1, Whitewater, and Wister Unit.
Comments: This species is a regular spring migrant in the area but was uncommon on the counts.

Yellow-rumped Warbler *Dendroica coronata*
Status: Common visitor
Counts: 1 (September) - 382(January). Seen on most counts and in all months except July and August. Seen at most sites (not Bombay Beach or NWRHq). Largest concentrations at Wister Unit; the Avenues, Ramer and Finney Lakes were also favored sites.
Comments: This species was a large fall and winter presence around the sea October - February when upwards of 200 were seen on counts. It favored sites with trees and shrubs.

Black-throated Gray Warbler *Dendroica nigrescens*
Status: Rare migrant
Counts: 1 - 2 birds seen 3 times in May and September at Finney and Ramer Lakes.
Comments: This species is a more common migrant through the area than was indicated by its appearance on the counts.

Townsend's Warbler *Dendroica townsendi*
Status: Migrant
Counts: 3 sightings of 1 - 2 birds in March and May at Wister Unit,

Finney and Ramer Lakes.

Comments: This species is a more common migrant through the area than was indicated by its appearance on the counts.

Hermit Warbler *Dendroica occidentalis*
Status: Rare migrant
Counts: Single bird seen once in May at Finney Lake

American Redstart *Setophaga ruticilla*
Status: Rare visitor
Counts: Single bird seen once in September 1999 at Wister Unit.
Comments: This species is out of range in California.

MacGillivray's Warbler *Oporornis tolmiei*
Status: Rare migrant
Counts: Single bird seen once in May at Ramer Lake

Common Yellowthroat *Geothlypis trichas*
Status: Common resident
Counts: 5 (January) - 123 (June). Seen on all counts and at all sites except West Side; most abundant at Wister Unit; goodly numbers also at Ramer and Finney Lakes, Whitewater.
Comments: This resident warbler was present wherever there was dense vegetation (emergent aquatic plants and shoreline shrubs). Nesting was documented at Finney and Ramer Lakes, Whitewater, and presumably occurred at other sites where there was freshwater marsh.

Wilson's Warbler *Wilsonia pusilla*
Status: Uncommon migrant
Counts: 1 - 35 (May). Seen on 6 counts in April, May, September, and November; many more in spring than in fall. Seen at Fig Lagoon, Finney Lake, Johnson Street, NWRHq, Ramer Lake, SSSRA, Whitewater, and Wister Unit. Largest group at one site was a flock of 29 in May at Finney Lake.
Comments: A common migrant through the California desert region in spring, this warbler has been banded in large numbers at Morongo Valley in the Mohave Desert (C.T. Collins, pers. comm.) and at the Salton Sea

(Shuford *et. al.* 2000). It is a more regular migrant through the area than was indicated by its appearance on the counts.

Yellow-breasted Chat *Icteria virens*
Status: Rare summer (breeding) visitor
Counts: 1 - 2 birds on counts April - July at Finney Lake, Ramer Lake, Whitewater, and Wister Unit.
Comments: This reclusive warbler was more often heard than seen. Its presence in June at the sites listed above indicated probable breeding.

Summer Tanager *Piranga rubra*
Status: Rare visitor
Counts: 1 bird seen once in July 1999 at SSSRA.
Comments: The presence of a female in July indicates possible nesting in the vicinity.

Western Tanager *Piranga ludoviciana*
Status: Rare migrant
Counts: 1 - 7 birds seen on 3 counts in May and September at Alamo, Finney Lake, Ramer Lake and Wister Unit.
Comments: This species is a more common migrant through the area than was indicated by its appearance on the counts.

Spotted Towhee *Pipilo maculatus*
Status: Rare visitor
Counts: 2 sightings of 1 - 2 birds in March and December at Whitewater.
Comments: A common resident of chaparral and oak woodlands to the west, this species is rare in southeastern California.

Abert's Towhee *Pipilo aberti*
Status: Common resident
Counts: 8 - 67 (July). Seen on all counts and all sites except SSSRA, Unit 1, and West Side. Most abundant at Whitewater, but also favored Finney Lake, Ramer Lake and Wister Unit.
Comments: This species favored sites with thick shrubby vegetation and trees. Nesting presumably occurred at many sites, but was not documented.

Chipping Sparrow *Spizella passerina*
Status: Rare visitor
Counts: Single bird seen once in April at Obsidian Butte.

Brewer's Sparrow *Spizella breweri*
Status: Rare migrant
Counts: 1 - 3 seen on 3 counts: 3 birds in May at Whitewater and Wister Unit, 1 in September at Fig Lagoon.

Lark Sparrow *Chondestes grammacus*
Status: Rare visitor
Counts: 1 - 5 seen on 4 counts in January, May, June, and October at the Avenues, Wister Unit, Whitewater.
Comments: This ground-hugging species is resident in southern California, but an erratic visitor to the Salton Sea. Nesting has been documented locally.

Black-throated Sparrow *Amphispiza bilineata*
Status: Rare visitor
Counts: Single bird seen once in August at Alamo.
Comments: There is little natural habitat for this desert resident around the sea.

Sage Sparrow *Amphispiza belli*
Status: Rare visitor
Counts: 1 - 7 seen on 6 counts in summer, fall, winter but mostly in winter. Seen at the Avenues, Bombay Beach, Whitewater and Wister Unit; most often at Whitewater.
Comments: This species is a resident of the arid brushlands southern California (Garrett and Dunn 1981), but has been an erratic visitor to the Salton Sea.

Savannah Sparrow *Passerculus sandwichensis*
Status: Fairly common fall and winter visitor
Counts: 2 (June) - 57 (October). Largest numbers (20 - 57) September - January, few in spring. Seen at most sites (not at Finney Lake, Ramer Lake, Red Hill, or Unit 1); concentrated at Obsidian Butte.

Comments: The large-billed subspecies *P. s. rostratus* was seen on 6 counts in March, September - December and was also concentrated at Obsidian Butte; largest numbers in September and October (45 - 50). A few were seen at Alamo, West Side.

Song Sparrow *Melospiza melodia*
Status: Common resident
Counts: 17 (November) - 135 (June). Seen on all counts and at all sites except West Side. Most common at Wister Unit and Whitewater; many also at Alamo, Unit 1, Obsidian Butte.
Comments: Associated with wet places, this sparrow nested at Obsidian Butte, Whitewater and presumably Wister Unit and several other sites.

Lincoln's Sparrow *Melospiza lincolnii*
Status: Uncommon fall and winter visitor
Counts: 1 - 3 seen on counts October - March. Seen at the Avenues, NWRHq, Ramer Lake, SSSRA, Whitewater and Wister Unit.
Comments: This species winters in southern California in marshy fields and other wet places.

White-crowned Sparrow *Zonotrichia leucophrys*
Status: Common visitor; no summer
Counts: 1 (May) - 275 (January). Seen September - May at all sites except Johnson Street; most abundant at Finney Lake.
Comments: This sparrow winters throughout southern California and Mexico; it is most associated with desert scrub at the Salton Sea.

Golden-crowned Sparrow *Zonotrichia atricapilla*
Status: Rare fall visitor
Counts: 2 sightings: single bird in October at Obsidian Butte, flock of 20 in November at SSSRA.
Comments: This species winters on the coast but is out-of-range in southeastern California.

Dark-eyed Junco *Junco hyemalis*
Status: Rare fall and winter visitor
Counts: 1 - 5 birds seen on 3 counts; in January and February at Finney

Lake, in October at Red Hill and Wister Unit.

Comments: This species resides in chaparral, oak and pine woodlands. It descends to the lowlands only in winter.

Black-headed Grosbeak *Pheucticus melanocephalus*
Status: Rare migrant
Counts: 1 sighting of 3 birds in April at Wister Unit.
Comments: This species is a more common migrant through the area than was indicated by its appearance on the counts.

Blue Grosbeak *Guiraca caerulea*
Status: Rare spring and summer (breeding?) visitor
Counts: 1 - 2 birds seen on 5 counts from April - August. Seen at NWRHq, Ramer Lake, Whitewater, and Wister Unit.
Comments: Although nesting was not documented, the presence of this species through the breeding season was indicative of at least a few breeding pairs.

Lazuli Bunting *Passerina amoena*
Status: Rare migrant
Counts: Single bird seen once in May at Finney Lake.
Comments: This species is a more common migrant through the area than was indicated by its appearance on the counts.

Red-winged Blackbird *Agelaius phoeniceus*
Status: Common resident
Counts: 88 - 7,100 (March). Seen on all counts and at all sites. Heaviest concentration at Ramer Lake, large numbers also at Finney Lake and Wister Unit.
Comments: Large breeding colonies present in cattails and reeds at Ramer and Finney Lakes, NWRHq, Obsidian Butte and other sites.

Tricolored Blackbird *Agelaius tricolor*
Status: Rare visitor
Counts: 1 sighting of 10 birds in March at Wister Unit.
Comments: This species is a rare spring migrant in the area.

Western Meadowlark *Sturnella neglecta*

Status: Fairly common resident
Counts: 1 - 41 (January). Seen in all months except July and August and at most sites (not Alamo, West Side, or Whitewater). Most common at the Avenues.
Comments: This species is a resident of the area, but was found more often in agricultural fields than in the habitat at the count sites. Nesting was probable at Wister Unit.

Yellow-headed Blackbird *Xanthocephalus xanthocephalus*
Status: Fairly common spring and summer (breeding) visitor
Counts: 5 (September) - 173 (June). Present on counts February - September at Alamo, Finney Lake, Johnson Street, Obsidian Butte, NWRHq, Ramer Lake, SSSRA, Whitewater and Wister Unit. Largest numbers at Ramer Lake, Wister Unit, and Obsidian Butte.
Comments: This species arrived in late winter to breed in reeds and cat-tails in ponds along with the Red-winged Blackbird. Nesting was documented at NWRHq, Obsidian Butte, Ramer Lake, Wister Unit.

Brewer's Blackbird *Euphagus cyanocephalus*
Status: Common resident
Counts: 4 - 1,070 (September). Present all months except August; at the Avenues, Finney Lake, NWRHq, Ramer Lake, Red Hill, SSSRA, West Side, Whitewater and Wister Unit. One huge flock of 1000 in October at Red Hill.
Comments: More common in fall and winter; this blackbird has bred locally but suitable habitat is restricted.

Great-tailed Grackle *Quiscalus mexicanus*
Status: Common resident
Counts: 60 - 298 (October). Seen on all counts and at all sites. Most abundant at Obsidian Butte, Ramer Lake and Wister Unit.
Comments: This species was in evidence during the breeding season but not during the winter months. It presumably stayed in the Imperial Valley, joining the huge flocks of "blackbirds" around the cattle feed lots. Nesting was documented at Obsidian Butte, SSSRA, and Wister Unit.

Brown-headed Cowbird *Molothrus ater*

Status: Common resident
Counts: 6 - 148 (July). Seen on counts from March - August at all sites except Red Hill and West Side. Largest numbers at Finney and Ramer Lakes.
Comments: Courting pairs were observed at Obsidian Butte. This species lays eggs in the nests of small passerines; a juvenile was seen at SSSRA being fed by a Black-tailed Gnatcatcher.

Hooded Oriole *Icterus cucullatus*
Status: Uncommon migrant
Counts: 1 - 5 seen on counts from March - August at the Avenues, Alamo, Finney Lake, NWRHq, Ramer Lake, SSSRA and West Side.
Comments: This species has been known to nest in the area (Shuford *et. al.* 1999).

Bullock's Oriole *Icterus bullockii*
Status: Uncommon spring and summer (breeding) visitor
Counts: 1 - 20 (May and June). Seen on counts from March - June at the Avenues, Finney Lake, Ramer Lake, Whitewater and Wister Unit. Most at Whitewater
Comments: Nesting was documented at Whitewater.

Scott's Oriole *Icterus parisorum*
Status: Rare visitor
Counts: Single bird seen once in January at the Avenues
Comments: This species is a rare migrant and winter visitor in the area.

House Finch *Carpodacus mexicanus*
Status: Common resident
Counts: 2 - 122 (December). Seen on most counts and in all months; seen at most sites (not Alamo, Bombay Beach, or Johnson Street). Most common at Unit 1.
Comments: Nesting was documented at NWRHq and Wister Unit; and was presumed at other sites.

Lesser Goldfinch *Carduelis psaltria*

Status: Uncommon resident
Counts: 1 - 12 seen on 12 counts, a few present in all seasons, very local. Seen at the Avenues, Finney Lake, Ramer Lake and Unit 1; mostly at Unit 1.
Comments: Nesting was not documented.

Lawrence's Goldfinch *Carduelis lawrencei*
Status: Rare visitor
Counts: 1 sighting of 5 birds in January at the Avenues.

American Goldfinch *Carduelis tristis*
Status: Rare visitor
Counts: Single bird seen once in June at Obsidian Butte.

House Sparrow *Passer domesticus*
Status: Fairly common resident
Counts: 1 - 37 (May). Seen in all months, on most counts and at most sites (not at Fig Lagoon, Red Hill, Unit 1, Whitewater, or Wister Unit). Most common at Finney Lake and West Side.
Comments: This species was introduced into the United States from Europe long ago, and occurs ubiquitously throughout the country.

Nonnative species

Flamingo spp.

There is a small group of flamingos in residence at the Salton Sea, presumably escapees, but their history is obscure. The first reference to them was on the 1968 Audubon Christmas Count when "American Flamingo" was listed among the non-natives seen at the south end (Salton Sea [south] 1969). References since then have mostly been by word-of-mouth. During our count period 2 - 7 birds were seen on 6 counts in all seasons, mostly out on the sand bars far off the Alamo River Delta. Usually when seen they were too far away to be more than pink splashes among the White Pelicans with which they fraternized; but occasionally they were close enough to identify as to species. No evidence of nesting has been found. On the counts there were 3 sightings of unidentified flamingos in 1998: 6 in July, 7 in August, 4 in October at Alamo. There were 3 sightings of identifiable species as follows:

Lesser Flamingo (*Phoeniconaias minor*)
Status: Resident (non-breeding, escapees)
Counts: 1 sighting of 4 birds in January 1999 at Red Hill.

Chilean Flamingo (*Phoenicopterus chilensis*)
Status: Resident (non-breeding, escapees)
Counts: 2 sightings: 3 birds in March 1998 at the Avenues, 4 in July 1999 at Wister Unit.

Mute Swan Cygnus olor
Status: Accidental
Counts: Single bird seen once in July at Alamo.
Comments: This bird was probably an escapee; it is an introduced species that frequents ponds in northeastern United States, but is not often seen in the west.

Black-throated Magpie-Jay *(Callocitta colliei)*
Status: Escapee
Counts: A single bird was seen during the counts - at Finney Lake in May 1998. The species is resident in central Mexico. It is kept as a caged bird, and this was undoubtedly an escapee. There have been other sightings in the Imperial Valley, most recently a single bird observed flying around a residential neighborhood in El Centro in late 2000. A pair nested in the Tijuana River Valley on the California coast south of San Diego in spring 2000, and one was seen there again in March 2001. This species might become established on the coast or at the Salton Sea.

RARE SPECIES SEEN DURING THE COUNT PERIOD

The Salton Sea has long been known as a special region for finding rare and out-of-range birds. As such, it has been visited on a regular basis by many rare bird enthusiasts and records have been kept of the sightings. Guy McCaskie has compiled these records for many years, and they have appeared in *Audubon Field Notes* (through 1997), *Field Notes* (1998) and *North American Birds* (1999 on) under the heading "Southern Pacific Coast Region." After the Internet came into popular use, sightings were posted on Web pages and sent by e-mail to subscribers.

The information in this chapter was gathered from both Internet and published sources. It is a compilation of rare-bird sightings for the count period covered in this book. There has been no attempt to make it all-encompassing; it is intended rather to show the range of unusual species found around the Salton Sea. If a species was seen on the counts, it is not included here, and there is only one listing per species, although some were seen subsequent to the date(s) given.

Rare-bird sightings from Internet sources (1998 and 1999)

The information in table below was obtained from CALBIRD (calbird.kiwi.net) and John Green's e-mail service (bewickwren@EARTHLINK.NET), and was compiled by Barbara Massey and Bob Miller.

1998

Species	Month	Site
Blue-footed Booby	Feb	NWR
Neotropic Cormorant	Apr - Jun	Lack & Lindsey
Red-tailedHawk (Harlan's)	Jan	Wister Unit
Rough-legged Hawk	Feb	near Finney Lake
Black Turnstone	Feb, Mar, Jun	Obsidian Butte, Wister Unit
Thayer's Gull	Jan - Mar	Obsidian Butte
Lesser Black-backed Gull	Jan	Obsidian Butte
Black Swift	May	Finney Lake
Dusky-capped Flycatcher	Jan	Finney Lake
Bronzed Cowbird	Jun	West Side

1999

Species	Month	Site
Black Storm-Petrel	Aug	Southeast Shore
Neotropic Cormorant	Nov	Obsidian Butte
White-winged Scoter	Jul	Johnson Rd
Solitary Sandpiper	Feb	Obsidian Butte
Wandering Tattler	Oct	Obsidian Butte

Ruff	Jan - Mar	Obsidian Butte
Red Phalarope	Jun	Wister Unit
Mew Gull	Feb, Sep	Obsidian Butte
Glaucous Gull	Jan	Obsidian Butte
Acorn Woodpecker	Jul	Wister Unit
Eastern Kingbird	Jun	Wister Unit
Black and White Warbler	Jun	Wister Unit
Rose-breasted Grosbeak	Nov	Wister Unit
Purple Finch	Oct	Finney Lake

Published sources

Additional sightings were culled by Dennis Vroman and Barbara Massey from reports published in Field Notes (McCaskie 1998) and North American Birds (McCaskie 1999a and b; 2000). The exact locations were not given; the sea was divided into north-end (NESS Riverside County) and south-end (SESS Imperial County). Although the north end contains excellent waterbird habitat, approximately 80% of the sea lies south of the county line.

Rare bird sightings from published sources

1998

Species	Month	Site
Pacific Loon	Jan	NESS
Reddish Egret	Jul	NESS
Winter Wren	Dec	SESS
Northern Parula	Nov	SESS
Orchard Oriole	Jan	SESS

1999

Species	Month	Site
Lesser Black-backed Gull	Sep	SESS
Elegant Tern	May	NESS

Species of Concern

The species listed here are considered at risk by USFWS, CDFG, or both, and are on an official published list as endangered, threatened or of special concern.

These species are: (1) State and Federally Endangered or Threatened Species, (2) Species of Special Concern in California (CDFG 1992), and (3) Migratory Nongame birds of Management Concern in the United States (USFWS 1995), a category which includes visitors that spend significant time at the Salton Sea during seasons in which they are considered at risk as well as resident birds.

Species of concern

	ES	TS	SC	MC
American White Pelican			X	
Brown Pelican	X			
Double-crested cormorant			X	
White-faced Ibis			X	X
Wood Stork			X	

continued on next page

	ES	TS	SC	MC
Fulvous Whistling-duck			X	
Snowy Plover			X	X
Mountain Plover			X	X
Long-billed curlew			X	
Laughing Gull			X	
California Gull			X	
Gull-billed Tern			X	
Black Tern			X	X
Black Skimmer			X	
Snowy Plover			X	X
Mountain Plover			X	X
Long-billed Curlew			X	X
Yuma Clapper Rail	X			
Black Rail		X		X
American Bittern			X	
Least Bittern			X	X
Burrowing Owl			X	X

Key:
ES=Endangered Species (state and/or federal)
TS=Threatened Species (state and/or federal)
SC=Bird Species of Special Concern in California (CDFG 1992)
MC=Migratory birds of Management Concern in the U.S. (USFWS 1995

PLANT LIST

This list identifies the trees, shrubs and grasses at the Salton Sea that are noted in the 15 site chapters on the census sites. Scientific names follow The Jepson Manual (Hickman 1993).

Scientific Name	Common Name
Allenrolfea occidentalis	Iodine bush
Arundo donax	Giant Reed
Atriplex canescens	Saltbush or Shad scale
Atriplex lentiformis	Saltbush or Quail bush
Cercidium sp.	Palo verde spp.
Cyperus spp.	Sedge spp.
Distichlis spicata	Alkali saltgrass
Helianthus spp.	Western sunflower spp.
Hymenoclea salsola	Burrobush
Isocoma acradenia	Desert goldenbush
Lycium spp.	Box thorn spp.
Phoradendron californicum	Desert mistletoe
Phragmites australis	Common reed
Pluchea sericea	Arrowweed
Popolus fremontii	Cottonwood
Prosopis pubescens	Screwbean mesquite
Prosopis glandulosa	Honey mesquite
Salix spp.	Willow spp.
Scirpus spp.	Bulrush spp.
Suaeda moquinii	Bush seepweed

Tamarix aphylla	Tamarisk or salt cedar or athel
Tamarix chinensis	Tamarisk or salt cedar
Typha angustifolia	Narrowleaf cattail
Typha latifolia	Soft flag

Compiled by Pat Flanagan in consultation with Larry Hendrickson, San Diego Natural History Museum, San Diego, California

LITERATURE CITED

American Ornithologists' Union. 1998. *Check-list of North American Birds, 7th Edition.*

California Department of Fish and Game. 1992. Bird species of special concern. Unpublished list, Calif. Dept. Fish & Game, Sacramento, CA.

Cody, M. 1998. California Thrasher. In *The Birds of North America,* No. 323 (A. Poole, P. Stettenheim, and F. Gill, Eds.). The Birds of North America Inc., Philadelphia, PA.

deBuys, William and Joan Myers. 1999. *Salt Dreams: Land and water in low-down California.* Univ. of New Mexico Press, Albuquerque, NM.

Earnst, S.L., L. Neel, G.L. Ivey, and T. Zimmerman. 1998. *White-faced Ibis in the Great Basin area: A population trend summary, 1985-1997.* Report for U.S. Fish & Wildl. Serv., Office of Migratory Birds, Region 1, Portland, OR.

Evens, J.G., G.W. Page, S.A. Laymon, and R.W. Stallcup. 1991. *Distribution, relative abundance and status of the Black Rail in western North America.* Condor 93:952-966.

Garrett, K. & J. Dunn. 1981. *Birds of southern California.* Los Angeles Audubon Society, Los Angeles CA.

Grinnell, Joseph. 1908. *Birds of a voyage on Salton Sea*. The Condor 10:185-191.

Hickman, J.C. ed. 1993. *The Jepson Manual: Higher plants of California*. University of California Press, Berkeley, CA.

Hunter, W.C., R.D. Ohmart, and B.W. Anderson. 1988. *Use of exotic saltcedar (Tamarix chinensis) by birds in riparian systems*. Condor 90:113-123.

James, George Wharton. 1911. *The Wonders of the Colorado Desert*. Little Brown, Boston MA.

Jehl, J.R. Jr. 1988. *Biology of the Eared Grebe and Wilson's Phalarope in the nonbreeding season; a study of adaptations of saline lakes*. Studies Avian Biol. 12:1-74.

Massey, B.W. 1998. *Guide to Birds of the Anza-Borrego Desert*. Anza-Borrego Desert Natural History Association. P.O. Box 310. Borrego Springs CA 92004-0310.

McCaskie, G. 1992. *The Summer Season: Southern Pacific Coast region*. Am. Birds 46:1177-1180.

McCaskie, G. 1996. *The Summer Season: Southern Pacific Coast region*. Natl. Aud. Soc. Field Notes 50:995-998.

McCaskie, G. 1998. *The Winter Season: Southern Pacific Coast region*. Natl. Aud. Soc. Field Notes 52:256-260.

McCaskie, G. 1999a. *Southern Pacific Region in Field Notes* 52(1,4).

McCaskie, G. 1999b. *Southern Pacific Region in North American Birds* 53(4):433.

McCaskie, G. 2000. *Southern Pacific Region in North American Birds* 54(1).

McCaskie, G., S. Liston, and W. Rapley. 1974. *First nesting of Black Skimmers in California*. Condor. 76:337-338.

Molina, K.C. 1996. *Population status and breeding biology of Black Skimmers at the Salton Sea*, California. West. Birds 27:143-158.

Pemberton, J.R. 1927. *The American Gull-billed Tern breeding in California*. The Condor 29:253-258.

Salton Sea (north) and Salton Sea (south). 1966. in *Amer. Birds*. 20:453.

Salton Sea (south). 1969. In *Amer. Birds*. 23:422-423.

Shuford, W.D., G.W. Page, and C.M Hickey. 1995. *Distribution and abundance of Snowy Plovers wintering in the interior of California and adjacent states*. West. Birds 26:82-98.

Shuford, W.D., C.M. Hickey, R.J. Safran, and G.W. Page. 1996. *A review of the status of the White-faced Ibis in winter in Calfifornia*. West. Birds 27:169-196.

Shuford, W.D., N. Warnock & K.C. Molina. 1999. *The avifauna of the Salton Sea: A synthesis*. Report for EPA Contract No. R826552-01-0 to the Salton Sea Authority, 78401 Highway 111, Suite T, La Quinta, CA 92253. Contribution No. 715 of Point Reyes Bird Observatory, 4990 Shoreline Hwy., Stinson Beach CA 94970.

Shuford, W.D., N. Warnock, K.C. Molina, B. Mulrooney, and A.E. Black. 2000. *Avifauna of the Salton Sea: Abundance, distribution, and annual phenology*. Final report for EPA Contract No. R826552-01-0 to the Salton Sea Authority, 78401 Highway 111, Suite T, La Quinta, CA 92253. Contribution No. 931 of Point Reyes Bird Observatory, 4990 Shoreline Hwy., Stinson Beach CA 94970.

Storer, P.W. and G. L. Neuchterlein. 1992. Western and Clark's Grebe.

In *The Birds of North America,* No. 26 (A. Poole and F. Gill, eds.). The Birds of North America Inc., Philadelpia, PA.

Tetra Tech Inc. 2000. Draft *Salton Sea Restoration Project* EIS/EIR, prepared for the Salton Sea Authority and Bureau of Reclamation.

U.S. Fish & Wildlife Service. 1995. *Migratory nongame birds of the United States: The 1995 list.* Office of Migratory Bird Management, U.S. Fish & Wildlife Service, Washington D.C.

About the
Participants

Kennon Corey

Ken grew up in the small college town of Claremont in eastern Los Angeles County and was birdwatching by the age of 9. His traveling began with birding trips in southern California, Arizona, Mexico, and Costa Rica under the auspices of the Audubon Society and the San Bernardino County Museum during junior high and high school. He took his bachelor's degree at University of California, Davis and master's degree at California State University, Long Beach under Charlie Collins. He worked on several field jobs specifically related to gathering information on bird diversity and abundance throughout the country prior to joining USFWS in the Carlsbad, California office. To this day his travels locally and around the world revolve around birdwatching and documenting field observations.

John Fitch

A native Californian, John started birding in 1988. Currently he is leading an active life in retirement, serving as president of El Dorado Audubon Society and doing volunteer work for several organizations, including Audubon and Seal Beach National Wildlife Refuge.

Pat Flanagan

Pat received her bachelor's degree from California State University, Long Beach, and has had a diverse career as a biologist, conservationist and educator. She is currently Conservation Outreach Director at the San Diego Natural History Museum.

Paul Jorgensen

Born and raised in San Diego County, Paul has worked as a biologist in natural resource management since 1975. He has been a Resource Ecologist for California State Parks since 1983; first as manager of the National Estuarine Research Reserve at Tijuana Estuary, and since 1993 with his brother Mark as resource manager for seven state parks in southern California: Salton Sea, Picacho, Indio Hills Palms, Mt. San Jacinto, Palomar, Rancho Cuyamaca, and Anza-Borrego Desert. His specialties include estuaries, sensitive birds and riparian restoration.

Doug Julian

Doug has been birding for about 25 years. He has been president of the Imperial Valley Birders since 1997 and acts as a guide with the Salton Sea Bird Festival. He has recently retired to Portal, Arizona.

Kathy Keane

Kathy's interest in birds led her to take a bachelor's degree in ecology at Cornell University and a master's degree in biology at California State University, Long Beach under Charlie Collins. She has owned and operated her own biological consulting firm since 1995 and feels very fortunate to have carved a niche for herself watching birds for a living. She has monitored, banded and done research on 3 endangered species: California Least Tern, Western Snowy Plover and California Gnatcatcher. In addition to working with birds, she has led and participated in several birding expeditions for the Natural Science Section of the Sierra Club, Angeles Chapter, including several to the Salton Sea, and taught biology at Cerritos Community College. When doing surveys of the northern half of the Wister Unit she often camped there to enjoy the gorgeous sunsets over the Anza-Borrego Desert and snow goose flocks greeting the rose-pink skies of dawn over the Chocolate Mountains.

John Konecny

John has been an ornithologist and ecologist in southern California since 1981. He has worked with and helped promote the recovery of several endangered or threatened avian species; including the California Least Tern, Least Bell's Vireo, California Gnatcatcher, Southwestern

Willow Flycatcher, Yuma Clapper Rail, and Light-footed Clapper Rail. He worked as a wildlife biologist with the USFWS in Carlsbad, California, for six years. In 1998, he established his own biological consulting company in Escondido, California. When not working, he enjoys birding, nature, and ecology, particularly that of seabirds in the Hawaiian Islands and Pacific Rim areas.

Clarann Levakis

Clarann has been an active birder and conservationist for many years. She has been closely involved with El Dorado Audubon, particularly as Conservation Chair.

Barbara Massey

After a 20 year stint as a medical research technician, Barbara returned to school in 1970 as a middle-aged student to pursue a second career as a field biologist. She received her master's degree at California State University, Long Beach under Charlie Collins. Her thesis was on the breeding biology of the California Least Tern, which led to continuing research on the tern and other endangered coastal birds in southern California. She also became an ardent advocate for conservation, was a founding member and early president of El Dorado Audubon in Long Beach, and in 1988 co-founded *pro esteros*, a bi-national group dedicated to the preservation of Baja California's wetlands. Now retired, she is working harder than ever on a third career as an author. Her first book was on the birds of the Anza-Borrego Desert. A third book is underway, a guide to birds of the Rogue Valley, Oregon where she now lives.

Chet McGaugh

A wildlife biologist specializing in ornithological studies, Chet lives in Riverside California, with wife Irma and daughter Carly. He has been the compiler of the Salton Sea-North Christmas Bird Counts for many years.

Bob Miller

Born and raised near the Salton Sea, Bob grew up camping and exploring the deserts and mountains of the Southwest. He is a graduate of the great outdoors and for 22 years was a professional driver who spent all of his free time getting away from the highway. He now makes his living as a bird guide and naturalist sharing his backyard with others.

Kathy Molina

Kathy is a Los Angeles based biologist specializing in studies of the Gull-billed Tern and Black Skimmer at the Salton Sea. She is currently the curator of the Dickey Ornithological Collection at the University of California, Los Angeles.

Carol Roberts

Carol has a bachelor's degree in biology from the University of Cincinnati and a master's degree from the University of California, Irvine in Biological Sciences. After a period of work as a contract consultant, she joined USFWS and for 8 years was an environmental contaminants specialist dealing with impacts of contaminants on wildlife in a variety of arenas including military installation clean ups, discharge permits, and special studies. For the past year her activities have focused on issues related to the Salton Sea, including working with the Salton Sea Authority and BR on the restoration program.

Pete Sorenson

After graduating from Humboldt State with a degree in wildlife management, Pete worked for BLM for 4 years before joining USFWS (Office of Ecological Services in Sacramento and Carlsbad, California) where he has been for over 20 years.

Mark Wimer

Mark left California in 2000 for Laurel, Maryland, to work for the American Bird Conservancy, building the web-based North American Bird Point Count Database at the USGS Patuxent Wildlife Research Center. He earned his master's degree in biology in 1995 at California State University, Long Beach under Charlie Collins, studying song variation in the Rufous-crowned Sparrow. He is co-authoring the Los Angeles County Breeding Bird Atlas, after coordinating the data-gathering phase of the project for five years. He also taught Zoology at a community college and spent six summers as a field biologist studying the California Least Tern.

Richard Zembal

Dick was introduced to the out-of-doors in high school by his older sister's boyfriend who accompanied him through gold prospecting adventures on the Yuba River, treks through the Sierra, fishing, hunting, exploring, photography, and finally observation and study. Field classes at California State University, Long Beach, where he got a master's degree under Charlie Collins, sent him off permanently in the direction of study of, and advocacy for, the natural world. Barbara and Dick first collaborated on a natural resources assessment at Point Mugu and enjoyed the association so much that they have continued off and on since. Together they unfolded some of the mysteries of a secretive endangered bird of the coastal wetlands of CA and Baja California, Mexico: the Light-footed Clapper Rail. Dick spent over 20 years working for the USFWS as a wildlife biologist, office manager, and then on special assignments. He is now working on endangered and multiple species planning and management through the Santa Ana River Watershed Program, which he helped found, as the Natural Resources Director for the Orange County Water District.

Southwest Birding Opportunities for the Ecotourist

Pat Flanagan
Conservation Outreach Director
San Diego Natural History Museum

One of the richest wintering areas for birds in the United States, the Salton Sea is also a starting point for multiple southwest birding adventures, including trips across the border into Mexico.

Each year on President's Day weekend the Salton Sea Bird Festival draws a national and international audience to not only experience the rich bird life but also to learn from many experts through lectures, workshops, and on field trips. Visit their web site for information. http://www.imperialcounty.com/birdfest/

Building from the festival, the SouthWest Birders, a group of friends and birders, have joined together to offer year round birding guide service for the southwest. Founded by two confessed birdaholics, Henry Detwiler of Yuma, Arizona and Bob Miller of Brawley, California, they specialize in the Salton Sea, southern California, and southern Arizona. They know the birds, ecology, and natural history of their backyards well. Their web site gives touring information, but also celebrates the region by providing photos, bird lists for various trips, and links to area resources. <http://www.southwestbirders.com> The San Diego Bay Bird Festival takes place the weekend prior to President's Day and also includes regional ecotourist field trips including down into Baja California. For information consult <http://www.flite-tours.com/festival.htm.

Feeding, resting and nesting habitats join the Salton Sea with the Gulf of California to the south. These bodies of water are separated by the delta of the Colorado River. The delta region, a complicated blend of habitats for humans and birds, is located in two Mexican states: Baja California and Sonora. The largest portion is in Baja California and includes the Mexicali Valley, most of the mainstream from Morelos Dam to the mouth of the river, the Rio Hardy and its floodplain, the Cucapah Range and the Laguna Salada Basin. The rich delta muds are the basis for the agricultural economy which supports Mexicali, the capital of Baja California. Many other smaller cities, ejidos (a type of communal settlement), and the Cucapah Indian communal land that includes the Laguna Salada floodplain and basin, also lie atop the delta.

The Upper Gulf of California and Colorado River Delta Biosphere Reserve, one of the largest reserves in Mexico, includes the lower floodplain of the river (as well as a large area of the waters in the upper Gulf) and is home to 280 bird species using a variety of ecosystems including riparian zones, intertidal mud flats, brackish and freshwater wetlands. The lower delta supports a variety of water and wetland uses such as small scale fishing (mostly tilapia, largemouth bass, catfish, gulf corvina, and shrimp), hunting, recreation, aquaculture, and ecotourism.

Of importance to birders, the 50,000 acre Ciènega de Santa Clara, lying within the protected core area of the reserve, is a critical component of the Colorado River Delta. Its vast lagoons support thousands of overwintering migratory waterfowl and endangered species such as the Yuma Clapper Rail and the Desert Pupfish. The Ejido Luis Encinas Johnson, an ecotourism project, includes a visitor center and trained guides with canoes and pangas or fishing boats for exploration. There is an observation tower by the campground where you can see Vs of geese and ducks, pelicans, osprey, bald eagle, or any number of heron and egret species pass overhead. With a guide you can paddle quietly through lagoons in a canoe or visit the mouth of the Colorado River and watch the 12-plus-foot tides and flocks of shorebirds come and go.

To visit the Cièneg de Santa Clara you can contact La Ruta de Sonora, a nonprofit organization that creates authentic, meaningful, and responsible travel experiences through personal encounters with the people and places of the Sonoran Desert and The Gulf of California. La Ruta fosters understanding, appreciation, and conservation of nature and culture. Through the promotion of ecotourism, La Ruta supports the economies of local communities and the different resource conservation efforts. To contact the La Ruta office, call: 1-800-806-0766, email: information@laruta.org, or visit http://www.laruta.org for an interesting description of the Sonoran borderlands including a detailed map of the Salton Sea Gulf of California region.

For additional opportunities in Sonora, visit the Southeastern Arizona Bird Observatory (SABO) on line. Noted for hummingbird research, SABO was created to address the growing needs for educational activities, ecotourism development and conservation-oriented research on both public and private lands in southeastern Arizona. Based on their award winning Southeastern Arizona Birding Trail Map with 50 great birding spots, they received a contract for the Sonora Ecotourism Project. The two maps (La Ruta and SABO) are similar in that each spot has a habitat description, signature birds, travel directions, and tourist facilities, and can be downloaded free from their web site: http://www.sabo.org.

The Intercultural Center for the Study of Deserts & Oceans (CEDO) operates from Puerto Peasco, Sonora Mexico. Throughout the year they offer excellent natural history explorations of the desert and sea by expert guides for modest fees. To get on their mailing list for upcoming programs email at: info@cedointercultural.org.

Ecotourism is conservation through ecologically responsible travel at home and abroad. It offers a positive incentive to local communities to protect their natural resources. Your commitment to tread lightly and leave a positive impact should include spending locally on food and lodging, using local guides and outfitters whenever possible, supporting citizen organizations and government agencies with stewardship responsibilities through membership and/or participation in service projects.

INDEX TO SPECIES ACCOUNTS

Abert's Towhee	177
American Avocet	152
American Bittern	136
American Coot	149
American Crow	168
American Golden-Plover	150
American Goldfinch	183
American Kestrel	147
American Pipit	173
American Redstart	176
American White Pelican	135
American Wigeon	141
Anna's Hummingbird	164
Ash-throated Flycatcher	167
Baird's Sandpiper	155
Bald Eagle	146
Bank Swallow	170
Barn Owl	163
Barn Swallow	170
Belted Kingfisher	165
Bewick's Wren	171
Black Phoebe	166
Black Rail	148
Black Scoter	144
Black Skimmer	161
Black Tern	161
Black-bellied Plover	150
Black-crowned Night-Heron	138
Black-headed Grosbeak	180
Black-necked Stilt	151
Black-tailed Gnatcatcher	172
Black-throated Gray Warbler	175
Black-throated Magpie	184
Black-throated Sparrow	178
Blue Grosbeak	180
Blue-gray Gnatcatcher	172
Blue-winged Teal	142
Bonaparte's Gull	158
Brant	141
Brewer's Blackbird	181
Brewer's Sparrow	178
Brown Pelican	135
Brown-headed Cowbird	182
Bufflehead	144
Bullock's Oriole	182
Burrowing Owl	163
Bushtit	170
Cactus Wren	171
California Gull	158
California Thrasher	172
Canada Goose	140
Canvasback	143
Caspian Tern	160
Cassin's Kingbird	167
Cassin's Vireo	168
Cattle Egret	137
Cedar Waxwing	174
Chilean Flamingo	184
Chipping Sparrow	178
Cinnamon Teal	142
Clapper Rail	148
Clark's Grebe	134
Cliff Swallow	170
Common Goldeneye	145
Common Ground-Dove	163
Common Loon	133
Common Moorhen	149
Common Raven	168
Common Snipe	156
Common Tern	161
Common Yellowthroat	176
Cooper's Hawk	146
Costa's Hummingbird	165
Crissal Thrasher	173
Dark-eyed Junco	179
Double-crested Cormorant	135
Dowitcher spp.	156
Dunlin	155
Eared Grebe	133
Eastern Phoebe	167
Empidonax spp.	166
Eurasian Wigeon	141
European Starling	173
Flamingo spp.	183
Forster's Tern	161
Franklin's Gull	157
Fulvous Whistling-Duck	139
Gadwall	141
Gambel's Quail	148
Glaucous-winged Gull	160
Golden-crowned Sparrow	179
Great Blue Heron	136
Great Egret	137
Great Horned Owl	163
Great-tailed Grackle	181
Greater Roadrunner	163
Greater Scaup	144
Greater White-fronted Goose	140
Greater Yellowlegs	152
Green Heron	138
Green-winged Teal	143
Gull spp.	160
Gull-billed Tern	160
Heermann's Gull	158
Hermit Warbler	176
Herring Gull	159
Hooded Oriole	182
Horned Grebe	133
Horned Lark	169
House Finch	182
House Sparrow	183
House Wren	171
Inca Dove	163
Killdeer	151
Ladder-backed Woodpecker	165
Lark Sparrow	178
Laughing Gull	157
Lawrence's Goldfinch	183

Lazuli Bunting	180	Sage Sparrow	178
Least Bittern	136	Sage Thrasher	172
Least Sandpiper	155	Sanderling	154
Least Tern	161	Sandhill Crane	150
Lesser Black-backed Gull	159	Savannah Sparrow	178
Lesser Flamingo	184	Savannah Sparrow (Large-billed)	178
Lesser Goldfinch	183	Say's Phoebe	167
Lesser Nighthawk	164	Scott's Oriole	182
Lesser Scaup	144	Semipalmated Plover	151
Lesser Yellowlegs	152	Sharp-shinned Hawk	146
Lincoln's Sparrow	179	Snow Goose	140
Little Blue Heron	137	Snowy Egret	137
Little Gull	158	Snowy Plover	150
Loggerhead Shrike	168	Song Sparrow	179
Long-billed Curlew	153	Sora	149
Lucy's Warbler	175	Spotted Dove	162
MacGillivray's Warbler	176	Spotted Sandpiper	153
Magnificent Frigatebird	136	Spotted Towhee	177
Mallard	142	Sprague's Pipit	173
Marbled Godwit	154	Stilt Sandpiper	155
Marsh Wren	171	Summer Tanager	177
Merlin	147	Surf Scoter	144
Mountain Bluebird	172	Thayer's Gull	159
Mountain Plover	151	Townsend's Warbler	175
Mourning Dove	162	Tree Swallow	169
Mute Swan	184	Tricolored Blackbird	180
Nashville Warbler	174	Turkey Vulture	139
Northern Flicker	165	Vaux's Swift	164
Northern Harrier	146	Verdin	170
Northern Mockingbird	172	Vermilion Flycatcher	167
Northern Pintail	143	Violet-green Swallow	169
Northern Rough-winged Swallow	169	Virginia Rail	149
Northern Shoveler	142	Virginia's Warbler	174
Orange-crowned Warbler	174	Warbling Vireo	168
Osprey	145	Western Bluebird	172
Pacific-slope Flycatcher	166	Western Grebe	134
Parasitic Jaeger	157	Western Gull	159
Peeps (Calidris spp.)	156	Western Kingbird	168
Peregrine Falcon	147	Western Meadowlark	181
Phainopepla	174	Western Sandpiper	154
Pied-billed Grebe	133	Western Tanager	177
Plumbeous Vireo	168	Western Wood-Pewee	166
Prairie Falcon	147	Whimbrel	153
Red Knot	154	White-crowned Sparrow	179
Red-breasted Merganser	145	White-faced Ibis	138
Red-naped Sapsucker	165	White-tailed Kite	146
Red-necked Phalarope	157	White-throated Swift	164
Red-shouldered Hawk	147	White-winged Dove	162
Red-tailed Hawk	147	Willet	153
Red-winged Blackbird	180	Willow Flycatcher	166
Redhead	143	Wilson's Phalarope	157
Ring-billed Gull	158	Wilson's Warbler	176
Ring-necked Duck	143	Wood Stork	139
Ring-necked Pheasant	148	Yellow Warbler	175
Rock Dove	162	Yellow-breasted Chat	177
Ross's Goose	140	Yellow-footed Gull	159
Ruby-crowned Kinglet	171	Yellow-headed Blackbird	181
Ruddy Duck	145	Yellow-rumped Warbler	175
Ruddy Turnstone	154		
Sabine's Gull	160		

CHAPTER TABLES

The following tables give information about each species seen at each site. Seasonal occurrence, breeding status and range in numbers of individuals seen on the counts are included. Abbreviations and symbols are used as follows:

Spr = Spring (Mar, Apr, May)
Sum = Summer (Jun, Jul, Aug)
Aut = Autumn (Sep, Oct, Nov)
Win = Winter (Dec, Jan, Feb)

dot =present

+ = breeding verified; p = breeding probable

Number (month) - number (month) = Range in number of birds of a species on a count - lowest number and month of occurrence followed by highest number and month of occurrence

> = more than; < = less than; ≥ = equal to or more than; ≤ = equal to or less than

occ = occasional

Alamo River Delta

	Spr	Sum	Aut	Win	Br	Comments
Pied-billed Grebe	•	•	•	•		1-8 birds seen on 4/18 counts July-Sep
Eared Grebe	•	•	•	•		3-1,100 (Jan); on 14/18 counts; highest numbers Oct-Mar
Western Grebe	•	•	•	•		2-101 (July); on 7/18 counts May-Oct
Clark's Grebe	•	•	•	•		1-28 (June); on 5/18 counts Mar-Oct
Aechmophorus spp.	•	•	•			Distant flocks of 30-327 large (Western/Clark's) grebes 3x July-Sep
American White Pelican	•	•	•	•		63 (Mar) - 2000 (Jan); on 17/18 counts; numbers variable
Brown Pelican	•	•	•	•		1 (Apr) - 500 (Aug); on 14/18 counts, largest numbers May-Sep
Double-crested Cormorant	•	•	•	•		1 (Jan) - 7500 (Dec); on 17/18 counts; usually >1,000
Great Blue Heron	•	•	•	•		3 (Jan) -195 (Aug); on all counts; largest numbers July-Nov
Great Egret	•	•	•	•		1-248 (July); on 17/18 counts; largest numbers June-Sep
Snowy Egret	•	•	•	•		1 (Jan) - 353 (July); on 15/18 counts; largest numbers June-Sep
Cattle Egret	•	•	•			4 (Mar) - 566 (July); on 8/18 counts Mar-Aug
Green Heron	•	•	•	•		1-6 birds seen on 7/18 counts Mar-Aug
Black-crowned Night-Heron	•	•	•	•		1 (Sep) - 35 (June); on 11/18 counts; most numerous in June-July
White-faced Ibis	•	•	•	•		1 (Sep) - 68 (May); on 11/18 counts; usually ≤12
Wood Stork		•	•			3 sightings: 3 birds in June, 2 in July, 13 in Sep
Turkey Vulture	•	•	•			1-32 (July); on 9/18 counts, usually ≤10
Flamingo spp.		•	•			3 sightings: 6 birds in July, 7 in Aug, 4 in Oct; too far away to speciate
Snow Goose			•	•		3 sightings: 1 bird in Jan, 1 & 36 in Nov

	Spr	Sum	Aut	Win	Br	Comments
Ross's Goose			•			10 birds seen 1x in Nov
White Goose (Snow/Ross's)				•		Distant flock of 5,000 white geese seen 1x in Dec
Canada Goose			•			Flock of 15 seen 1x in Nov
Brant	•	•		•		3 sightings: 5 birds in Feb, 1 in May, 12 in June
Mute Swan		•				3 birds seen 1x in July
Gadwall	•		•	•		1-25 (Feb); on 7/18 counts Sep-May
American Wigeon			•			5 birds seen 1x in Oct
Mallard	•		•	•		3 sightings: 5 birds in May, 3 in July, 1 in Sep
Blue-winged Teal	•			•		2 birds seen 2x in Jan & May
Cinnamon Teal	•		•	•		3-30 (Mar); on 7/18 counts Jan-July; usually ≤16
Teal spp.	•		•			Distant flocks of 15-708 seen on 4/18 counts July-Nov
Northern Shoveler	•		•	•		1 (May) - 6,600 (Jan); on 14/18 counts, usually >3,000
Northern Pintail	•		•	•		2 (May) - 372 (Jan); on 11/18 counts; 1 large flock, usually <50
Green-winged Teal	•		•	•		40 (Sep) - 1,210 (Jan); on 11/18 counts
Canvasback	•		•	•		2 sightings: 30 birds seen in Jan, 1 in Nov
Redhead	•	•	•	•		1 (Nov) - 77 (May); on 9/18 counts Mar-Nov; usually <15
Lesser Scaup	•		•	•		2 (Jan) - 454 (Nov); on 8/18 counts Oct-Mar; usually ≤30
Bufflehead				•		1 bird seen 1x in Feb
Common Goldeneye		•				1 bird seen 1x in July
Ruddy Duck	•	•	•	•		2 (July) - 2,000 (Nov); on 15/18 counts; few July-Sep
Osprey			•	•		Single birds seen on 6/18 counts July-Feb
Northern Harrier	•		•	•		1-13 (Nov); on 9/18 counts Sep-Mar

	Spr	Sum	Aut	Win	Br	Comments
Cooper's Hawk			•			1 bird seen 1x in Oct
Red-tailed Hawk			•			3 sightings of single birds in Oct-Nov
American Kestrel		•	•	•		1-4 birds seen on 10/18 counts
Merlin				•		1 bird seen 2x in Jan, Feb
Peregrine Falcon	•		•	•		1-2 birds seen on 11/18 counts
Clapper Rail	•	•		•		3 sightings of 1-2 birds in May, July, Aug
Sora		•		•		2 sightings: 2 birds in Jan, 1 in Aug
Common Moorhen	•	•	•	•		4 sightings of 1-2 birds in Jan, May, July, Sep
American Coot	•	•	•	•		6 (July) - 2,520 (Jan); on 17/18 counts; usually ≥1,000 but few Apr-July
Black-bellied Plover	•	•	•	•		1 (Aug) - 266 (Feb); on 17/18 counts; several flocks but usually <50
Snowy Plover	•	•	•	•	+	2-83 (Nov); on 11/18 counts; largest numbers Nov-Jan; nested on salt pans
Semipalmated Plover	•	•	•	•		2-61 (July); on 11/18 counts; usually <20
Killdeer	•	•	•	•	+	1-36 (Dec); on 17/18 counts; numbers variable
Black-necked Stilt	•	•	•	•	+	25 (Nov) - 2,560 (July); on all counts; >1,000 in summer months
American Avocet	•	•	•	•		83-4,120 (Mar); on all counts
Greater Yellowlegs	•	•	•	•		1-11 birds seen on 9/18 counts
Willet	•	•	•	•		2-39 birds seen on 15/18 counts; numbers variable
Spotted Sandpiper	•			•		1 bird seen 2x in Jan, Apr
Whimbrel	•	•				3 sightings of 3-5 birds in May-June
Long-billed Curlew	•	•	•	•		1-541 (Sep); on 13/18 counts; often in flocks >100

	Spr	Sum	Aut	Win	Br	Comments
Marbled Godwit	•	•	•	•		1-342 (Feb); on 17/18 counts; usually <100
Western Sandpiper	•	•	•	•		1 (June) - 10,600 (July); on 16/18 counts; largest numbers July-Aug
Least Sandpiper	•	•	•	•		5 (Sep) - 270 (Feb); on 12/18 counts; largest numbers Dec-Feb
Dunlin	•	•	•	•		1-56 (Jan); on 7/18 counts; usually ≤15
Stilt Sandpiper	•	•	•	•		1 (Feb) - 73 (Nov); on 7/18 counts; highest numbers Nov-Jan
Peep (*Calidris* spp.)	•	•	•	•		Distant flocks of 635 & 770 small sandpipers in Jan, Sep
Dowitcher spp.	•	•	•	•		2 (May) - 3,250 (Mar); on 17/18 counts; largest numbers Mar-Apr & July-Sep
Wilson's Phalarope	•	•	•			1-446 (July); on 5/18 counts; usually in flocks >140
Red-necked Phalarope		•	•			3 sightings of 6-30 birds July-Sep
Laughing Gull	•	•	•			1-30 (July); on 7/18 counts May-Oct; numbers variable
Bonaparte's Gull	•	•	•	•		1-243 (May); on 5/18 counts; two large flocks, other sightings <10
Ring-billed Gull	•	•	•	•		3 (Apr) - 1,260 (Aug); on all counts
California Gull	•	•	•	•		1 (Nov) - 129 (Aug); on 13/18 counts
Herring Gull	•	•	•	•		1-365 (Jan); on 10/18 counts Sep-Mar; occ flocks, usually ≤12
Western Gull				•		1 bird seen 1x in Feb 1998
Yellow-footed Gull	•	•	•	•		2 (Oct) - 49 (June); on 8/18 counts Mar-Oct
Gull spp.	•	•	•	•		Distant flocks of 35-1,200 gulls seen on 10/18 counts
Gull-billed Tern	•	•	•			2-12 birds seen on 5/18 counts Mar-July
Caspian Tern	•	•	•	•		1-296 (Aug); on 11/18 counts; 1 large flock, usually <20
Forster's Tern	•	•	•	•		2 (Sep) - 393 (June); on 11/18 counts May-Nov; occ flocks, usually ≤40
Black Tern	•	•	•			1 (Oct) -327 (Aug); on 9/18 counts May-Oct; numbers variable

	Spr	Sum	Aut	Win	Br	Comments
Black Skimmer	•	•	•			1-21 birds seen on 5/18 counts May-Nov
White-winged Dove			•			2 birds seen 1x in Sep
Mourning Dove	•	•	•	•	p	1 (Sep) - 17 (June); on 7/18 counts May-Sep
Common Ground-Dove	•	•	•			1-4 birds present on 6/18 counts May-Sep
Lesser Nighthawk		•				1 bird seen 1x in June
Belted Kingfisher			•	•		2 sightings: 3 birds in Oct, 1 in Nov
Black Phoebe	•	•	•	•	p	1-4 birds seen on 15/18 counts
Say's Phoebe	•	•	•	•		1-5 birds seen on 8/18 counts July-Dec
Western Kingbird	•	•	•		p	1-8 birds seen on 5/18 counts May-Aug
Loggerhead Shrike	•	•	•	•	p	1-7 birds seen on 10/18 counts
Tree Swallow	•					3 birds seen 1x in May
No. rough-winged Swallow	•			•		4 sightings of 2-3 birds Feb-May
Cliff Swallow	•					1 bird seen 1x in Mar
Barn Swallow	•		•			5 birds seen 1x in Sep
Verdin	•	•	•	•	p	1-17 birds seen on 16/18 counts; usually ≤8
Marsh Wren	•	•	•	•	+	3-9 birds seen on 15/18 counts
Ruby-crowned Kinglet			•	•		4 birds seen 1x in Oct
American Pipit	•		•	•		4-18 birds seen on 5/18 counts Oct-Mar
Orange-crowned Warbler	•	•	•			1-6 birds seen on 7/18 counts Sep-Mar
Yellow-rumped Warbler	•		•	•		2-36 (Nov); on 9/18 counts Oct-Mar; numbers variable
Common Yellowthroat	•	•	•	•	+	1-12 (Sep); on 11/18 counts
Western Tanager	•					1 bird seen 1x in May

	Spr	Sum	Aut	Win	Br	Comments
Abert's Towhee	•	•	•	•	p	1-3 birds seen on 6/18 counts
Black-throated Sparrow		•				1 bird seen 1x in Aug 1998
Savannah Sparrow			•			2 sightings of 1 & 2 birds; in Sep
Savannah Sparrow (Large-billed)			•	•		2 sightings: 1 bird in Sep, 3 in Dec
Song Sparrow	•		•	•	+	1-12 birds seen on 13/18 counts
White-crowned Sparrow			•	•		2 sightings of single birds; in Jan, Nov
Red-winged Blackbird	•		•	•	+	2 (Mar) - 85 (Sep); on 10/18 counts
Yellow-headed Blackbird		•				Flock of 16 birds seen 1x in June
Great-tailed Grackle	•		•	•		1-151 (Nov); on 11/18 counts
Brown-headed Cowbird	•		•			1 (Sep) - 21 (June); on 5/18 counts May-Sep
Hooded Oriole			•			1 bird seen 1x in Aug 1998

The Avenues

	Season				Avenue				Br	Comments
	Spr	Sum	Aut	Win	76	79	81	84		
Pied-billed Grebe	•	•		•			•	•		1-3 on 5/13 counts; mostly at 81st Ave
Eared Grebe	•	•	•	•	•	•	•	•		13 (July) - 10,300 (Jan); on 9/10 counts; highest numbers Dec-Feb
Western Grebe	•		•	•	•		•	•		2 (Jan) - 37 (Mar); on 7/13 counts
Clark's Grebe	•	•			•					1 (May) - 31 (Aug); on 5/13 counts
American White Pelican	•	•	•	•	•	•	•	•		7 (Aug) - 2,300 (Feb); on all 10 counts; few in Sum
Brown Pelican	•	•	•	•		•	•			5 (Mar) - 160 (Aug); on 6/13 counts; usually <15
Double-crested Cormorant	•	•	•	•	•	•	•	•		302 (May) - 2,900 (Feb); on all 10 counts; usually >1,000
Magnificent Frigatebird	•				•					2 birds seen 1x, in June 1998
Least Bittern		•	•				•			1 bird seen 2x in Aug, Nov
Great Blue Heron	•	•	•	•	•	•	•	•	+	11 (Oct) - 169 (Jan); on all 13 counts; fewer in Spr
Great Egret	•	•	•	•	•	•	•	•	+	11 (May) - 230 (Jan); on all 13 counts
Snowy Egret	•	•	•	•	•	•	•	•	+	3 (Oct) - 240 (Apr); on all 13 counts
Cattle Egret	•	•	•	•	•	•	•	•		8-75 birds seen on 4/13 counts Apr-Aug
Green Heron	•	•	•	•	•	•	•	•		1-2 birds seen on 10/13 counts
Black-crowned Night-Heron	•	•	•	•	•	•	•	•	+	2 (Feb) - 25 (June/July); on 8/13 counts Jan-Aug
White-faced Ibis	•	•	•	•	•	•	•	•		2-33 birds seen on 10/13 counts
Turkey Vulture	•	•	•			•				3 sightings of single birds; in Feb, Apr, Aug
Chilean Flamingo				•						3 birds seen 1x in Mar 1998

216

	Season				Avenue				Br	Comments
	Spr	Sum	Aut	Win	76	79	81	84		
Snow Goose	•			•	•					2 birds seen 1x in Dec
Canada Goose		•		•	•					6 birds seen 1x in Dec
Brant	•				•					1-22 birds seen on 4/10 counts May-Aug
Gadwall				•		•				2 sightings: 3 birds in Dec, 1 in Jan
American Wigeon				•	•					1 bird seen 1x in Jan
Mallard	•	•		•	•	•	•			1-5 birds seen on 5/10 counts Jan-July
Cinnamon Teal	•			•	•	•		•		3-7 birds seen on 4/10 counts
Northern Shoveler	•		•	•		•	•	•		13-570 (Jan); on 7/10 counts
Northern Pintail	•	•	•	•	•	•	•	•		3 (Mar) - 56 (Jan); on 7/10 counts Aug-Mar
Green-winged Teal	•			•		•	•	•		1-4 birds seen on 3 counts Jan-Mar
Redhead	•	•		•	•	•	•	•		1 (Mar) - 106 (Dec); on 7/10 counts; most in Dec-Jan
Greater Scaup				•		•				3 birds seen 1x in Jan 1998
Lesser Scaup	•	•		•	•	•	•	•		38-146 birds seen on 5/10 counts Dec-Feb (and 1 bird in June)
Surf Scoter	•	•			•	•		•		1-5 birds seen on 3 counts in May, July, Aug
Black Scoter		•			•					2 birds seen 1x in July 1998
Bufflehead				•			•	•		2 sightings of 1 & 3 birds in Dec
Common Goldeneye				•	•					1 bird seen 1x in Dec
Red-breasted Merganser	•	•		•	•	•	•	•		1-9 birds seen on 6/10 counts Dec-July
Ruddy Duck	•	•	•	•	•	•	•	•		2 (July) - 5,900 (Feb); on 9/10 counts; few in Sum

	Season				Avenue				Br	Comments
	Spr	Sum	Aut	Win	76	79	81	84		
Osprey	•	•	•	•	•	•	•	•		1-10 birds seen on all 13 counts
White-tailed Kite				•	•	•				2 sightings of single birds in Jan 1999
Northern Harrier				•	•					1 bird seen 1x in Jan
Cooper's Hawk				•	•	•	•			1-3 birds seen 3x in Dec, Jan
Red-shouldered Hawk	•	•	•	•				•		1-3 birds seen on 8/13 counts scattered throughout the year
Red-tailed Hawk	•			•	•		•			1-3 birds seen on 4/13 counts Jan-Mar
American Kestrel	•	•	•	•	•	•	•	•	p	2-7 birds seen on 12/13 counts
Peregrine Falcon		•		•	•		•			2 sightings: 2 birds in Feb, 1 in June
Gambel's Quail	•	•	•	•	•		•	•	p	2-24 (Dec); on 6/10 counts
Virginia Rail				•				•		1 bird seen 1x in Dec
Sora				•		•				2 birds seen on 2 counts; in Jan, Feb
Common Moorhen	•	•	•	•	•		•			1-13 birds seen on 11/13 counts
American Coot	•	•	•	•	•		•	•		2 (Aug) - 875 (Apr); on 11/13 counts; few in Sum
Black-bellied Plover	•	•	•	•	•			•		2-48 (Aug); on 9/13 counts
Snowy Plover	•	•			•				p	1-8 on 5/13 counts Mar-Aug
Semipalmated Plover	•	•	•		•					4-12 birds seen 4x in Apr, Aug, Oct
Killdeer	•	•	•	•	•	•	•	•	+	3 (Mar) - 19 (Aug); on all 13 counts
Black-necked Stilt	•	•	•	•	•	•	•	•	+	9 (Mar) - 811 (July); on all 13 counts
American Avocet	•	•	•	•	•	•	•	•	+	85 (Aug) - 580 (Apr); on all 13 counts
Greater Yellowlegs	•	•	•	•	•	•	•	•		1-9 seen on 10/13 counts

	Season				Avenue				Br	Comments
	Spr	Sum	Aut	Win	76	79	81	84		
Lesser Yellowlegs	•	•				•	•			1 and 3 birds seen on 2 counts; in Feb, Aug
Willet	•	•	•	•	•	•	•	•		1 (Jan) - 155 (Apr); on 11/13 counts; highest numbers Apr, Aug
Spotted Sandpiper		•		•			•			2 sightings: 2 birds in Aug, 1 in Dec
Whimbrel	•	•	•		•					3 sightings: 3 birds in Mar, 16 in Apr, 31 in Aug
Long-billed Curlew	•	•	•		•					3 sightings of 1-4 birds; in Apr, May, Aug
Marbled Godwit	•	•	•	•	•					1 (Aug) - 66 (Oct); on 11/13 counts
Sanderling	•				•					1 bird seen 1x in May 1998
Western Sandpiper	•	•	•	•	•		•			22 (Dec) - 730 (Aug); on 7/13 counts
Least Sandpiper	•	•	•	•	•		•	•		1-95 (Dec); on 9/13 counts
Dunlin	•		•		•					3 sightings: 17 birds in Apr, 4 in Nov, 1 in Dec
Dowitcher spp.	•	•	•	•	•		•			1 (Jan) - 520 (Apr); on 9/13 counts
Common Snipe	•			•		•				Single bird seen 2x in Feb, Mar
Wilson's Phalarope	•	•	•		•		•			3 sightings: 1 bird in May, 60 in July, 165 in Aug
Red-necked Phalarope	•				•					1 flock of 400; in May
Laughing Gull		•		•	•			•		3 sightings: 2 birds in Jan, 4 in June, 1 in Aug
Bonaparte's Gull	•	•	•	•	•	•				2 sightings: 252 in May, 4 in Nov
Ring-billed Gull	•	•	•	•	•	•	•	•		2 (June) - 14,000 (Nov); on all 13 counts; usually <300
California Gull	•	•	•	•	•		•	•		(June) - 3,750 (Nov); on 13/13 counts; usually <500
Herring Gull	•	•	•	•	•	•	•	•		15 (Apr) - 550 (Nov); on 6/13 counts Nov-Apr; usually <70

	Season				Avenue				Br	Comments
	Spr	Sum	Aut	Win	76	79	81	84		
Thayer's Gull			•		•					1 bird seen 1x in Nov 1999
Yellow-footed Gull		•				•				14 birds seen 1x in Aug
Glaucous-winged Gull				•	•	•				Single bird seen 2x in Dec, Jan
Gull spp.		•	•	•	•	•	•	•		Distant flocks of 55-3,600 seen on 5/10 counts
Gull-billed Tern	•	•	•		•	•	•			2-8 birds seen on 4 counts in May-July
Caspian Tern	•		•	•	•	•	•	•		4 (Dec) - 190 (Aug); on all 13 counts
Common Tern			•		•		•			6 birds each at 2 sites on the same count in Aug 1998
Forster's Tern	•		•	•	•	•	•	•		1 (Dec) - 70 (Aug); on 11/13 counts
Least Tern		•				•				1 bird seen 1x in June 1998
Black Tern	•	•				•	•	•		1-72 (May); on 5/13 counts May-Aug
Black Skimmer		•				•	•			1-8 birds seen on 3 counts June-Aug
Rock Dove				•	•					Flock of 80 seen 1x in Dec
Spotted Dove	•									2 birds seen 1x in Mar 1998
White-winged Dove	•	•					•	•		3 sightings of 7, 14, & 64 birds in June-July
Mourning Dove	•	•	•	•	•	•	•	•	p	2 (Feb) - 85 (July); on 8/10 counts Dec-Aug
Common Ground-Dove	•		•	•	•	•	•	•	p	1-10 birds seen on 9/10 counts
Greater Roadrunner	•		•	•	•	•	•	•	p	1-3 birds seen on 8/10 counts
Lesser Nighthawk	•	•			•	•	•		p	2-6 birds seen on 3 counts, May-July
Anna's Hummingbird			•	•	•	•				1-2 birds seen on 3 counts; in Jan, Feb, Oct
Belted Kingfisher			•	•	•	•		•		1-3 birds seen on 4 /10 counts Oct-Jan

	Season				Avenue					
	Spr	Sum	Aut	Win	76	79	81	84	Br	Comments
Ladder-backed Woodpecker		•	•		•		•	•		1-4 birds seen on 4/10 counts in Jan, Feb, Oct
Northern Flicker			•	•		•				1 bird seen 1x in Jan
Black Phoebe	•		•	•	•	•	•	•	p	1-9 birds seen on 8/10 counts
Eastern Phoebe				•		•				1 bird seen 2x, in Dec 1998 & Jan 1999
Say's Phoebe			•	•	•	•		•		1-8 birds seen on 5/10 counts
Western Kingbird	•	•			•	•	•	•	p	5-14 birds seen on 4 counts May-Aug
Loggerhead Shrike	•	•	•	•	•	•	•	•	p	1-7 birds seen on 7/10 counts
Common Raven			•	•	•	•	•	•		2-9 birds seen on 6/10 counts
Horned Lark				•		•	•			Flock of 35 seen 1x, in Dec
Tree Swallow	•			•	•	•				3 sightings: 35 birds in Jan, single birds in Mar, Dec
Violet-green Swallow	•						•			1 bird each at 2 sites on same count in Mar
No. rough-winged Swallow	•		•		•	•	•			1-12 birds seen on 6/10 counts Dec-May
Barn Swallow			•		•	•				Seen on 2 counts at 3 sites; 8 birds in Oct, 4 in Dec
Verdin	•	•	•	•	•	•	•	•	p	2-15 birds seen on 10/10 counts
Cactus Wren		•	•	•	•	•	•			2-8 (Jan); on 6/10 counts
Bewick's Wren				•	•	•				2 sightings: 2 birds in Jan, 1 in Feb
Marsh Wren	•		•	•	•	•	•	•	p	1-15 (Jan); on 9/10 counts
Ruby-crowned Kinglet				•	•					1 bird seen 1x: in Dec
Blue-gray Gnatcatcher			•	•	•	•				2 sightings: 2 birds in Dec, 1 in Jan
Black-tailed Gnatcatcher			•	•	•	•		•	p	1-3 birds seen on 5/10 counts

	Season				Avenue				Br	Comments
	Spr	Sum	Aut	Win	76	79	81	84		
Northern Mockingbird	•	•	•	•	•	•	•	•	p	1-10 birds seen on all 10 counts
Sage Thrasher			•	•	•					1 bird seen 1x, in Jan 1998
European Starling	•			•	•	•	•	•	p	5 (Mar) - 338 (Jan); on 8/10 counts; mostly in Win
American Pipit			•	•	•	•	•	•		1-8 birds seen on 4/10 counts Dec-Feb
Phainopepla				•	•	•	•			1-9 birds seen on 4 counts Dec-Feb
Orange-crowned Warbler				•	•					1 bird seen 1x in Dec
Yellow-rumped Warbler			•	•	•		•	•		1 (Oct) - 85 (Dec); on 6/10 counts Oct-Mar
Common Yellowthroat		•	•	•	•	•	•	•	p	1-4 birds seen on 8/10 counts
Abert's Towhee		•			•	•	•		p	1-5 seen on 7/10 counts
Lark Sparrow	•	•					•	•		3 sightings of 3-5 birds; in Jan, May, June
Sage Sparrow				•		•	•			2 sightings: 3 birds in Dec, 2 in Jan
Savannah Sparrow	•			•	•	•	•			Seen on 2 counts at 3 sites; 1 bird in Jan, 2 in Mar
Song Sparrow	•		•	•	•	•		•	p	1-9 birds seen on 8/10 counts
Lincoln's Sparrow	•			•	•	•				1-2 birds seen on 3 counts, Jan-Mar
White-crowned Sparrow	•		•	•	•		•	•		3 (Mar) - 44 (Dec); on 6/10 counts Dec-Mar
Red-winged Blackbird	•			•	•	•				2 sightings: 200 birds in Jan, 2 in May
Western Meadowlark	•		•	•	•	•	•			2 (May) - 33 (Jan); on 4/10 counts Dec-May
Brewer's Blackbird		•		•	•		•			2-45 birds seen on 7/10 counts Dec-June
Great-tailed Grackle		•	•	•	•			•		1-16 birds seen on 8/10 counts
Brown-headed Cowbird	•	•			•	•		•		2-35 birds seen on 3 counts May-July; at all avenues in July

	Season				Avenue				Br	Comments
	Spr	Sum	Aut	Win	76	79	81	84		
Hooded Oriole	•	•			•					3 sightings of 1-2 birds, in Mar, May, June
Bullock's Oriole	•	•			•	•	•	•		3 sightings of 1-10 birds: 1 in Mar, 1 in May, 10 in June
Scott's Oriole				•	•					1 bird seen 1x in Jan
House Finch	•		•	•	•	•	•	•	p	1 (Aug) - 112 (Jan); on all 10 counts
Lesser Goldfinch	•			•						2 sightings: 2 birds in Feb, 1 in Mar
Lawrence's Goldfinch				•		•				5 birds seen 1x in Jan 1998
House Sparrow	•	•		•	•		•			1-5 seen on 5/10 counts

Bombay Beach

	Spr	Sum	Aut	Win	Comments
Eared Grebe	•	•	•	•	1 (June) - 6,000 (Feb); on 7/11 counts from Nov-June
American White Pelican	•		•	•	1-311 (Mar); on 6/11 counts
Brown Pelican		•	•	•	1-40 (Sep); on 4/11 counts
Double-crested Cormorant	•	•	•	•	1-125 (Nov); on 7/11 counts
Great Blue Heron	•	•	•	•	1-45 (Sep); on 10/11 counts; usually <15
Great Egret	•	•	•	•	1-9 (Aug); on 7/11 counts; usually 1-2
Snowy Egret	•	•	•	•	1-13 (Sep); on 6/11 counts
Black-crowned Night-Heron	•	•			3 sightings: 40 in Mar, 3 in Apr, 1 in Jul
Turkey Vulture		•			1 bird seen 1x in Aug
Brant	•	•			3 sightings of 1-4 birds in Mar, May, June
Gadwall				•	2 birds seen 1x in Jan
Mallard	•				2 birds seen 1x in Mar
Cinnamon Teal	•	•		•	1-30 (Aug); on 4/11 counts
Northern Shoveler	•	•	•	•	22-700 (Apr); on 6/11 counts
Northern Pintail	•	•		•	5-39 (Mar); on 4/11 counts
Green-winged Teal	•			•	7-280 (Mar); on 4/11 counts; usually <20, 1 large flock
Redhead	•		•	•	5-301 (Jan); on 4/11 counts; large flocks in Jan, Mar
Ring-necked Duck				•	4 birds seen 1x in Jan
Lesser Scaup				•	2 sightings: 30 birds in Jan, 23 in Dec
Surf Scoter		•			1 bird seen 1x in Aug

	Spr	Sum	Aut	Win	Comments
Common Goldeneye			•	•	2 sightings: 1 bird in Nov, 7 in Dec
Ruddy Duck	•		•	•	40-251 (Apr); on 6/11 counts
Osprey		•	•		Single bird seen 2x in Aug-Sep
Northern Harrier	•				1 bird seen 1x in Mar
American Kestrel		•			1 bird seen 1x in June
Common Moorhen			•		1 bird seen 1x in Sep
American Coot	•	•	•	•	5-104 (Mar); on 7/11 counts
Black-bellied Plover	•	•	•	•	2-41 (Mar); on 8/11 counts
Snowy Plover	•	•	•	•	3-30 (June); on 6/11 counts Feb-Aug
Semipalmated Plover	•	•	•	•	1-28 (July); on 5/11 counts Jan-July
Killdeer	•	•	•	•	1-10 (Mar); on 8/11 counts
Black-necked Stilt	•	•	•	•	10-210 (Sep); on all counts
American Avocet	•	•	•	•	5-317 (Sep); on 10/11 counts
Willet	•	•	•	•	1-26 (Sep); on 5/11 counts
Spotted Sandpiper	•	•			1 bird seen 1x in Aug
Marbled Godwit			•		1 bird seen 1x in Sep
Red Knot	•				5 birds seen 1x in Apr 1998
Western Sandpiper	•	•	•	•	25-580 (Aug); on 7/11 counts
Least Sandpiper	•	•	•	•	2-73 (Feb); on 8/11 counts; usually >25
Dunlin	•				5 birds seen 1x in Mar
Peep (*Calidris* spp.)	•				Distant flocks of <200 small sandpipers in Mar, Apr
Dowitcher spp.	•	•	•	•	1-155 (Sep); on 8/11 counts

	Spr	Sum	Aut	Win	Comments
Wilson's Phalarope		•			2 sightings: 57 birds in July, 1 in Aug
Red-necked Phalarope		•			Flock of 40 seen 1x, in June
Parasitic Jaeger			•		1 bird seen 1x in Aug 1998
Bonaparte's Gull	•		•	•	2-41 (Apr); on 4/11 counts
Ring-billed Gull	•	•	•	•	5-150 (Apr); on 9/11 counts
California Gull	•	•	•	•	1-150 (Apr); on 6/11 counts
Herring Gull	•		•	•	2-40 (Jan); on 5/11 counts
Yellow-footed Gull	•				2 birds seen 1x in Apr
Gull spp.	•	•	•	•	Distant flocks of 150-2,050 on 5/11 counts
Caspian Tern	•	•	•	•	1-100 (Apr); on 9/11 counts
Forster's Tern	•	•	•		3-36 (Sep); on 4/11 counts
Black Tern	•	•	•		Single bird seen 2x, in Aug, Sep
Rock Dove	•	•	•	•	1-20 (Feb); on 6/11 counts
Lesser Nighthawk	•	•		•	1-29 (July); on 3/11 counts; nested in Jul
Black Phoebe			•		1 bird seen 1x, in Sep
Say's Phoebe	•	•		•	1-2 birds seen 3x, in May, Aug, Dec
Common Raven	•	•			5 birds seen 1x in June
Tree Swallow	•	•		•	1-20 (June); on 4/11 counts
Bank Swallow		•			1 bird seen 1x in July 1998
Cliff Swallow		•			1 bird seen 1x in July
Barn Swallow	•		•		2 sightings: 4 birds seen in Aug, 2 in Sep
Verdin		•	•		2 sightings: 1 bird seen in Aug, 3 in Sep

	Spr	Sum	Aut	Win	Comments
Marsh Wren	•		•		2 sightings: 8 birds seen in Mar, 2 in Sep
American Pipit	•			•	2 birds seen 2x in Jan, Mar
Orange-crowned Warbler			•		2 birds seen 1x in Sep
Common Yellowthroat		•	•		5 birds seen 2x in Aug, Sep
Abert's Towhee	•	•	•	•	1-6 (Sep); on 6/11 counts
Sage Sparrow		•		•	2 sightings: 1 bird seen in July, 3 in Dec
Savannah Sparrow	•	•	•	•	1-7 (Aug); on 5/11 counts
Song Sparrow	•	•	•	•	2-19 (Apr); on 6/11 counts
White-crowned Sparrow	•		•	•	2-5 birds seen on 3 counts; in Jan, Apr, Sep
Red-winged Blackbird		•	•		2 birds seen 1x in Sep
Western Meadowlark			•		6 birds seen 1x, in Sep
Great-tailed Grackle	•				2 sightings: 1 bird seen in Mar, 3 in May
Brown-headed Cowbird	•	•		•	1-20 (Feb); on 5/11 counts
House Sparrow	•	•	•		1-6 (June); on 4/11 counts

Fig Lagoon

	Spr	Sum	Aut	Win	Br	Comments
Common Loon	•					1 bird seen 1x in Mar
Pied-billed Grebe	•	•	•	•	p	3 (Sep) - 48 (Jan); on 13/15 counts
Eared Grebe	•		•	•		1-12 birds seen on 10/15 counts Sep-May
Western Grebe	•	•	•	•		1-18 birds seen on 13/15 counts
Clark's Grebe	•			•		2 sightings: 2 birds in Jan, 1 in Mar
American White Pelican				•		1 bird seen 1x in Jan
Brown Pelican		•	•			4 sightings of 1-6 birds in Aug, Sep, Oct
Double-crested Cormorant	•		•	•		2 (May) - 125 (Nov); on 14/15 counts
American Bittern				•		1 bird seen 1x in Jan
Great Blue Heron	•	•	•	•		1-10 birds seen on all counts
Great Egret	•	•	•	•		2-18 birds seen on all counts
Snowy Egret	•	•	•	•		2-24 birds seen on 14/15 counts
Cattle Egret	•	•	•	•		1-27 (Aug); on 12/15 counts; usually <10
Green Heron	•		•	•		1-4 on 11/15 counts
Black-crowned Night-Heron	•	•	•	•		1-28 (Oct); on 11/15 counts; usually ≤6
White-faced Ibis	•		•	•		1-50 (Feb); on 6/15 counts, usually ≤10
Turkey Vulture	•	•	•			1-2 birds seen 3x in Mar, June, Sep
Mallard	•			•		2-6 birds seen on 4 counts; in Jan, Mar, May, Nov
Cinnamon Teal	•	•		•		1-73 (Jan); on 8/15 counts; usually <20
Northern Shoveler				•		3 birds seen 1x in Jan

	Spr	Sum	Aut	Win	Br	Comments
Green-winged Teal	•		•	•		1-13 birds seen on 4 counts; in Jan, Mar, Nov
Redhead	•			•		2 sightings: 5 birds in Jan, 1 in Mar
Lesser Scaup				•		1-2 birds seen 2x in Jan
Surf Scoter	•					Flock of 15 birds seen 1x in Mar
Bufflehead	•					1 bird seen 1x in Mar
Ruddy Duck	•	•	•	•		2-68 (Jan); on 12/15 counts
Osprey				•		1 bird seen 1x in Jan
Northern Harrier	•	•	•	•		Single birds seen on 6/15 counts
Cooper's Hawk	•					1 bird seen 1x in Mar
Red-tailed Hawk	•				•	2 sightings: 2 birds in Jan, 1 in Mar
American Kestrel	•	•	•		•	1-2 birds seen on 10/15 counts
Merlin			•			1 bird seen 1x in Sep
Gambel's Quail	•					1 bird seen 1x in Apr
Common Moorhen	•	•		•		1-3 birds seen on 5/15 counts; in Jan, Mar, Apr, Sep
American Coot	•	•	•	•		3 (May) - 37 (Nov); on all counts
Killdeer	•		•			4 sightings of 1-2 birds, in Apr, May, Sep
Black-necked Stilt	•	•			•	2-18 birds seen on 5/15 counts
American Avocet	•				•	3 sightings: 1 bird in Feb, 17 in Mar, 2 in May
Long-billed Curlew			•		•	3 sightings: 1 & 14 birds in Jan, 1 in Oct
Western Sandpiper				•		Flock of 15 seen 1x in Feb
Dowitcher spp.				•		Flock of 26 seen 1x in Jan
Heermann's Gull		•				Flock of 13 seen 1x in June

	Spr	Sum	Aut	Win	Br	Comments
Ring-billed Gull	•	•	•	•	•	1-17 birds seen on 6/15 counts
Herring Gull		•		•	•	2 sightings: 1 bird in Jan, 3 in June
Caspian Tern		•	•			2 sightings: 1 bird in July, 2 in Aug
Forster's Tern	•	•	•	•		1-12 birds seen on 12/15 counts
White-winged Dove	•	•	•			2 sightings: 2 birds in May, 1 in June
Mourning Dove	•	•	•	•		3-14 birds seen on 9/15 counts Mar-Oct
Common Ground-Dove	•		•	•		3 sightings of 1-2 birds in Jan, Mar, Sep
Greater Roadrunner	•	•	•	•		1-2 birds seen on 6/15 counts
Burrowing Owl	•					5 birds seen 1x in May
Lesser Nighthawk	•					1 bird seen 1x in May
Belted Kingfisher			•	•		1-3 birds seen on 5/15 counts Sep-Mar
Western Wood-Pewee	•					1 bird seen 1x in May
Willow Flycatcher			•			1 bird seen 1x in Sep
Black Phoebe	•	•	•	•		1-4 birds seen on 13/15 counts
Say's Phoebe	•		•	•		3 sightings of 1-2 birds in Jan, Sep, Oct
Western Kingbird	•	•				4 sightings of 1-5 birds, Apr-July
Loggerhead Shrike	•		•			4 sightings of 1-2 birds in May, Sep, Oct
Common Raven	•	•				1-11 birds seen on 4 counts Mar-July
Tree Swallow			•	•		3 sightings: 85 in Jan, 6 in Feb, 35 in Oct
No. rough-winged Swallow	•	•	•	•		1-30 birds seen on 7/15 counts, Jan-June
Cliff Swallow	•	•	•			5-80 (June); on 5/15 counts, Mar-Aug
Barn Swallow			•			8 birds seen 1x in Oct

	Spr	Sum	Aut	Win	Br	Comments
Verdin	•			•		1-4 birds seen on 9/15 counts Sep-May
Marsh Wren	•	•	•	•		1-3 birds seen on 8/15 counts
Blue-gray Gnatcatcher	•					1 bird seen 1x in Apr
Black-tailed Gnatcatcher	•					1 bird seen 1x in Mar
Mountain Bluebird	•					1 bird seen 1x in Apr 1998
Northern Mockingbird	•		•	•		1-2 birds seen on 4 counts; in Jan, Mar, Apr, Sep
European Starling	•	•				2 sightings: 3 birds in Mar, 15 in Aug
Phainopepla	•					1 bird seen 1x in Mar
Orange-crowned Warbler	•		•			2-4 birds seen on 3 counts in Mar, May, Sep
Yellow Warbler	•		•			2 sightings: 2 birds in May, 1 in Sep
Yellow-rumped Warbler	•			•		1-16 (Oct); on 8/15 counts, Oct-Apr
Common Yellowthroat	•	•				4 sightings of 1-3 birds from Apr-June
Wilson's Warbler	•					2 birds seen 1x in Apr
Abert's Towhee	•	•	•	•	p	2-8 birds seen on 11/15 counts
Brewer's Sparrow			•			2 birds seen 1x in Sep 1999
Savannah Sparrow			•			11 birds seen 1x in Sep
Song Sparrow	•					2 birds seen 1x in Mar
White-crowned Sparrow	•			•		2 sightings: 9 birds in Jan, 3 in Apr
Red-winged Blackbird	•	•				6-52 (July); on 9/15 counts, Jan-Sep
Western Meadowlark	•		•	•		1-4 birds seen on 6/15 counts
Great-tailed Grackle	•	•	•	•		1-10 birds seen on 8/15 counts
Brown-headed Cowbird	•					4 sightings of 1-6 birds Apr-June

	Spr	Sum	Aut	Win	Br	Comments
House Finch	•					1 bird seen 1x in Apr

Finney Lake

	Spr	Sum	Aut	Win	Br	Comments
Pied-billed Grebe	•	•	•	•	+	1 (Feb) - 20 (Oct); on 17/19 counts; juvs in May, Oct
Eared Grebe	•		•	•		1-6 birds seen on 14/19 counts
Western Grebe	•	•	•	•	+	1-33 (Nov); on 16/19 counts; juvs in June-July
Clark's Grebe	•	•	•	•	+	1-7 birds seen on 11/19 counts; juvs in June-July
Brown Pelican		•				Group of 12 birds seen 1x in Sep
Double-crested Cormorant	•	•	•	•		1-956 birds seen on all counts; usually ≤36 but occ large flocks
Magnificent Frigatebird		•				1 bird seen 1x overhead; in July 1998
Least Bittern	•		•	•	p	1-5 birds seen on 8/19 counts May-Oct
Great Blue Heron	•	•	•	•		1-13 birds seen on 17/19 counts; usually ≤5
Great Egret	•	•	•	•		1-87 birds seen on all counts; few Jan-June; highest numbers July, Nov
Snowy Egret	•	•	•	•		1-107 (July); on 16/19 counts; occ roosted at night
Cattle Egret	•	•	•	•		1-192 (July); on 17/19 counts; occ roosted at night
Green Heron	•	•	•	•	+	1-15 (July); on 17/19 counts; in all months; juvs in June
Black-crowned Night-Heron	•	•	•	•		1-24 (July); on 18/19 counts; 24 in July, usually <10
White-faced Ibis	•	•	•	•		1-51 (Jan); on 13/19 counts; occ roosted at night
Turkey Vulture	•	•	•	•		1-3 birds seen on 10/19 counts Mar-Nov
Fulvous Whistling-Duck	•	•			+	1-7 adults seen 4x Apr-July; pair with 10 chicks in July 1999
Canada Goose			•			1 bird seen 1x in Nov
Gadwall	•					2 birds seen 2x in Mar-Apr

	Spr	Sum	Aut	Win	Br	Comments
American Wigeon	•			•		3 birds seen 1x in Mar
Mallard	•	•	•	•		1-5 birds seen on 7/19 counts
Blue-winged Teal	•		•			1-2 birds seen 2x in Apr, Oct
Cinnamon Teal	•	•	•	•	+	1-89 (Jan); on 15/19 counts; numbers variable; 3 juvs in June
Northern Shoveler	•	•	•	•		1-42 (Dec); on 10/19 counts; highest numbers Nov-Dec
Northern Pintail			•	•		2-24 birds seen 3x in Jan, Sep, Nov
Green-winged Teal	•	•	•	•		1-27 (Jan); on 7/19 counts Sep-Apr
Redhead	•		•	•		1-4 birds seen on 6/19 counts Apr-July, Nov
Ruddy Duck	•		•	•	+	1-26 (June); on 16/19 counts; juvs in June
Osprey			•	•		Single bird seen 2x in Feb, Nov
Northern Harrier			•	•		1-4 birds seen on 8/14 counts Oct-Feb
Sharp-shinned Hawk			•	•		1-2 birds seen 3x in Jan, Feb, Oct
Cooper's Hawk			•	•		1-2 birds seen on 4/19 counts in Oct, Nov, Jan, Feb
Red-shouldered Hawk				•		1 bird seen 1x in Jan
Red-tailed Hawk	•		•	•		1-4 birds seen on 7/19 counts Oct-Mar
American Kestrel		•	•	•		1-3 birds seen on 9/19 counts June-Jan
Ring-necked Pheasant	•					1 bird seen 1x in May
Gambel's Quail	•	•	•	•	p	1-18 (Sep); on 8/19 counts; usually <10
Clapper Rail	•	•		•	p	1-4 birds seen on 7/19 counts Mar-Aug
Virginia Rail			•	•		1-2 birds heard 3x in July, Sep, Dec
Sora	•		•	•	p	1-3 birds heard on 10/19 counts
Common Moorhen	•	•	•	•	+	1 (Jan) - 27 (July); on 16/19 counts; highest numbers June-Aug; juvs in June

	Spr	Sum	Aut	Win	Br	Comments
American Coot	•	•	•	•	+	18-171 (Jan); on all counts; juvs in May-June
Killdeer	•	•	•	•	+	1-14, 14 in June; on 16/19 counts; in most months; juvs in June
Black-necked Stilt	•	•	•	•		5-52 (July); on 18/19 counts
American Avocet	•	•	•	•		2-50 (Aug); on 12/19 counts July-Feb
Greater Yellowlegs	•	•	•	•		1-37 (Oct); on 6/19 counts Sep-Mar; usually ≤8
Lesser Yellowlegs			•	•		1 bird seen 2x in Jan, Sep
Willet	•		•			1 bird seen 2x in May, Oct
Spotted Sandpiper	•	•	•	•		1-5 birds seen on 9/19 counts throughout the year
Whimbrel	•	•				1-2 birds seen 3x in Mar, May, July
Long-billed Curlew	•					1 bird seen 1x in June
Western Sandpiper	•	•	•	•		2-75 (Oct); on 5/19 counts July-Dec
Least Sandpiper	•	•	•	•		2-59 (Sep); on 5/19 counts Sep-Mar
Dunlin			•			2 birds seen 1x in Nov
Dowitcher spp.	•	•	•	•		6 (July) - 109 (Jan); on 11/19 counts
Common Snipe		•	•			1 bird seen 1x in Sep
Red-necked Phalarope		•				3 birds seen 1x in June
Laughing Gull		•				3 birds seen 1x in July
Ring-billed Gull	•		•	•		7-21 (Nov); on 4/19 counts
Gull-billed Tern	•					1 bird seen 1x in Apr
Caspian Tern	•	•	•	•		1-6 birds seen on 12/19 counts
Forster's Tern	•	•	•	•		1-17 (Sep, Oct); on 13/19 counts; higher numbers in Aut
Black Tern	•	•	•			3-20 (Aug); on 6/19 counts; May-Sep

	Spr	Sum	Aut	Win	Br	Comments
Black Skimmer		•				2 sightings: 1 bird seen in June, 2 in July
Rock Dove	•					10 birds seen 1x in Apr
White-winged Dove	•	•	•	•	p	4-52 (May); on 6/19 counts; present May-July
Mourning Dove	•	•	•	•	+	1-59 (May); on 17/19 counts; in all months; nest with eggs in June
Inca Dove			•			1 bird seen 1x in Sep 1999
Common Ground-Dove	•	•	•	•	p	1-9 birds seen on 11/19 counts; not seen Jan-Apr
Greater Roadrunner	•	•	•		p	1-3 birds seen on 10/19 counts; nested locally
Barn Owl	•	•				1-2 birds seen 3x in June, July, Aug
Burrowing Owl	•	•				1-2 birds seen 2x in Mar, June
Lesser Nighthawk	•	•	•	•	+	1-11 birds seen on 9/19 counts; mostly May-Aug; juvs in Aug
Belted Kingfisher	•		•	•		1-2 birds seen on 8/19 counts May-July
Red-naped Sapsucker	•					1 bird seen 1x in Apr 1998
Ladder-backed Woodpecker	•			•		1 bird seen 2x in May, Dec
Northern Flicker			•	•		1-2 birds seen on 4/19 counts Oct-Jan
Western Wood-Pewee	•					4 birds seen 1x in May
Willow Flycatcher	•					1 bird seen 1x in May
Pacific-slope Flycatcher	•		•			2 sightings: 4 birds seen in May, 1 in Sep
Black Phoebe	•	•	•	•	p	1-16 (Dec); on 18/19 counts
Say's Phoebe	•		•	•		1-5 birds seen on 5/19 counts; nested locally
Ash-throated Flycatcher	•				p	2 sightings: 1 bird seen in May, 2 in July; nested locally
Western Kingbird	•	•			p	2-7 birds seen on 7/19 counts Apr-July; nested locally
Loggerhead Shrike	•		•	•		1-5 birds seen on 6/19 counts July-Dec

	Spr	Sum	Aut	Win	Br	Comments
Warbling Vireo	•					4 birds seen 1x in May
Tree Swallow	•	•	•	•		1 (Mar) - 550 (Jan); on 8/19 counts Aug-Feb
No. rough-winged Swallow	•			•		2-151 (Mar); on 8/19 counts Nov-June
Bank Swallow	•					Flock of 10 seen in Apr 1999
Cliff Swallow	•	•	•	•	+	2->1,000 (June-July); on 7/19 counts; nesting colony, see text
Barn Swallow	•	•	•			2 sightings; 3 birds seen in Mar, 58 in Sep
Verdin	•	•	•	•	+	2-36 (July); on 18/19 counts; juvs in June
Cactus Wren	•	•	•	•	p	1-8 (May); on 15/19 counts; nested locally
Bewick's Wren			•	•		1 bird seen 2x in Feb, Sep
House Wren	•		•			2 birds seen 1x in Sep
Marsh Wren	•		•	•	+	2 (July) - 200 (Jan); on 18/19 counts; nested in cattails
Ruby-crowned Kinglet	•		•	•		1-2 birds seen on 4/19 counts Nov-Jan
Blue-gray Gnatcatcher			•	•		2-7 birds seen 3x in Jan, Sep, Dec
Black-tailed Gnatcatcher	•	•	•	•	p	1-4 birds seen on 11/19 counts; nested locally
Northern Mockingbird			•	•		1-5 birds seen on 5/19 counts
California Thrasher	•					1 bird seen 1x in May 1998
Crissal Thrasher		•	•		+	2-3 birds seen 3x in July, Sep, Oct; pair feeding one juv in June 1998
Phainopepla			•	•		1-8 birds seen on 6/19 counts Oct-Jan
European Starling	•	•	•	•	+	4-71 birds seen on 13/19 counts; numbers variable; nested locally
American Pipit			•			1 bird seen 1x in Nov
Orange-crowned Warbler	•		•			2 flocks seen 2x in migration; 26 in May, 12 in Sep
Nashville Warbler	•		•			1-2 birds seen 2x in Apr, Sep

	Spr	Sum	Aut	Win	Br	Comments
Lucy's Warbler		•				1 bird seen 1x in July 1998
Yellow Warbler	•	•	•			3 sightings: 1 & 17 birds seen in May, 2 in Sep
Yellow-rumped Warbler	•		•	•		2-54 (Feb); on 11/19 counts; mostly Oct-Feb; usually >20
Black-throated Gray Warbler	•		•			1-3 birds seen 2x in May, Sep
Townsend's Warbler	•					2 birds seen 1x in May
Hermit Warbler	•					1 bird seen 1x in May
Common Yellowthroat	•		•	•	+	1-26 (July); on 17/19 counts; nested in shoreline scrub
Wilson's Warbler	•					1 flock of 29 birds in migration in May
Yellow-breasted Chat	•	•			+	1-2 birds heard 3x in May, July; nested locally
Western Tanager	•		•			1 & 4 birds seen 2x in May, Sep
Abert's Towhee	•	•	•	•	p	1-13 (July); on 15/19 counts; nested locally
Song Sparrow	•	•	•	•	+	1-29 (July); on 14/19 counts; nested in shoreline scrub
White-crowned Sparrow	•		•	•		4-188 (Jan); on 9/19 counts Sep-Mar
Dark-eyed Junco				•		1-5 birds seen 2x in Jan, Feb
Lazuli Bunting	•					3 birds seen 1x in migration in May
Red-winged Blackbird	•	•	•	•	+	12 (Jan) - 1640 (Sep); on 17/19 counts; nested in cattails
Western Meadowlark	•	•	•	•		1-3 birds seen on 5/19 counts Feb-June
Yellow-headed Blackbird	•			•		2 sightings: flock of 60 in Mar, 1 bird in May
Brewer's Blackbird	•			•		2-13 birds seen 3x in Jan, Mar
Great-tailed Grackle	•	•	•	•		1-57 (July); on 17/19 counts; nested locally
Brown-headed Cowbird	•	•	•	•		3 (Sep/Oct) - 50 (July); on 10/19 counts Mar-Oct
Hooded Oriole	•					3 birds seen 1x in July

	Spr	Sum	Aut	Win	Br	Comments
Bullock's Oriole	•	•			p	1-3 birds seen on 4/19 counts Apr-June; nested locally
House Finch	•	•	•		p	1-18 (Sep); on 7/19 counts May-Nov; nested locally
Lesser Goldfinch	•		•			1-5 birds seen on 5/19 counts Mar-Nov
House Sparrow	•			•	p	5-12 birds seen on 5/19 counts; nested locally

Johnson Street

	Spr	Sum	Aut	Win	Br	Comments
Pied-billed Grebe	•	•	•	•	p	1-5 birds seen on 10/19 counts
Eared Grebe	•	•	•	•		3 (July) - 1,560 (Apr); on all counts; highest numbers Nov-Apr
Western Grebe	•	•	•	•		1 (Sep) - 49 (July); on 10/19 counts; numbers variable
Clark's Grebe	•	•	•			1-3 birds seen on 4/19 counts
American White Pelican	•	•	•	•		3 (Sep) - 551 (Apr); on 10/19 counts; 1 large flock, usually <50.
Double-crested Cormorant	•	•	•	•	+	119 (July) - 2,200 (Mar); on all counts; 2 nests in 1999
Least Bittern	•	•	•	•	p	1-2 birds seen on 6/19 counts May-Nov; in ponds
Great Blue Heron	•	•	•	•	+	6-179 (Jan); on all counts; 157 nests in 1999
Great Egret	•	•	•	•	+	1 (Dec) - 71 (Aug); on 17/19 counts; 26 nests in 1999
Snowy Egret	•	•	•	•	+	1-37 (July); on all counts; usually <10; 6 nests in 1999
Cattle Egret	•	•	•	•		1 (Mar) - 77 (June); on 13/19 counts
Green Heron	•	•	•	•	p	1-3 birds seen on 13/19 counts
Black-crowned Night-Heron	•	•	•	•	+	1 (Dec) - 72 (June); on 15/19 counts; 77 nests in 1999
White-faced Ibis	•	•	•	•		1 (Jan) - 47 (July); on 9/19 counts; usually 1-3 birds
Turkey Vulture	•	•	•			1-3 birds seen on 4/19 counts Apr-Aug
Fulvous Whistling-Duck			•			2 birds seen overhead 1x in Sep 1998
Snow Goose			•	•		Single bird seen 2x in Nov, Feb
Canada Goose				•		22 birds seen 1x in Feb
Brant	•	•				1-5 birds seen on 4/19 counts May-Aug

	Spr	Sum	Aut	Win	Br	Comments
Gadwall		•	•		p	2 sightings; 39 birds in July, 2 in Nov
American Wigeon	•	•	•	•		1-20 (Feb); on 5/19 counts Jan-July; usually ≤4
Mallard	•	•	•	•		1-7 seen on 8/19 counts Jan-Aug
Blue-winged Teal	•					3 birds seen 1x in Apr
Cinnamon Teal	•	•	•	•		1-58 (Feb); on 12/19 counts; usually ≤20
Northern Shoveler	•	•	•	•		6 (Apr) - 709 (Feb); on 11/19 counts; highest numbers Dec-Feb
Northern Pintail	•		•	•		1 (Sep) - 315 (Feb); on 8/19 counts July-Feb
Green-winged Teal	•		•	•		1-125 (Feb); on 8/19 counts; highest numbers Jan-Feb
Canvasback		•	•	•		3 sightings: 5 birds in Jan, 120 in Feb, 7 in Aug
Redhead	•	•	•	•		1-163 (Feb); on 13/19 counts; usually <20
Ring-necked Duck			•	•		2 sightings of 3 & 120 birds; in Jan
Lesser Scaup	•	•	•	•		1-552 (Mar); on 13/19 counts; highest numbers Jan-Mar
Surf Scoter	•	•	•	•		2 sightings of 1 & 2 birds; in Apr, Aug
Common Goldeneye				•		1 bird seen 1x in Jan
Bufflehead	•		•	•		2-13 birds seen on 7/19 counts Nov-Apr
Red-breasted Merganser	•		•	•		1-2 seen on 6/19 counts
Ruddy Duck	•	•	•	•		21 (May) - 2,340 (Feb); on all counts; highest numbers Jan-Apr
Osprey	•	•	•	•		1-2 birds seen on 12/19 counts
Northern Harrier	•			•		Single bird seen on 5/19 counts Jan-Mar, Oct
Cooper's Hawk				•		1 bird seen 1x in Jan
Red-tailed Hawk			•	•		3 sightings of single birds in Jan, Feb, Nov

	Spr	Sum	Aut	Win	Br	Comments
American Kestrel	•			•		Single bird seen on 5/19 counts
Prairie Falcon			•	•		1 bird seen 1x in Nov
Clapper Rail			•	•		1 bird heard 1x in Jan
Virginia Rail				•		2 birds heard 2x in Dec-Jan
Common Moorhen	•	•	•	•	p	1-5 birds seen on 15/19 counts
American Coot	•	•	•	•	p	2 (July) - 497 (Mar); on all counts; highest numbers Jan-Apr
Black-bellied Plover	•	•		•		1-15 birds seen on 9/19 counts
Snowy Plover	•	•			+	1-4 birds seen on 7/19 counts Mar-Aug
Semipalmated Plover	•	•				3 sightings of 3-17 birds; in Apr, July
Killdeer	•	•	•	•	p	1-12 birds seen on 18/19 counts
Black-necked Stilt	•	•	•	•	p	2 (Mar) - 326 (July); on all counts
American Avocet	•	•	•	•	p	1 (May) - 386 (Nov); on 18/19 counts
Greater Yellowlegs	•	•	•	•		1-3 birds seen on 11/19 counts
Lesser Yellowlegs	•		•	•		1-8 birds seen on 4/19 counts in Jan, Mar
Willet	•	•	•	•		1-31 (Jan); on 8/19 counts; usually ≤8
Spotted Sandpiper	•	•	•	•		1-3 seen on 8/19 counts Aug-Apr
Whimbrel	•	•				1 bird seen 1x in July
Marbled Godwit	•	•	•	•		2-46 (Aug); on 8/19 counts; mostly May-Sep
Western Sandpiper	•	•	•	•		5 (Jan) - 276 (Apr); on 12/19 counts; peaks in Apr, Sep
Least Sandpiper	•	•	•	•		1 (Aug) - 119 (Apr); on 15/19 counts; highest numbers Mar/Apr
Dunlin	•					8 birds seen 1x in Apr

	Spr	Sum	Aut	Win	Br	Comments
Dowitcher spp.	•	•	•	•		2 (July) - 131 (Nov); on 12/19 counts; numbers variable
Bonaparte's Gull	•	•	•	•		1-53 (June); on 9/19 counts; usually ≤11
Ring-billed Gull	•	•	•	•		14 (July) - 570 (Nov); on 18/19 counts; highest numbers Sep-Feb
California Gull	•			•		3 sightings: 1 bird seen 2x in Jan, flock of 30 in May
Herring Gull	•	•	•	•		1-56 (Nov); on 15/19 counts; numbers variable
Yellow-footed Gull	•		•			3 sightings: 1 bird seen in Apr & Oct, 16 in May
Gull spp.			•			2 flocks of 225 & 450 in Oct, Nov
Gull-billed Tern	•		•		+	1 (Aug) - 24 (May); on 7/19 counts Apr-Aug
Caspian Tern	•	•	•			1-321 (Sep); on 17/19 counts; usually <15
Common Tern		•				Flock of 29 birds seen 1x in July
Forster's tern	•	•	•	•		1 (Jan) - 38 (Apr); on 13/19 counts; usually <20
Black Tern	•	•	•			4 sightings: 35 & 287 in July, 4 in Aug, 22 in Sep
Black Skimmer	•	•			+	13 (Aug) - 152 (July); on 6/19 counts Apr-Aug
White-winged Dove	•	•				2-7 birds seen on 5/19 counts May-Aug
Mourning Dove	•	•	•	•	p	1-7 birds seen on 9/19 counts
Common Ground-Dove	•					1 bird seen 1x in Apr
Greater Roadrunner		•		•		2 birds seen 2x in June, Dec
Burrowing Owl				•		1 bird seen 1x in Jan
Lesser Nighthawk	•	•				2 sightings of 5 & 9 birds in Apr, June
Vaux's Swift	•					9 birds seen 1x in Apr
White-throated Swift	•					3 birds seen 1x in Apr

	Spr	Sum	Aut	Win	Br	Comments
Belted Kingfisher	•			•		1-3 birds seen on 8/19 counts Sep-Feb
Western Wood-Pewee		•				1 bird seen 1x in July
Black Phoebe	•	•	•	•	p	1-3 birds seen on 12/19 counts
Say's Phoebe	•	•	•	•	p	1-4 birds seen on 7/19 counts
Ash-throated Flycatcher	•					2 birds seen 1x in Apr
Cassin's Kingbird	•					2 sightings of 1-2 birds; in Apr-May
Western Kingbird	•	•			p	1-4 birds seen on 6/19 counts Apr-July; nested locally
Loggerhead Shrike	•		•	•	p	1-2 birds seen on 10/19 counts June-Feb
American Crow	•					Flock of 50 seen 1x in May
Common Raven	•			•		Single bird seen 2x in Feb, Mar
Tree Swallow	•			•		3-46 birds seen on 4/19 counts Jan-Apr
No. rough-winged Swallow	•			•		2-22 birds seen on 6/19 counts Mar-May
Cliff Swallow	•		•	•		1-33 birds seen on 7/17 counts
Barn Swallow	•					3 sightings of 1-2 birds Mar-May
Verdin	•		•	•	p	1-4 birds seen on 17/19 counts
Cactus Wren	•	•				Single birds seen 3x in Mar, Apr, July
House Wren				•		1 bird seen 1x in Feb
Marsh Wren	•		•	•	+	1-12 (May); on 18/19 counts; nested in cattails
Black-tailed Gnatcatcher	•	•				1-2 birds seen on 7/19 counts
Northern Mockingbird			•			2 birds seen 1x in Nov
American Pipit	•			•		1-3 birds seen on 9/19 counts Oct-Apr

	Spr	Sum	Aut	Win	Br	Comments
Phainopepla				•		1 bird seen 1x in Jan; in mesquite
Orange-crowned Warbler	•					2 birds seen 1x in Apr
Yellow Warbler			•			2 birds seen 1x in Nov
Yellow-rumped Warbler	•		•	•		1-5 birds seen on 6/19 counts Nov-Apr
Common Yellowthroat	•	•	•	•		1-2 birds seen on 4/19 counts
Wilson's Warbler	•					1 bird seen 1x in Apr
Abert's Towhee		•	•			1 bird seen 2x in Aug/Sep
Savannah Sparrow			•	•		2 sightings: 1 bird in Jan, 5 in Nov
Song Sparrow	•	•	•	•	p	2-10 (May); on 14/19 counts
Red-winged Blackbird	•		•	•		1-35 (Jan); on 6/19 counts; usually ≤6
Western Meadowlark				•		2 sightings of 1-2 birds; in Dec, Jan
Yellow-headed Blackbird	•		•		p	6-13 (June); on 8/19 counts Mar-Aug
Great-tailed Grackle	•	•	•	•	p	1-147 (Jan); on all counts; 1 large flock; usually <20
Brown-headed Cowbird	•		•	•		1-4 birds seen on 5/19 counts May-Aug
House Sparrow	•					2 birds seen 1x in Apr

Obsidian Butte

	Spr	Sum	Aut	Win	Br	Comments
Pied-billed Grebe	•	•	•	•	+	1-6 birds seen on 9/17 counts
Horned Grebe			•	•		2 sightings, 1 bird in Sep 1999, 2 in Feb 1999
Eared Grebe	•	•	•	•		2 (Aug) - 4,790 (Mar); on 14/17 counts; few in Sum
Western Grebe	•	•	•	•		1-9 birds seen on 5/17 counts
Clark's Grebe			•			1 bird seen 1x in Nov
American White Pelican	•	•	•	•		2 (May) - 885 (Oct); on 14/17 counts; numbers variable
Brown Pelican	•	•	•	•	+	69 (Aug) - 1,100 (Oct); on 14/17 counts; nesting attempts in Apr
Double-crested Cormorant	•	•	•	•		9 (Aug) - 592 (Dec); on all counts
Great Blue Heron	•	•	•	•		6 (Feb) - 48 (Nov); on all counts
Great Egret	•	•	•	•		1 (Feb) - 34 (Oct); on all counts
Snowy Egret	•	•	•	•		1 (Jan) - 80 (Aug); on 16/17 counts
Cattle Egret	•	•	•	•		1 (Oct) - 80 (May); on 13/17 counts
Green Heron	•	•	•	•	p	1-10 birds seen on 12/17 counts
Black-crowned Night-Heron	•	•	•	•		1-22 birds seen on 16/17 counts
White-faced Ibis	•	•	•	•		1-7 birds seen on 8/17 counts
Turkey Vulture			•			1 bird seen 1x in Sep
Snow Goose				•		2 sightings: 33 birds in Feb, 90 in Dec
Brant	•					2 birds seen 1x in Apr
Gadwall		•				1 bird seen 1x in June
American Wigeon	•		•	•		Seen on 4/17 counts: a flock of 183 in Feb; 2-7 in Feb, Apr, Nov

	Spr	Sum	Aut	Win	Br	Comments
Mallard	•		•	•		2-5 birds seen on 4/17 counts
Blue-winged Teal			•	•		2 sightings: 2 birds in Feb, 1 in Nov
Cinnamon Teal	•	•	•	•	+	1-31 birds seen on 12/17 counts; usually ≤10
Northern Shoveler	•		•	•		4-122 (Feb); seen on 8/17 counts; usually <20
Northern Pintail	•		•	•		1-11 birds seen on 6/17 counts
Green-winged Teal	•			•		2 sightings: 3 birds in Feb, 4 in Mar
Redhead	•			•		1-7 birds seen on 4/17 counts in Mar, Apr, Sep, Nov
Lesser Scaup	•			•		6-61 (Mar); seen on 6/17 counts; most in Mar, Nov
Bufflehead				•		7 birds seen 1x in Feb
Red-breasted Merganser	•	•		•		1-42 (Sep); seen on 6/17 counts; usually ≤3
Ruddy Duck	•	•	•	•		1 (July, Aug) - 1,380 (Mar); on 13/17 counts; few in Sum
Osprey		•	•	•		1-4 birds seen on 10/17 counts June-Jan
Northern Harrier		•	•	•		1-2 birds seen on 7/17 counts July-Feb
Red-tailed Hawk			•			1 bird seen 1x in Nov
American Kestrel	•	•	•	•		1-5 birds seen on 7/17 counts
Peregrine Falcon			•	•		1 bird seen on 5/17 counts, Nov-Feb
Ring-necked Pheasant			•			2 birds seen 1x in Oct
Sora				•		1 bird seen 1x in Feb
Common Moorhen	•	•	•	•		1-19 (Aug); on 13/17 counts; juvs in July
American Coot	•	•	•	•	+	1-263 (Feb); seen on all counts; nested in May; highest numbers Nov-Mar
Black-bellied Plover	•	•	•	•		1 (Feb) - 30 (Oct); on 10/17 counts; usually ≤10

	Spr	Sum	Aut	Win	Br	Comments
Semi-palmated Plover	•	•				3 sightings of 1-2 birds in Apr, July, Aug
Killdeer	•	•	•	•	+	1-30 birds seen on all counts; juvs in July; usually ≤10
Black-necked Stilt	•	•	•	•	+	55 (Feb) - 359 (Aug); on all counts; usually >100; juvs in June
American Avocet	•	•	•	•		6-156 (Oct); on 15/17 counts; numbers variable
Greater Yellowlegs	•	•	•	•		1-12 seen on 12/17 counts
Lesser Yellowlegs	•	•	•	•		2-26 seen on 8/17 counts; numbers variable
Willet	•	•	•	•		2 (July) - 96 (Jan); on 14/17 counts; usually >20
Spotted Sandpiper	•	•	•	•		1-5 birds seen on 8/17 counts
Whimbrel	•	•				3 birds seen 1x in June
Long-billed Curlew	•		•	•		1 (July) -16 (Nov); on 6/17 counts; usually ≤7
Marbled Godwit		•	•	•		4 sightings of 2-25 birds July-Sep
Ruddy Turnstone		•	•	•		1-8 birds seen on 5/17 counts Aug-Nov
Sanderling		•				1 bird seen 1x in Aug 1998
Western Sandpiper	•		•	•		1 (July) - 226 (Sep); on 11/17 counts; highest numbers Spr, Aut
Least Sandpiper	•		•	•		2 (Aug) - 204 (Jan); on 14/17 counts; highest numbers Oct-Mar
Baird's Sandpiper		•				1 bird seen 1x in Aug 1998
Dunlin	•		•	•		3 sightings: 17 birds in July, 7 & 15 in Nov
Dowitcher spp.	•		•	•		1 (July) - 49 (Jan); on 10/17 counts
Wilson's Phalarope	•	•	•	•		2-375 birds seen on 10/17 counts; flocks of 375 in Aug, 102 in Nov
Red-necked Phalarope				•		2 sightings: 1 bird in Jan, 4 in Feb
Laughing Gull		•	•			4 sightings: 35 & 46 birds in July, 1 & 2 in Sep
Bonaparte's Gull	•		•	•		3 (Sep) - 609 (Apr); on 8/17 counts; numbers variable

	Spr	Sum	Aut	Win	Br	Comments
Heermann's Gull	•	•	•	•		4 sightings of single birds; in Feb, Apr, May, Sep
Ring-billed Gull	•		•	•		60 (Mar) - 720 (Oct); on all counts; usually >150
California Gull	•	•	•	•	+	1 (May) - 213 (Dec); on 15/17 counts; usually >50
Herring Gull	•		•	•		1-48 birds seen on 13/17 counts; highest numbers Feb-Apr, Oct, Nov
Yellow-footed Gull	•	•	•	•		1 (Dec) - 170 (July); on 14/17 counts; largest numbers July/Aug
Sabine's Gull			•			1 bird seen 1x in Nov 1998
Gull-billed Tern	•	•				3 (Mar) - 14 (July); on 7/17 counts Mar-July
Caspian Tern	•		•	•		2-97 (Sep); on 12/17 counts
Forster's Tern	•		•	•		1-160 birds seen on 10/17 counts; usually <50, except 1 flock of 160 in July
Black Tern	•	•				2 sightings; 111 birds in July, 5 in Aug
Black Skimmer	•	•				3 sightings of 1-3 birds in June, July
Rock Dove	•			•		3 sightings of 1-3 birds in Feb, May, Aug
Mourning Dove	•	•	•	•	p	2-36 birds seen on 13/17 counts; highest numbers Feb-May
Common Ground-Dove	•		•			2-3 birds seen on 5/17 counts Apr-Oct
Greater Roadrunner		•	•			3 sightings of 1-2 birds in Jan, Feb, July
Burrowing Owl	•	•				1 bird seen 2x in Apr, July
Lesser Nighthawk	•	•			+	4 sightings of 2-4 birds, Apr-July; one juv in May
Belted Kingfisher	•		•	•		1-6 birds seen on 7/17 counts Sep-Mar
Black Phoebe	•	•	•		+	1-9 birds seen on 13/17 counts; nested in Apr
Say's Phoebe			•	•		1-6 birds seen on 6/17 counts Oct-Feb
Western Kingbird	•	•			+	2-13 birds seen on 7/17 counts Apr-July; hatchlings in June

	Spr	Sum	Aut	Win	Br	Comments
Loggerhead Shrike	•	•	•	•		1-4 birds seen on 6/17 counts
Tree Swallow	•	•	•	•		3-77 birds seen on 8/17 counts
No. rough-winged Swallow	•	•	•	•		3-6 birds seen on 5/17 counts Feb-July
Cliff Swallow	•	•	•			3 sightings of 1-10 birds in June, July, Sep
Barn Swallow	•	•	•			1-60 birds seen on 6/17 counts Mar-May, Sep
Verdin		•	•	•	+	4 sightings of 1-3 birds; juvs in July
Bushtit		•				1 bird seen 1x in June
Marsh Wren				•		2 sightings of 1 & 2 birds in Feb, Dec
European Starling	•	•	•		+	1-10 birds seen on 7/17 counts
American Pipit			•	•		3 flocks sighted: 75 birds in Oct, 42 in Nov, 141 in Dec
Orange-crowned Warbler			•			1 bird seen 1x in Oct
Virginia's Warbler	•					1 bird seen 1; in Apr 1998
Yellow-rumped Warbler	•		•	•		4-17 birds seen on 8/17 counts Oct-Apr
Common Yellowthroat	•		•	•	p	1-7 birds seen on 9/17 counts
Abert's Towhee	•		•	•	p	4 sightings of 1-2 birds in May, Sep, Oct, Dec
Chipping Sparrow	•					1 bird seen 1x in Apr
Savannah Sparrow			•	•		2-51 (Oct); seen on 7/17 counts Sep-Feb
Savannah Sparrow (Large-billed)			•	•		4 sightings: 45 birds in Sep, 50 in Oct, 1 in Nov, 9 in Dec
Song Sparrow	•	•	•	•	+	2-20 birds seen on 15/17 counts; nesting in Apr
White-crowned Sparrow	•		•	•		9-24 birds seen on 5/17 counts Oct-Mar
Golden-crowned Sparrow			•			1 bird seen 1x in Oct
Red-winged Blackbird	•	•	•	•	+	2 (Feb) - 574 (May); on 15/17 counts; highest numbers Feb-Sep; nested in Apr

	Spr	Sum	Aut	Win	Br	Comments
Western Meadowlark	•	•	•			4 sightings of 1-3 birds in Apr, May, June, Nov
Yellow-headed Blackbird	•	•	•		+	3-103 (June); on 5/17 counts Apr-Aug; nested in May
Great-tailed Grackle	•	•	•	•	+	1 (Dec) - 81 (May); on 14/17 counts; nested in May
Brown-headed Cowbird	•	•	•		+	1-9 birds seen on 6/17 counts Apr-Oct; courting pair in Apr
House Finch	•	•	•			3 sightings of 1-4 birds in May, Oct, Nov
American Goldfinch				•		1 bird seen 1x in June
House Sparrow	•	•	•		+	1-8 birds seen on 7/17 counts; nested in Apr

Ramer Lake

	Spr	Sum	Aut	Win	Br	Comments
Pied-billed Grebe	•	•	•	•	+	1-28 birds seen on 17/19 counts; usually <10; juv in May
Eared Grebe	•	•	•	•		1-20 birds seen on 12/19 counts; usually <5
Western Grebe	•	•	•	•	+	1-51 (Jan); seen on all counts; usually >10; 8 juvs in June
Clark's Grebe	•	•	•	•	+	1-7 birds seen on 15/19 counts; in most months; juvs in July
American White Pelican				•		3 flocks, all in Jan, with 50, 78, & 930 birds in Jan
Brown Pelican	•			•		2 sightings of 1 & 3 birds in Jan, May
Double-crested Cormorant	•	•	•	•	+	1 (Jan) - 2,000 (Sep) on 17/19 counts
Least Bittern	•	•	•	•	p	1-4 birds seen 3x in May, June, Oct
Great Blue Heron	•	•	•	•		1-9 birds seen on 12/19 counts; in most months
Great Egret	•	•	•	•	+	1-121 (Sep); on all counts; usually <15; nested in June
Snowy Egret	•	•	•	•		1-188 (Sep); on 17/19 counts; highest numbers Mar-Sep; usually <30
Cattle Egret	•	•	•	•	+	13-17,200 (Sep); seen on 18/19 counts; thousands roosted at night; major nest site in spring
Green Heron	•	•	•	•	p	1-5 birds seen on 15/19 counts
Black-crowned Night-Heron	•	•	•	•	p	1-50 (Jan); on 14/19 counts; usually <10
White-faced Ibis	•	•	•	•	+	3-8,270 (Oct); on 17/19 counts; thousands roosted at night; minor nest site
Turkey Vulture	•	•				1-4 birds seen 3x May-July
Fulvous Whistling-Duck	•	•			p	3-6 birds seen 3x in May/June; presumed nesting
Greater White-fronted Goose				•		Group of 27 seen 1x in Jan 2000

	Spr	Sum	Aut	Win	Br	Comments
Snow Goose			•			Group of 9 seen 1x in Nov
Canada Goose				•		1 bird seen 1x in Jan
Gadwall				•		5 birds seen 1x in Jan
American Wigeon	•		•	•		4 sightings of 1-8 birds Feb, Mar, Oct, Nov
Mallard		•	•	•		1 (Dec) - 17 (Sep); on 16/19 counts; usually <10
Blue-winged Teal	•					Flock of 14 seen 1x in May
Cinnamon Teal	•	•	•	•		1 (Jan) - 102 (Sep); on 18/19 counts
Northern Shoveler	•	•	•	•		1 (Sep) - 362 (Nov); on 17/19 counts; usually <25
Northern Pintail	•	•	•	•		2-14 birds seen on 5/19 counts Aug-Feb
Green-winged Teal	•		•	•		1-30 birds seen on 7/19 counts Nov-Mar
Redhead		•	•	•		1-4 birds seen 3x in Jan, June, Sep
Bufflehead			•	•		2 sightings: 2 birds in Jan, 4 birds in Nov
Ruddy Duck	•	•	•	•	p	3 (Sep) - 195 (Nov); on all counts; highest numbers Oct-Nov
Northern Harrier	•	•	•	•		1-4 birds seen on 11/19 counts Oct-June
Sharp-shinned Hawk			•			1 bird seen 1x in Oct
Cooper's Hawk	•		•	•		1-2 birds seen on 7/19 counts Oct-Mar
Red-tailed Hawk			•	•		1 bird seen 2x in Jan, Nov
American Kestrel	•		•	•		1-3 birds seen on 11/19 counts
Merlin				•		1 bird seen 1x in Jan
Gambel's Quail	•	•	•	•		1-11 birds seen on 6/19 counts
Clapper Rail	•					1 bird heard 1x in Apr
Virginia Rail			•			1 bird heard 2x in Sep, Nov

	Spr	Sum	Aut	Win	Br	Comments
Sora	•		•	•		1-5 birds seen on 9/19 counts Sep-Apr
Common Moorhen	•	•	•	•	+	1-29 birds seen on all counts; nested in May
American Coot	•	•	•	•	+	39-782 (Sep); on all counts; usually >100; juvs in July
Killdeer	•	•	•	•	+	1 (Nov) - 18 (May); on 17/19 counts; juvs in June
Black-necked Stilt	•	•	•		+	5-51 (July); on 10/19 counts; numbers variable; nested in June
American Avocet	•					2 birds seen 1x in Mar
Greater Yellowlegs			•	•		1-4 birds seen 3x in Feb, Sep
Willet	•					1 bird seen 1x in June
Spotted Sandpiper	•		•	•		1-3 birds seen on 14/19 counts July-Mar; in most months
Whimbrel	•					11 birds seen 1x in May
Western Sandpiper	•		•	•		1-75 (Apr); on 8/19 counts July-Mar
Least Sandpiper	•	•	•	•		1-34 (Mar); seen on 10/19 counts; usually ≤15
Dowitcher spp.	•		•			2-55 (Apr); on 8/19 counts Mar-Nov
Common Snipe			•			1-2 birds seen 3x Oct-Dec
Wilson's Phalarope		•				25 birds seen 1x in Aug
Laughing Gull			•			1 bird seen 3x in Aug-Sep
Bonaparte's Gull	•					36 birds seen 1x in Apr
Ring-billed Gull	•		•	•		1 (Aug) - 64 (Dec); on 9/19 counts; highest numbers Nov-Jan
Herring Gull	•		•	•		2 sightings: 43 in Jan, 6 in Mar
Gull spp.			•	•		3 flocks of 60-300 unidentifiable gulls Nov-Jan
Caspian Tern	•	•	•	•		1-56 (Sep); on 16/19 counts; usually <10
Forster's Tern	•	•	•	•		1-65 (Sep); on 12/19 counts; usually ≤6

	Spr	Sum	Aut	Win	Br	Comments
Black Tern	•	•	•			1-12 birds seen on 8/19 counts Jan-Sep; usually 1-2
Black Skimmer	•	•				4 sightings of 1-9 birds May-Sep
White-winged Dove	•	•	•		p	1-30 (May); on 8/19 counts; usually ≤5; summer visitor
Mourning Dove	•	•	•	•	p	1 (Jan) - 95 (May); on 15/19 counts; highest numbers May-July
Inca Dove	•					2 birds seen 1x in May 1999
Common Ground-Dove	•	•	•	•		1-11 birds seen on 12/19 counts; usually ≤5
Greater Roadrunner	•	•	•			1-2 birds seen on 5/19 counts May-Sep
Barn Owl	•					1-2 birds seen 2x in May
Great Horned Owl	•					1 bird seen 1x in May
Burrowing Owl	•					2 birds seen 1x in May
Lesser Nighthawk	•	•	•		+	1-2 birds seen on 5/19 counts May-Sep; juv in June
Belted Kingfisher			•	•		1-5 birds seen on 10/16 counts Sep-Feb
Ladder-backed Woodpecker	•		•			1 bird seen 2x in May, Oct
Northern Flicker			•	•		4 sightings of 1-2 birds in Jan, Oct, Nov
Western Wood-Pewee	•					1 bird seen 1x in migration in May
Willow Flycatcher	•					4 birds seen 1x in migration in May
Pacific Slope Flycatcher	•					1 bird seen 1x in migration in May
Black Phoebe	•		•	•	p	1 (Feb) - 17 (Oct); on 17/19 counts
Say's Phoebe		•	•	•		1-3 birds seen 3x in Aug, Nov, Dec
Vermilion Flycatcher			•	•		1-2 birds seen on 4/19 counts; present in both winters
Ash-throated Flycatcher	•	•				1 bird seen 2x in May-June
Western Kingbird	•	•			+	1-5 birds seen on 6/19 counts Apr-July; nested in June

	Spr	Sum	Aut	Win	Br	Comments
Loggerhead Shrike	•		•	•		1-2 birds seen 3x in Nov, Dec, Jan
Tree Swallow	•	•	•	•		2-1,260 (Aug); on 8/19 counts; large flocks in Jan, Aug, Nov
No. rough-winged Swallow	•			•		2-17 birds seen on 5/19 counts Jan-May
Bank Swallow			•			Flock of 20 birds seen 1x in Sep 1999
Cliff Swallow	•	•	•		+	1-2,020 (Jul); seen on 11/19 counts; large numbers June-July; nested locally
Barn Swallow	•					Flock of 23 seen 1x in May
Verdin	•	•	•	•	+	1 (Nov) - 24 (May); seen on all counts; nested in May
Cactus Wren	•	•	•	•		1-5 birds seen on 6/19 counts scattered through the year
Marsh Wren	•	•	•	•	+	2 (Aug) - 45 (Feb); on all counts; nested in reeds
Ruby-crowned Kinglet			•	•		1-7 birds seen on 6/19 counts Oct-Feb
Blue-gray Gnatcatcher			•	•		1-5 birds seen on 5/19 counts Nov-Feb
Black-tailed Gnatcatcher	•	•	•	•	p	1-9 birds seen on 6/19 counts; nested locally
Northern Mockingbird		•	•	•		1-3 birds seen on 5/19 counts
Crissal Thrasher			•			2 sightings: 1 bird in Oct, 2 in Dec
European Starling	•	•	•	•	+	2 (July) - 53 (Dec); on 15/19 counts; highest numbers Dec-Jan
American Pipit			•	•		1 bird seen 2x in Jan, Oct
Phainopepla	•		•	•		1-10 birds seen on 8/19 counts; 2 birds in May, the rest Oct-Jan
Warbling Vireo	•					2 sightings: 1 bird in Apr, 9 in May
Orange-crowned Warbler	•		•	•		1-23 birds seen on 6/19 counts; 23 in May, 1-2 usually in Aut, Win
Nashville Warbler	•					1 bird seen 1x in migration in May
Yellow Warbler	•	•				2 sightings: 10 birds in May, 1 in Aug

	Spr	Sum	Aut	Win	Br	Comments
Yellow-rumped Warbler	•		•	•		5-244 birds seen on 9/19 counts Oct-Mar; 244 in Nov
Black-throated Gray Warbler	•					1 bird seen 1x in migration in May
Townsend's Warbler	•					1 bird seen 1x in migration in May
MacGillivray's Warbler	•					1 bird seen 1x in migration in May
Common Yellowthroat	•	•	•	•	+	1-20 birds seen on all counts; nested in lake reeds
Wilson's Warbler	•					3 birds seen 1x in migration in May
Yellow-breasted Chat	•	•			p	1 bird seen 2x in Apr, June
Western Tanager	•					2 birds seen 1x in migration in May
Abert's Towhee	•	•	•	•	p	1-13 birds seen on 16/19 counts
Song Sparrow	•	•	•	•	p	1-29 (Jul); seen on 14/19 counts
Lincoln's Sparrow	•		•	•		1 bird seen 3x in Jan, Oct, Dec
White-crowned Sparrow	•		•	•		3-42 birds seen on 9/19 counts Oct-Mar
Blue Grosbeak	•	•			p	4 sightings of single birds Apr-Aug
Red-winged Blackbird	•	•	•	•	+	38-5,000 (Mar); seen on all counts; highest numbers Feb-Mar, Sep; nested in lake reeds
Western Meadowlark	•					1 bird seen 1x in May
Yellow-headed Blackbird	•	•	•	•	+	1 (Aug) - 90 (Feb); on 8/19 counts Feb-Sep; nested in lake reeds
Brewer's Blackbird	•		•	•		4-22 birds seen 3x in Feb, May, Dec
Great-tailed Grackle	•	•	•	•	p	2 (Mar) - 115 (May); on 16/19 counts
Brown-headed Cowbird	•	•	•	•	p	2 (Feb) - 45 (July); on 7/19 counts; mostly in breeding season
Hooded Oriole	•					1 bird seen 1x in Apr
Bullock's Oriole	•	•			+	1-2 birds seen 3x in May, June

	Spr	Sum	Aut	Win	Br	Comments
House Finch		•		•		2-9 birds seen 3x in Jan, June, July
Lesser Goldfinch				•		5 birds seen 1x in Feb
House Sparrow		•	•			2 &12 birds seen 2x in May, June

Red Hill

	Spr	Sum	Aut	Win	Br	Comments
Pied-billed Grebe				•		3 sightings of 1-3 birds Oct-Dec
Eared Grebe		•	•	•		10 (Sep) - 1040 (May); on 15/17 counts; few in Sum
Western Grebe	•	•	•	•		1-11 birds seen on 7/17 counts Apr-Nov
Clark's Grebe	•		•			2 sightings of 2 & 3 birds in May, Sep
American White Pelican	•	•	•	•		11 (Sep) - 680 (Oct); on 12/17 counts
Brown Pelican	•	•	•			6 (Apr) - 200 (July); on 8/17 counts, Apr-Nov
Double-crested Cormorant	•	•	•	•		2 (Mar) - 700 (Oct); on 15/17 counts; usually >100
Great Blue Heron	•	•	•	•		3 (Mar) - 63 (May); on all counts
Great Egret	•	•	•	•		1-57 (Jun); seen on 11/17 counts Mar-Nov; <10 most months, more in Sum
Snowy Egret	•	•	•	•		1-64 birds seen on 12/17 counts Mar-Nov; >50 May-July
Cattle Egret	•	•	•	•		1 (Nov) - 621 (Sep); on 7/17 count; very variable
Green Heron	•	•	•			1 bird seen 2x, in July, Oct
White-faced Ibis	•	•	•			1 (Mar) - 550 (Sep); on 5/17 counts Mar-Oct
Turkey Vulture	•	•				4 sightings of 1-7 birds Mar-June
Lesser Flamingo				•		4 birds seen 1x in Jan 1999
Snow Goose				•		Flock of 950 seen 1x in Jan
Gadwall				•		2 birds seen 1x in Jan
Mallard	•				•	3 sightings of 1-2 birds in May, Sep, Oct
Blue-winged Teal					•	4 birds seen 2x in Jan

	Spr	Sum	Aut	Win	Br	Comments
Cinnamon Teal		•	•			3 sightings of 15-78 birds Aug-Oct
Northern Shoveler	•	•	•	•		37-1,800 (Nov); seen on 12/17 counts Aug-Mar; usually >500
Northern Pintail	•	•	•	•		7-104 (Jan); seen on 7/17 counts Aug-Jan
Green-winged Teal	•	•	•	•		7-88 (Mar); seen on 8/15 counts Aug-Mar
Canvasback				•		Flock of 18 seen 1x in Jan
Redhead	•	•	•			4 sightings of 2-10 birds in Mar, May, June, Oct
Lesser Scaup	•		•	•		1-235 (Jan) seen on 8/15 counts Oct-Mar; usually <10; 1 large flock
Bufflehead				•		1 bird seen 1x in Jan
Red-breasted Merganser				•		2 birds seen 1x in Jan
Ruddy Duck	•		•	•		17 (July) - 7,700 (Oct); on 13/17 counts; largest flocks Oct-Nov
Osprey	•		•			1 bird seen 3x in Mar, Nov
Northern Harrier			•	•		1 bird seen 2x in Jan, Nov
American Kestrel	•		•			1 bird seen 3x, in May, Oct, Nov
Merlin				•		1 bird seen 1x in Jan
Peregrine Falcon				•		1 bird seen 1x in Dec
Prairie Falcon			•			1 bird seen 1x in Nov
Gambel's Quail	•					1 bird seen 2x in Mar, May
Common Moorhen		•	•			1 bird seen 2x in June, Oct
American Coot	•		•	•		2-215 (Oct); seen on 15/17 counts; numbers variable
Black-bellied Plover	•		•	•		1-49 (Jan); seen on 13/17 counts; highest numbers Sep-Jan
Semipalmated Plover	•		•			2 sightings: 15 birds in Apr, 1 in Oct
Killdeer	•	•	•	•	p	1-17 (Mar, Oct); on 15/17 counts; usually ≤5

	Spr	Sum	Aut	Win	Br	Comments
Mountain Plover	•					1 bird seen 1x in Mar
Black-necked Stilt	•	•	•	•	+	17 (May) - 798 (July); on all counts; usually >80
American Avocet	•	•	•	•	+	10-2,120 (Oct); seen on all counts; numbers variable; highest Sep-Jan
Greater Yellowlegs	•	•	•	•		1-5 birds seen on 5/17 counts Aug-Jan
Lesser Yellowlegs	•		•	•		3 sightings of 1-2 birds; in Jan, Mar, Aug
Willet	•	•	•	•		2 (Aug) - 56 (Oct); on 14/17 counts; highest numbers Sep-Dec
Spotted Sandpiper	•	•		•		1 bird seen 2x in Jan, Aug
Whimbrel	•		•	•		3 sightings: 1 bird in Jan, 3 in June, 6 in Sep
Long-billed Curlew	•	•	•	•		1 (Mar) - 635 (Nov); on 9/17 counts; highest numbers Sep-Nov
Marbled Godwit	•	•	•	•		4 (Mar) - 425 (Oct); on 13/17 counts; numbers variable
Western Sandpiper	•	•	•	•		1 (Mar) - 555 (Apr, Oct); on 12/17 counts; peaks during migration
Least Sandpiper	•	•	•	•		1-73 (Mar); seen on 8/17 counts Sep-Mar
Dunlin				•		1 bird seen 1x in Dec
Peep (*Calidris* spp.)	•	•	•	•		Distant flocks of 60-825 on 6/17 counts
Dowitcher spp.	•	•	•	•		31-706 (Jan); on 13/17 counts; highest numbers Sep-Mar
Laughing Gull		•	•			3 sightings: 5 birds in June, 8 in Aug, 2 in Oct
Bonaparte's Gull	•		•	•		1-55 (Mar); on 6/17 counts usually ≤10
Ring-billed Gull	•	•	•	•		43-1,600 (Jan); on all counts; lowest numbers Mar-June
California Gull	•	•	•	•		1-550 (Oct); seen on 7/17 counts; numbers variable
Herring Gull	•	•	•	•		2 (May) - 364 (Jan); on 12/17 counts; highest numbers Oct-Jan
Western Gull	•					2 sightings: 1 bird in Apr, 3 in May
Yellow-footed Gull		•	•			4 sightings of 1-15 birds May-Sep

	Spr	Sum	Aut	Win	Br	Comments
Glaucous-winged Gull	•					1 bird seen 1x in May
Gull spp.	•	•	•	•		Distant flocks of 28-1500 on 9/17 counts
Gull-billed Tern	•	•	•			2 sightings: 1 bird in May, 43 in June
Caspian Tern	•	•	•	•		2 (Nov) - 115 (July); on 12/17 counts; highest numbers May-Sep
Forster's Tern	•	•	•	•		1-215 (Sep); on 8/17 counts June-Nov
Black Tern		•	•			3 sightings: 140 birds in June, 254 in July, 165 in Aug
Black Skimmer		•	•			3 sightings: 2 birds in June & Sep, 29 in July
Mourning Dove	•	•	•			4 sightings of 1-7 birds Mar-Sep
Common Ground-Dove		•	•			2 sightings: 4 birds in July, 1 in Sep
Burrowing Owl		•	•			1 bird seen 1x in Sep
Belted Kingfisher			•			1 bird seen 1x in Nov
Black Phoebe	•		•	•		1-3 birds seen on 8/17 counts
Say's Phoebe		•	•	•		1-3 birds seen 3x in Jan, Oct, Nov
Western Kingbird	•	•			+	1-2 birds seen 4x Mar-July; nested in 1998
Loggerhead Shrike			•			2 sightings: 2 birds in Oct, 1 in Nov
Tree Swallow			•			7 birds seen 1x: in Oct
No. rough-winged Swallow	•					2 birds seen 1x: in May
Cliff Swallow	•					2 sightings: 8 birds in Mar, 1 in May
Verdin		•				1-2 birds seen 3x in Apr, May, Oct
Western Bluebird	•					6 birds seen 1x in Mar
Yellow-rumped Warbler	•		•			4 sightings of 1-16 birds in Jan, Mar, Oct, Dec
Common Yellowthroat		•				1 bird seen 2x in Mar, July

	Spr	Sum	Aut	Win	Br	Comments
Abert's Towhee	•					1 bird seen 1x in Mar
Song Sparrow	•	•	•	•	p	1-4 birds seen on 6/17 counts
White-crowned Sparrow			•			1 bird seen 1x in Oct
Dark-eyed Junco			•			2 birds seen 1x in Oct
Red-winged Blackbird			•			Flock of 39 seen 1x in Sep
Western Meadowlark			•			1 bird seen 1x in Nov
Brewer's Blackbird			•			Flock of 1,000 birds seen 1x in Oct
Great-tailed Grackle	•	•	•	•		2-29 (Jan); on 13/17 counts
House Finch	•					5 birds seen 1x in Mar

Salton Sea State Recreation Area

	Spr	Sum	Aut	Win	NSM	SPHq	SCr	Br	Comments
Pied-billed Grebe	•	•	•	•	•	•	•	p	Single birds seen on 3 counts; in Jan, May, June
Eared Grebe	•	•	•	•	•	•	•		10 (Aug) - 27,000 (Jan); on 17/19 counts; few July-Sep
Western Grebe	•	•	•	•	•	•	•		1 (Jan-Feb) - 98 (Apr); on 13/19 counts; highest numbers Apr-May
Clark's Grebe	•			•	•	•	•		Single birds seen on 6/19 counts Mar-May, Oct, Nov
American White Pelican	•		•	•	•	•	•		15 (Apr) - 1,590 (Nov); on 12/19 counts; usually >100
Brown Pelican	•		•	•	•	•	•		3 sightings: 1 bird in Jan, 48 in Mar, 210 in Sep
Double-crested Cormorant	•	•	•	•	•	•	•		4 (May) - 290 (Nov); on 12/19 counts Sep-May
Great Blue Heron	•	•	•	•	•	•	•	+	1-28 birds seen on 17/19 counts; nested in snags
Great Egret	•	•	•	•	•	•	•		1-23 birds seen on 13/19 counts
Snowy Egret	•	•	•	•	•	•	•		1-26 birds seen on 15/19 counts
Green Heron	•	•	•	•	•	•	•	p	1-6 on 12/17 counts; nested locally
Black-crowned Night-Heron	•	•	•	•	•	•	•	+	4-48 (May); seen on 16/19 counts; highest numbers Apr-June
White-faced Ibis			•				•		1 bird seen 1x in Sep
Turkey Vulture	•		•				•		1 bird seen 2x in May, Sep
Snow Goose			•		•				6 birds seen 1x in Nov

	Spr	Sum	Aut	Win	NSM	SPHq	SCr	Br	Comments
Canada Goose			•		•				14 birds seen 1x in Nov
American Wigeon				•	•	•	•		35 birds seen 1x at 2 sites; in Dec
Mallard	•		•	•	•	•	•		2-7 birds seen on 6/19 counts Nov-May
Blue-winged Teal				•			•		2 sightings: 2 birds in Nov, 5 birds in Jan
Cinnamon Teal	•	•		•	•		•		3 sightings of 5-10 birds; 2x in Jan, 1x in Aug
Northern Shoveler	•		•	•	•	•			1 (Apr) - 192 (Jan); on 9/19 counts Nov-Mar
Northern Pintail	•		•	•	•	•	•		1-50 (Dec); seen on 8/19 counts Nov-Apr; usually ≤7
Green-winged Teal				•	•		•		2 sightings of 5 & 6 birds; in Dec, Jan
Redhead	•			•	•		•		5-22 seen on 5/19 counts Dec-May
Lesser Scaup	•			•	•	•	•		1-3 birds seen on 3 counts; in Jan, Mar
Surf Scoter	•		•		•	•			1 bird seen 2x in Apr, Nov
Common Goldeneye				•			•		2 sightings of 1 & 4 birds; in Dec, Jan
Red-breasted Merganser	•	•		•	•		•		1-9 seen on 7/19 counts Nov-July
Ruddy Duck	•	•		•	•	•	•		1 (June) - 780 (Jan); on 15/19 counts; not in July/Aug
Northern Harrier			•	•			•		1 bird seen 2x in Jan, Nov
Red-tailed Hawk		•		•	•				1 birds seen 2x in Dec, Jan
American Kestrel		•		•		•			1 bird seen 1x in Dec
Clapper Rail	•					•			1 bird seen 1x in May
Sora	•						•		1 bird seen 1x in Apr
Common Moorhen	•	•	•	•			•	+	1-7 birds seen on 6/19 counts; chicks in June

	Spr	Sum	Aut	Win	NSM	SPHq	SCr	Br	Comments
American Coot	•		•	•	•	•	•	+	2-110 birds on 11/19 counts Oct-May
Black-bellied Plover	•	•	•	•	•	•	•		1-7 birds seen on 12/19 counts
Snowy Plover	•	•	•				•		1-3 birds seen on 3 counts in Apr, July, Sep
Semipalmated Plover	•				•	•	•		8 birds seen on 1 count, several at each site in Apr
Killdeer	•	•	•	•	•	•	•	+	1-6 birds seen on all counts; chicks in June
Black-necked Stilt	•	•	•	•	•	•	•	+	6 (May) -190 (Oct); on all counts; usually >25; chicks in June
American Avocet	•		•	•	•	•	•		1-20 birds seen on 6/19 counts Sep-Mar
Greater Yellowlegs	•		•	•	•	•	•		1-4 birds seen on 9/19 counts
Willet	•		•		•	•	•		1-5 birds seen on 8/19 counts Mar/Apr and Aug-Nov
Spotted Sandpiper	•	•			•		•		2 sightings: 2 birds in May, 1 in Aug
Long-billed Curlew	•	•				•			2 birds seen 1x in Mar
Marbled Godwit			•		•				1 bird seen 1x in Sep
Sanderling	•						•		2 birds seen 1x in Apr
Western Sandpiper	•	•	•		•	•	•		1 (Aug) - 102 (Apr); on 5/19 counts Mar-Apr and Aug-Nov
Least Sandpiper	•		•		•	•	•		2 (Nov) - 32 (Mar); on 7/19 counts Mar-Apr and Sep-Nov
Dunlin	•						•		1 bird seen 1x in Nov
Dowitcher spp.		•	•			•			5-15 birds seen 3x in Mar-Apr
Laughing Gull		•	•		•	•			1-6 birds seen on 4/19 counts June-Sep

	Spr	Sum	Aut	Win	NSM	SPHq	SCr	Br	Comments
Franklin's Gull	•	•			•	•			1 bird seen 2x in Apr, June 1998
Bonaparte's Gull	•		•	•	•	•	•		1-72 (Mar); seen on 11/19 counts Oct-Apr; numbers variable
Ring-billed Gull	•	•	•	•	•	•	•		19 (May) - 1,760 (Jan); on 18/19 counts; highest numbers Sep-Apr
California Gull	•	•	•	•	•	•	•		1 (July) - 1,570 (Jan); on all counts; highest numbers Sep-Apr
Herring Gull	•	•	•	•	•	•	•		1 (Sep) - 990 (Dec); on 11/19 counts; largest numbers Nov-Jan
Thayer's Gull				•		•	•		2 birds seen 1x in Feb 1998
Lesser Black-backed Gull			•	•		•			1 bird seen 1x in Jan 2000
Yellow-footed Gull	•		•			•	•		1-2 birds seen 2x in May, Sep
Glaucous-winged Gull	•						•		1 bird seen 1x in Mar
Caspian Tern	•	•	•		•	•	•		4 (Jan) - 190 (Sep); on 13/19 counts; usually ≤8
Common Tern		•	•		•	•	•		12 birds seen on count in Sep 1998: at all 3 sites
Forster's Tern	•	•	•		•	•	•		1-38 (Sep); on 7/19 counts May-Sep
Black Tern		•	•		•				3 sightings: 10 birds in Aug, 5 & 250 in Sep
Black Skimmer		•	•		•				2 birds seen 1x in June
Rock Dove	•		•	•	•		•	+	1-17 birds seen on 18/19 counts; a flock in residence at NSM
White-winged Dove	•	•				•			1 bird seen 2x in May, July
Mourning Dove			•		•	•		+	1-2 birds on 2 counts; in July, Sep; nested locally
Common Ground-Dove					•	•			1 bird seen 1x in Jan

	Spr	Sum	Aut	Win	NSM	SPHq	SCr	Br	Comments
Lesser Nighthawk	•	•			•		•		Seen on 2 counts: 11 birds in May, 2 in June
White-throated Swift	•					•	•		5 birds overhead 1x in May
Costa's Hummingbird				•		•	•		1 bird seen 1x in Dec
Western Wood-Peewee		•					•		1 bird seen 1x in Aug
Willow Flycatcher	•	•			•				1-2 birds seen 2x in May, June
Black Phoebe	•		•	•	•	•	•		1-2 birds seen on 9/19 counts July-Jan
Say's Phoebe	•	•	•	•	•	•	•	+	1-3 birds seen on 10/19 counts; nested at SPHq
Western Kingbird	•		•		•	•	•		1-3 birds seen on 3 counts; in Mar, Apr, July
Loggerhead Shrike	•		•	•			•		1 bird seen on 3 counts; in Jan, Mar, Sep
Common Raven	•	•		•					1-15 (Oct); on 6/19 counts
Horned Lark		•	•		•		•		Seen on 2 counts: 2 birds in Sep, 1 in Nov
Tree Swallow	•	•			•		•		2-53 (Mar); on 4/19 counts in Jan, Mar, July
Violet-green Swallow	•					•			2 & 30 birds seen on 2 counts in Mar
No. Rough-winged Swallow	•	•			•		•		4-95 (Jul); seen on 7/19 counts; numbers variable
Cliff Swallow	•	•	•		•	•	•		6-35 birds seen on 3 counts; in Mar, May, June
Barn Swallow	•	•	•		•	•	•		1-30 birds seen on 7/19 counts
Verdin	•	•	•	•	•	•	•	+	1-3 birds seen on 5/19 counts; nested at SPHq
Cactus Wren	•	•	•	•	•	•			1-3 birds seen on 3 counts; in Mar, Nov, Dec
Marsh Wren	•			•	•		•		1-7 (Jan); on 9/19 counts
Ruby-crowned Kinglet	•		•	•		•			2 sightings: 3 birds in Nov, 2 in Dec
Black-tailed Gnatcatcher		•				•			1 bird seen 1x in July
Northern Mockingbird	•	•	•	•	•	•	•	+	1-3 birds seen on 9/19 counts; nested at SPHq

	Spr	Sum	Aut	Win	NSM	SPHq	SCr	Br	Comments
European Starling	•	•	•	•	•	•		+	3 (July) - 70 (Jan); on all counts
American Pipit		•				•	•		1 bird seen 1x in Oct
Cedar Waxwing				•		•			Flock of 30 seen 1x in Jan 1999
Phainopepla			•	•	•	•	•		2 sightings: 6 birds in Oct, 1 in Dec
Orange-crowned Warbler		•			•		•		1 bird seen 1x in June
Yellow-rumped Warbler	•		•		•	•	•		1-5 birds seen on 4/19 counts; in migration in Mar, Oct, Nov
Common Yellowthroat			•	•		•			1-2 birds seen on 3 counts; in Nov, Dec, Jan
Wilson's Warbler	•				•	•	•		1 bird seen in migration on 2 May counts
Summer Tanager		•				•			1 bird seen 1x in July 1999
Savannah Sparrow			•				•		4 birds seen 1x in Sep
Song Sparrow	•			•		•			Single birds seen 3x in Jan, May
Lincoln's Sparrow			•			•			2 birds seen 1x in Nov
White-crowned Sparrow	•		•	•	•	•			1-10 birds seen on 5/19 counts Oct-Mar
Golden-crowned Sparrow			•			•			Flock of 20 birds seen 1x in Nov 1998
Red-winged Blackbird	•	•			•	•			6-20 birds seen on 4/19 counts Mar-July
Western Meadowlark			•	•	•		•		1-6 birds seen on 6/19 counts; Sep-Jan
Yellow-headed Blackbird	•						•		10 birds seen 1x in Apr
Brewer's Blackbird	•		•	•	•		•		8-90 (Jan) seen on 14/19 counts
Great-tailed Grackle	•		•	•	•	•	•	+	1-33 birds seen on 16/19 counts; nest-building in June
Brown-headed Cowbird	•	•			•	•	•		1-25 birds seen on 5/19 counts May-Oct; fledg-

	Spr	Sum	Aut	Win	NSM	SPHq	SCr	Br	Comments
Hooded Oriole	•	•					•		ling fed by Black-tailed Gnatcatcher in Aug / 2 sightings: 1 bird in May, 2 in July
House Finch	•		•	•		•	•		2-4 birds seen on 4/19 counts
House Sparrow	•	•	•			•	•		1-4 birds seen on 4/19 counts

Abbr: NSM = North Shore Marina
SPHq = State Park Hq
SCr = Salt Creek

National Wildlife Refuge Headquarters

	Spr	Sum	Aut	Win	Br	Comments
Pied-billed Grebe		•				1 bird seen 1x in June
Eared Grebe	•	•	•	•		10-1,250 (Feb); on 13/16 counts; highest numbers Nov-Feb
Western Grebe				•		4 birds seen 1x in Feb
American White Pelican	•	•	•	•		6-605 (Jan); on 8/16 counts; highest numbers Dec-Feb
Brown Pelican	•	•	•	•		1 (Dec) - 45 (Aug); on 10/16 counts
Double-crested Cormorant	•	•	•	•		1-283 (Feb); on 15/16 counts
American Bittern			•	•		1 bird seen 2x, in Nov, Jan; has nested in recent past
Great Blue Heron	•	•	•	•		1-14 birds seen on all counts
Great Egret	•	•	•	•		1-10 birds seen on 13/16 counts
Snowy Egret	•	•	•	•		1-24 birds seen on 9/16 counts
Cattle Egret	•	•	•	•		1-250 (Jan); on 11/16 counts
Green Heron	•	•	•	•	p	1-2 birds seen on 7/16 counts Feb-Aug
Black-crowned Night-Heron	•	•	•	•	p	1-19(June); on 15/16 counts
White-faced Ibis	•	•	•	•		1-1,010 (Nov); on 7/16 counts; usually <10, 1 large flock
Turkey Vulture	•	•	•	•		4 sightings: 1-3 birds overhead in May, July, Nov; 12 in Aug
Snow Goose	•		•	•		1-5,000 (Nov); on 9/16 counts Nov-Jan; often large flocks
Ross's Goose	•	•	•	•		3 sightings: 100 birds in Jan, 1 in June, 300 in Nov
Canada Goose			•	•		3 sightings: 1-2 in Oct, Jan; 165 in Jan
Gadwall		•	•			2 sightings: 6 birds in Aug, 4 in Nov
American Wigeon	•		•	•		1 (May) - 2,060 (Dec); on 9/16 counts Nov-May

	Spr	Sum	Aut	Win	Br	Comments
Mallard	•	•	•	•		2-45 (Dec); on 10/16 counts
Cinnamon Teal	•	•	•	•		1-88 (Aug); on 10/16 counts; highest numbers Aug-Oct
Northern Shoveler	•	•	•	•		1 (May) - 1600 (Oct); on 12/16 counts; highest numbers Oct-Jan
Northern Pintail	•		•	•		1 (May) - 900 (Nov); on 8/16 counts; highest numbers Oct-Jan
Green-winged Teal	•		•	•		2 (May) - 325 (Oct); on 6/16 counts; 1 large flock; usually <40
Canvasback				•		3 sightings: 1 bird in Nov-Dec, 21 in Jan
Redhead	•	•	•	•		1 (June) - 120 (Dec); on 6/16 counts; 1 large flock; usually ≤6
Lesser Scaup	•		•	•		1 (July) - 80 (Dec); on 6/16 counts; usually <25
Bufflehead				•		5 birds seen 1x in Jan
Common Goldeneye				•		7 birds seen 1x in Jan
Ruddy Duck	•			•	p	3 (July) - 2,300 (Nov); on 14/16 counts; few in summer
Osprey	•		•	•		2 sightings: 1 bird in Feb, 2 in Oct
Northern Harrier			•	•		3 sightings of 1-2 birds in Nov, Jan
Sharp-shinned Hawk				•		Single bird seen 2x in Jan
Cooper's Hawk				•		1 bird seen 1x in Jan
Red-tailed Hawk				•		1 bird seen 1x in Jan
American Kestrel	•		•	•		1-3 birds seen on 10/16 counts
Gambel's Quail	•	•	•			3 sightings of 1-6 birds in Apr, Oct, Nov
Clapper Rail	•	•	•		p	3 sightings of 1-4 birds in Mar, Apr, June
Sora	•		•	•		4 sightings of 1-2 birds in Apr, Aug, Nov
Common Moorhen	•	•	•	•	p	1-2 birds seen on 6/16 counts Feb-Oct
American Coot	•	•	•	•	p	9-264 (Feb); on 15/16 counts; 1 large flock; usually <70

	Spr	Sum	Aut	Win	Br	Comments
Black-bellied Plover	•	•	•	•		2 sightings: 1 bird in Aug, 5 in Oct
Semipalmated Plover		•				2 birds seen 1x in July
Killdeer	•	•	•	•	p	1-5 birds seen on 11/16 counts
Black-necked Stilt	•	•	•	•	p	3 (Jan) - 581 (July); on 14/16 counts; 1 large group, usually <40
American Avocet	•	•	•	•	p	15 (Dec) - 866 (July); on 15/16 counts; >350 July-Oct
Greater Yellowlegs	•	•	•	•		1-2 birds seen on 8/16 counts July-Mar
Willet	•	•	•	•		1-7 birds seen on 7/16 counts July-Feb
Spotted Sandpiper	•	•	•	•		3 sightings of 1-2 birds in Mar, Aug, Dec
Whimbrel	•					8 birds seen 1x in Apr
Long-billed Curlew	•	•	•			2 sightings: 1 bird seen in July, 36 in Oct
Marbled Godwit	•	•	•			4 sightings: flock of 300 in July; 1-10 June, Aug, Oct
Western Sandpiper	•	•	•			2 (Aug) - 3,270 (July); on 6/16 counts; 1 large flock; usually <50
Least Sandpiper	•	•	•			2 (Aug) - 32 (Feb); on 5/16 counts; usually <10
Dunlin				•		3 birds seen 1x in Dec
Stilt Sandpiper			•			1 bird seen 1x in Oct
Dowitcher spp.	•		•			14-574 (July); on 9/16 counts Mar-Nov; highest numbers Aug-Sep
Wilson's Phalarope	•					Flock of 120 seen 1x in Apr
Red-necked Phalarope		•				2 sightings: 18 in July, 50 in Aug
Bonaparte's Gull	•	•	•			4 sightings of 6-74 birds, 74 in Mar
Heermann's Gull	•					1 bird seen 1x in May
Ring-billed Gull	•		•	•		5 (May) - 575 (Feb); on 15/16 counts; numbers variable
California Gull	•	•	•	•		1-250 (Oct); on 7/16 counts; 1 large flock; usually <40

	Spr	Sum	Aut	Win	Br	Comments
Herring Gull	•	•	•	•		1-86 (Jan); on 10/16 counts; usually <10
Thayer's Gull	•					1 bird seen 1x in Apr 1998
Western Gull	•					2 birds seen 1x in May
Yellow-footed Gull	•	•				3-42 (July); on 6/16 counts May-Aug
Gull-billed Tern	•	•			+	1 (Aug) - 67 (Apr); on 5/16 counts Apr-Aug; nested on islands in pond
Caspian Tern	•	•	•	•	+	1 (Oct) - 638 (May); on 11/16 counts; nested in pond
Forster's Tern	•	•	•	•		Usually 1-2, but 335 in July; on 6/16 counts Feb-Aug
Black Tern	•	•	•			3 sightings: 4 birds in May, 95 in July, 3 in Aug
Black Skimmer	•	•	•	•	+	55-338 seen on 8/16 counts Apr-Sep; nested on islands in pond
Rock Dove	•	•	•	•		2 sightings: 28 birds in Apr, 7 in Sep
White-winged Dove	•	•				2 sightings: 7 birds in May, 3 in June
Mourning Dove	•	•	•	•	p	1-50 (Jan); on 14/16 counts; 1 flock of 50; other counts ≤10
Common Ground-Dove	•	•	•	•	p	1-12 birds seen on 7/16 counts
Greater Roadrunner	•	•	•	•	p	Single bird seen on 6/16 counts
Burrowing Owl	•	•	•			1 bird seen 2x in June, Aug
Vaux's Swift	•					4 birds seen 1x in Apr
Costa's Hummingbird	•	•				1 bird seen 1x in May
Belted Kingfisher				•		1 bird seen 1x in Feb
Ladder-backed Woodpecker	•	•				1 bird seen 2x in May, Aug
Northern Flicker			•	•		4 sightings of 1-5 birds Oct-Jan
Western Wood-Pewee	•					1 bird seen 1x in May

	Spr	Sum	Aut	Win	Br	Comments
Black Phoebe	•	•	•	•	p	1-3 seen on 12/16 counts
Say's Phoebe	•	•	•	•	p	1-2 birds seen on 7/16 counts
Ash-throated Flycatcher			•			1 bird seen 1x in Sep
Cassin's Kingbird	•					3 birds seen 1x in migration in Apr
Western Kingbird	•	•			p	1-5 birds seen on 6/16 counts Apr-Aug
Loggerhead Shrike		•	•	•		1-2 birds seen on 8/16 counts June-Jan
European Starling	•		•	•		4 sightings of 3-8 birds in Jan, May, Nov, Dec
Cassin's Vireo			•			1 bird seen 1x in migration in Sep
Tree Swallow				•		1 bird seen 1x in Feb
Violet-green Swallow	•			•		2 sightings: 10 birds seen in Jan, 1 in Aug
No. Rough-winged Swallow	•			•		2 sightings: 4 birds seen in Feb, 3 in May
Cliff Swallow	•	•				3 sightings of 20-55 birds in Mar, June, Aug
Barn Swallow	•					1 bird seen 1x in May
Verdin	•	•	•	•	+	2-13 (May); on 15/16 counts
Cactus Wren				•		1 bird seen 1x in Dec
Marsh Wren	•	•	•	•	+	2-15 (Aug); on 12/16 counts; nested in cattails
Ruby-crowned Kinglet			•	•		4 sightings of 1-4 birds Nov-Jan
Blue-gray Gnatcatcher			•	•		3 sightings of 2-3 birds in Nov, Jan
Black-tailed Gnatcatcher	•	•	•	•	p	4 sightings of 1-2 birds, in Jan, May, Aug, Sep
Northern Mockingbird	•	•	•	•	p	1-3 birds seen on 8/16 counts
American Pipit				•		2 winter flocks: 25 birds seen in Dec, 90 in Jan
Phainopepla			•			1 bird seen 1x in Oct

	Spr	Sum	Aut	Win	Br	Comments
Orange-crowned Warbler		•				1 bird seen 1x in Aug
Virginia's Warbler	•					1 bird seen 1x in Apr 1998
Yellow Warbler	•		•			3 sightings of single birds in migration in May, Sep
Yellow-rumped Warbler			•	•		1-55 (Jan); on 7/16 counts, Oct-Feb; numbers variable
Common Yellowthroat	•	•	•		p	1-6 seen on 5/16 counts
Wilson's Warbler	•					1 bird seen 1x in migration in Apr
Abert's Towhee	•		•	•	p	1-6 birds seen on 12/16 counts
Savannah Sparrow			•			1 bird seen 1x in Oct
Song Sparrow	•	•	•	•	p	1-9 birds seen on 6/16 counts
Lincoln's Sparrow			•			1 bird seen 1x in Nov
White-crowned Sparrow	•		•	•		1-19 (Nov); on 6/16 counts Oct-Mar
Blue Grosbeak	•					1 bird seen 1x in May
Red-winged Blackbird	•	•	•	•	+	2 (Aug) - 625 (Nov); on 14/16 counts; nesting colony in cattails
Western Meadowlark	•	•	•	•		1-3 birds seen 3x in May, June, Dec
Yellow-headed Blackbird	•	•	•		+	4 (Sep) - 24 (Aug); on 6/16 counts; nested in cattails
Brewer's Blackbird			•			1 bird seen 1x in Aug
Great-tailed Grackle	•	•	•	•		1 (Feb) - 30 (Apr); on 13/16 counts
Brown-headed Cowbird	•	•	•			3 sightings of 1-3 birds in Apr, May, Oct
Hooded Oriole	•	•				2 sightings: 1 bird in May, 5 in Aug
House Finch	•	•	•	•	+	1-7 seen on 5/16 counts Jul-Nov
House Sparrow	•	•	•	•	+	1-10 seen on 6/16 counts

Sonny Bono National Wildlife Refuge – Unit 1

	Spr	Sum	Aut	Win	Br	Comments
Pied-billed Grebe	•	•	•	•		8-42 (Nov); on 13/15 counts
Horned Grebe	•			•		1 bird seen 1x in Apr
Eared Grebe	•	•	•	•		5 (Aug) - 16,500 (Jan); on 14/15 counts; usually >3,500
Western Grebe	•	•	•	•		8 (Nov) - 42 (Apr); on 9/15 counts
American White Pelican	•	•	•	•		2 (July) - 2,120 (Feb); on all counts; numbers variable
Brown Pelican	•	•	•			7 (Aug) - 228 (June); on 6/15 counts May-Sep
Double-crested Cormorant	•	•	•	•	+	89 (July) - 980 (Jan); on all counts; usually >300
Great Blue Heron	•	•	•	•	+	14 (Feb) - 213 (Sep); on all counts
Great Egret	•	•	•	•	+	3 (Feb) - 175 (Sep); on all counts
Snowy Egret	•	•	•	•		2 (July) - 128 (Nov); on all counts
Cattle Egret	•	•	•	•		8 - 130 (May); on 13/15 counts; numbers variable
Green Heron	•	•	•	•		1-3 birds seen on 8/15 counts Sep-Mar
Black-crowned Night-Heron	•	•	•	•		6 (July) - 48 (Jan); on all counts
White-faced Ibis	•	•	•	•		1 (Mar) - 366 (Sep); on 11/15 counts
Turkey Vulture	•		•	•		3 sightings of 3-5 birds July-Sep
Snow Goose	•			•		4-8,800 (Jan); on 6/15 counts Nov-Feb
Ross's Goose				•		24 birds seen 1x in Jan
Canada Goose			•	•		2 flocks: 360 birds in Nov, 480 in Dec
Gadwall	•		•	•		3-48 (Dec); on 8/15 counts Oct-May
American Wigeon	•			•		4 (Sep) - 1,320 (Nov); on 11/15 counts Sep-May

	Spr	Sum	Aut	Win	Br	Comments
Mallard	•	•	•	•		5 (July) - 124 (Jan); on all counts
Cinnamon Teal	•	•	•	•		1-320 (Aug); on 13/15 counts
Northern Shoveler	•	•	•	•		3 (May-June) - 2,300 (Dec); on 14/15 counts; few in Sum
Northern Pintail	•		•	•		1 (Apr) - 1,400 (Dec); on 12/15 counts; not May-July
Green-winged Teal	•		•	•		6 (Sep) - 600 (Dec); on 10/15 counts
Canvasback	•		•	•		2-108 (Nov); on 5/15 counts in Mar/Apr and Oct-Nov
Redhead	•	•	•	•		2 (Sep) - 28 (Feb); on 9/15 counts Feb-Sep; usually ≤12
Lesser Scaup	•		•	•		22 (May) - 1,400 (Nov); on 10/15 counts Oct-Apr
Surf Scoter		•				1 bird seen 1x in June
Bufflehead	•		•	•		4 (Feb) - 82 (Nov); on 7/15 counts Nov-Apr
Common Goldeneye				•		2 birds seen 1x, in Jan
Red-breasted Merganser	•			•		2-4 birds seen on 5/15 counts Jan-May
Ruddy Duck	•	•	•	•		31 (June) - 4,500 (Dec/Jan); on 12/15 counts
Osprey	•		•	•		1-4 birds seen on 10/15 counts
Northern Harrier	•		•	•		1-2 birds seen on 6/14 counts Sep-Mar
Red-tailed Hawk				•		1 bird seen 1x, in Jan
American Kestrel	•		•	•		2-4 birds seen on 11/15 counts
Clapper Rail	•	•	•	•	p	1-5 birds seen on 11/15 counts
Sora	•		•	•		1-3 birds seen on 7/15 counts Aug-Mar
Common Moorhen	•	•	•	•	p	1-21 (Aug); on 6/15 counts Aug-Mar
American Coot	•	•	•	•	p	42 (June) - 380 (Nov); on 11/15 counts
Black-bellied Plover	•		•	•		5 (Aug) - 72 (Jan); on 14/15 counts

	Spr	Sum	Aut	Win	Br	Comments
Snowy Plover	•	•	•	•		2-4 birds on 7/15 counts Jan-Sep
Semipalmated Plover	•	•				2-15 (Aug); on 7/15 counts Mar-Aug
Killdeer	•	•	•	•	p	4-18 birds seen on all counts; higher numbers in Sum
Mountain Plover			•			4 birds seen 1x in Nov
Black-necked Stilt	•	•	•	•		45 (Feb) - 842 (July); on all counts; usually >300
American Avocet	•	•	•	•		60 (Jan) - 811 (July); on all counts; usually >400
Greater Yellowlegs	•	•	•	•		1 (Aug) - 26 (Mar, Oct, Nov); on 12/15 counts
Willet	•	•	•	•		2 (July) - 620 (Nov); on all counts; large flocks Nov-Jan
Spotted Sandpiper	•		•	•		1-4 birds seen on 5/15 counts; usually Feb-Apr
Whimbrel	•	•	•			1-5 birds seen on 5/15 counts Mar-July
Long-billed Curlew	•	•	•	•		1-47 (July); on 5/15 counts June-Dec; usually <10
Marbled Godwit	•	•	•	•		5 (Jan) - 135 (July); on 13/15 counts
Red Knot	•		•			2 sightings: 2 birds in Apr, 1 in Sep 1998
Sanderling	•					2 sightings: 2 birds in Apr, 5 in May
Western Sandpiper	•	•	•	•		4 (May-June) - 3,620 (July); on all counts; usually >100
Least Sandpiper	•	•	•	•		2-300 (Feb); on 7/15 counts Nov-Mar; numbers variable
Dunlin	•		•	•		2 (Mar) - 18 (Dec); on 6/15 counts Sep-Mar
Dowitcher spp.	•	•	•	•		18-420 (Feb); on 12/14 counts; usually <100
Common Snipe			•			1 bird seen 1x in Sep
Wilson's Phalarope	•					Flock of 36 seen 1x in Apr
Red-necked Phalarope	•	•				1-37 (July); on 4/15 counts May-Aug; usually ≤6
Laughing Gull			•			1 bird seen 1x in June

	Spr	Sum	Aut	Win	Br	Comments
Bonaparte's Gull	•					5-16 birds seen on 5/15 counts Mar-June
Ring-billed Gull	•	•	•	•		122 (June) - 2,900 (Sep); on all counts; >1000/count Aug-Jan
California Gull	•	•	•	•		1 (July) - 450 (Mar); on 14/15 counts; usually ≤40
Herring Gull	•		•	•		1 (Sep) - 110 (Jan); on 9/15 counts; numbers variable
Yellow-footed Gull	•	•	•	•		1 (Feb-Mar) - 74 (July); on 11/15 counts; highest numbers June-Sep
Glaucous-winged Gull				•		1 bird seen 1x in Sep
Gull spp.	•	•	•	•		Distant flocks of 108-1,700 (Sep); on 14/15 counts
Gull-billed Tern	•					2 sightings: 5 birds in Mar, 3 in May
Caspian Tern	•	•	•			1-388 (Aug); on 11/15 counts Mar-Nov; usually <30
Forster's Tern	•	•	•	•		1 (Jan) - 25 (Aug-Sep); on 12/15 counts; usually ≤10
Black Tern	•	•	•			3 (May) - 160 (Sep); on 6/15 counts May-Sep; postbreeding visitor
Black Skimmer	•					2 birds seen 1x in May
Mourning Dove	•	•	•	•		2 (May) - 52 (Dec); on 14/15 counts; usually >20
Common Ground-Dove		•	•			1-4 birds seen 3x in June, Aug, Sep
Greater Roadrunner	•	•	•	•		1-2 birds seen on 12/15 counts
Burrowing Owl	•	•	•	•	p	2-4 birds seen on 10/15 counts
White-throated Swift	•					4 birds seen 1x in Apr
Black Phoebe	•	•	•	•		1-5 birds seen on 10/15 counts Jan-Sep
Say's Phoebe				•		2 sightings: 6 birds in Dec, 5 in Jan
Ash-throated Flycatcher	•					1 bird seen 1x in Apr
Western Kingbird	•	•				2-8 (May); on 6/15 counts Mar-Oct
Loggerhead Shrike		•	•	•		1-4 birds seen on 6/15 counts July-Jan

	Spr	Sum	Aut	Win	Br	Comments
Common Raven	•			•		2-4 birds seen on 7/15 counts Jan-May
Tree Swallow	•			•		4 sightings of 6-12 birds Jan-Mar
No. Rough-winged Swallow	•	•				11-28 seen on 6/15 counts Apr-June
Cliff Swallow	•	•	•	•		1 (Sep) - 50 (Aug); on 9/15 counts Feb-Sep
Barn Swallow	•	•				4 sightings of 2-7 birds Apr-Aug
Verdin	•	•				2 birds seen 1x in Aug
Marsh Wren	•	•		•	P	2 (Jan) - 27 (Sep); on 14/15 counts; highest numbers Sep-Dec
Northern Mockingbird	•	•				2-3 birds seen on 6 counts Mar-June
Yellow Warbler	•					2 birds seen 2x in May
Common Yellowthroat	•	•				1-3 birds seen on 6 counts Apr-June
Song Sparrow			•			1 bird seen 1x in Sep
White-crowned Sparrow	•			•		4 sightings of 1-6 birds Jan-Mar
Red-winged Blackbird	•	•	•			13-55 (Aug); on 8/15 counts Mar-Sep
Western Meadowlark	•			•		1-2 birds on 7/15 counts Jan-May
Great-tailed Grackle	•	•				3-4 birds seen 3x in May/June
Brown-headed Cowbird	•	•				2-6 birds seen on 7/15 counts Mar-Aug
House Finch	•	•		•		12 (Feb/Mar) - 48 (June); on 8/15 counts Jan-June
Lesser Goldfinch	•	•		•		2-7 birds seen on 8/15 counts Jan-June

West Side

	Spr	Sum	Aut	Win	Desert Shores	Salton Sea Beach	Salton City	Br	Comments
Eared Grebe	•	•	•	•	•		•		3 (June) - 3,790 (Feb): on 10/13 counts Oct-June
Western Grebe	•	•	•	•	•	•	•		1-58 (Oct); on 6/13 counts Jan-Apr & Oct-Nov
Clark's Grebe	•					•	•		1 bird seen 1x in Mar
American White Pelican	•	•	•	•	•	•	•		2 (Mar) - 91 (Nov); on 6/13 counts
Brown Pelican		•	•	•		•	•		1-16 (Apr); on 9/13 counts
Double-crested Cormorant	•	•	•	•	•	•	•		1 (May) - 40 (Oct); on 9/13 counts; not July-Aug
Great Blue Heron	•	•	•	•	•		•		1-21 (Oct); on 10/13 counts
Great Egret	•	•	•	•	•	•	•		1-185 (Jan); on 6/13 counts Sep-Feb; 1 large flock; usually ≤6
Snowy Egret	•	•	•	•		•	•		1-15 (Oct); on 9/13 counts
Cattle Egret	•	•	•	•	•				2 sightings of 1 & 20 birds in Jan
Green Heron	•	•	•						2 sightings of 1 & 2 birds; in Apr, July
Black-crowned Night-Heron	•	•	•	•	•	•	•		1-19 (Aug); on 6/13 counts June-Jan
Turkey Vulture							•		Flock of 16 seen 1x in Sep at city park
Brant	•						•		1 bird seen 1x in Mar
Northern Shoveler	•		•	•		•	•		1-7 (Feb); on 5/13 counts
Northern Pintail			•	•		•			2 birds seen 1x in Feb

	Spr	Sum	Aut	Win	DS	SSB	SC	Br	Comments
Green-winged Teal				•	•				2 birds seen 1x in Jan
Redhead				•		•			5 birds seen 1x in Feb
Lesser Scaup				•	•	•	•		2 sightings: 7 birds in Jan, 30 in Feb
Surf Scoter		•					•		5 birds seen 1x in June
Black Scoter	•						•		2 birds seen 1x in May 1998
Bufflehead				•	•	•			15 birds seen 1x in Jan
Red-breasted Merganser	•			•	•	•			2-3 birds seen on 3 counts Jan-Mar
Ruddy Duck				•	•				6 birds seen 1x in Jan
American Kestrel			•		•		•		1-2 birds seen 2x in Oct/Nov
Merlin				•		•			1 bird seen 1x in Jan
American Coot	•				•				1 bird seen 1x in Mar
Black-bellied Plover	•	•	•	•	•	•	•		1 (July) - 20 (Oct); on 12/13 counts
Snowy Plover	•	•	•	•	•	•	•	+	1 (Sep) - 18 (May); on 6/13 counts Mar-Sep; nested at Desert Shores & Salton Sea Beach
Semipalmated Plover	•		•	•	•	•	•		Seen on 2 counts: 27 birds in Apr among the 3 sites, 1 in Nov
Killdeer	•	•	•	•	•	•	•	+	2 (Aug) - 16 (Mar); on all counts
Black-necked Stilt	•	•	•	•	•	•	•	+	39 (Dec) - 548 (Jan); on all counts; highest numbers at Salton City
American Avocet	•	•	•	•	•	•	•	p	9 (Oct) - 65 (Apr); on 10/13 counts Sep-May; highest numbers at Salton City
Greater Yellowlegs	•		•	•	•	•	•		1-8 birds seen on 8/13 counts Oct-Apr

	Spr	Sum	Aut	Win	DS	SSB	SC	Br	Comments
Lesser Yellowlegs	•	•		•	•	•	•	•	2-7 birds seen on 8/13 counts Oct-Apr
Willet	•	•	•	•	•	•	•		3 (Sep) - 127 (Jan); on 9/13 counts Aug-Apr; highest numbers at Salton City
Spotted Sandpiper	•		•	•	•	•	•		Single birds seen on 5/13 counts scattered through the year
Long-billed Curlew		•	•				•		1 bird seen 1x in Aug
Marbled Godwit	•	•	•		•		•		1-18 (Aug); on 5/13 counts; mostly at Salton City
Ruddy Turnstone	•						•		3 birds seen 1x in Apr
Red Knot	•				•	•			2 sightings of 7 & 3 birds in Apr 1998
Sanderling	•						•		20 birds seen 1x in May
Western Sandpiper	•	•	•	•	•	•	•		7 (Jan) - 655 (Apr); on 7/13 counts
Least Sandpiper	•	•	•	•	•	•	•		1 (Jan) - 46 (Feb); on 7/13 counts
Dunlin	•		•				•		1-2 birds seen 2x in Apr, Nov
Peep (*Calidris* spp.)	•		•		•	•	•		5-69 (Apr); on 6/13 counts Mar-Oct
Dowitcher spp.	•			•	•	•	•		1 (Dec) - 51 (Apr); on 6/13 counts Nov-Apr
Wilson's Phalarope	•	•			•	•	•		Seen on 3 counts: 27 birds in Apr, 3 in June, 70 in Aug
Red-necked Phalarope	•	•				•			2 sightings: flock of 260 in Aug, 2 in Oct
Bonaparte's Gull	•	•	•	•		•	•		1-426 (Jan); on 7/13 counts
Ring-billed Gull	•	•	•	•	•	•	•		25 (May) - 2,800 (Jan); on 12/13 counts; large numbers at all sites
California Gull	•	•	•	•	•	•	•		3 (May) - 329 (Mar); on 12/13 counts

	Spr	Sum	Aut	Win	DS	SSB	SC	Br	Comments
Herring Gull	•	•	•	•	•	•	•		1-299 (Jan); on 11/13 counts
Gull spp.	•	•	•	•	•	•	•		Distant flocks of ≤1,600 at all sites; on all counts
Gull-billed Tern		•					•		1 bird seen 1x in July
Caspian Tern	•	•	•	•	•	•	•		1 (Nov) - 67 (Aug); on 11/13 counts
Forster's Tern	•	•	•			•	•		10-53 birds seen on 4/13 counts in Apr, July-Sep
Black Tern		•			•	•	•		Seen on 2 counts: 2 birds in July, 3 in Aug
Black Skimmer		•					•		7 birds seen 1x in June
Rock Dove	•	•	•	•	•		•		1 (Sep) - 41 (Jan); on 9/13 counts
Mourning Dove	•	•	•	•		•	•		1-5 birds seen on 6/13 counts Feb-Nov
Common Ground-Dove	•	•				•			1 bird seen 2x in Apr, June
Lesser Nighthawk	•	•					•		1 bird seen 1x in June
Belted Kingfisher	•				•	•			1 bird seen 2x in Mar-Apr
Black Phoebe	•		•	•		•	•		1-2 birds seen on 3 counts in Mar, Nov, Dec
Say's Phoebe	•		•	•	•	•	•		1-4 birds seen on 5/13 counts Sep-May
Cassin's Kingbird		•					•		1 bird seen 1x in Aug
Western Kingbird		•					•		2 birds seen 1x in July
Loggerhead Shrike				•		•			3 sightings of 1-3 birds in June, Dec, Jan
Common Raven	•		•	•	•	•	•		1-5 birds seen on 4/13 counts in Jan, Mar, Apr, Nov
No. Rough-winged Swallow	•			•	•				1-6 birds seen on 5/13 counts Jan-May
Cliff Swallow	•						•		2 sightings: 1 bird in Mar, 4 in Apr

	Spr	Sum	Aut	Win	DS	SSB	SC	Br	Comments
Verdin			•				•		1 bird seen 1x in Nov
Northern Mockingbird	•	•			•	•			1 bird seen 2x in Mar, June
European Starling	•	•	•	•	•	•	•		1 (Apr) - 66 (Jan); on 11/13 counts
American Pipit		•					•		2 birds seen 1x in Nov
Yellow-rumped Warbler			•	•		•	•		Seen on 3 counts; 9 birds in Jan, 14 in Nov, 8 in Dec
Savannah Sparrow	•			•			•		3 sightings of 1-3 birds Jan-Mar
Savannah Sparrow (Large-billed)	•					•			1 bird seen 1x in Mar
White-crowned Sparrow		•					•		1-2 birds seen 1x in Nov
Brewer's Blackbird				•	•		•		1-5 birds seen 2x in Jan, Nov
Great-tailed Grackle	•	•	•	•	•	•	•		1 (Mar) - 41 (Aug); on 10/13 counts
Hooded Oriole		•	•	•		•			1 bird seen 1x in July
House Finch	•		•	•	•	•	•		1-5 birds seen on 4 counts in Jan, Mar, Nov, Dec
House Sparrow	•		•	•	•	•	•		1 (Jan) - 24 (May); on 7/13 counts

Whitewater River Delta

	Spr	Sum	Aut	Win	Br	Comments
Pied-billed Grebe	•	•	•	•	+	1-3 birds seen on 7/15 counts
Eared Grebe	•	•	•	•		4 (July) - 5,820 (Jan); on 12/15 counts; highest numbers Nov-Jan
Western Grebe	•	•	•			2-28 (July); on 10/15 counts Mar-Nov, usually <10
Clark's Grebe	•	•				3-7 birds seen 3x in May, July
American White Pelican	•	•	•	•		1-1,960 (Nov); on all counts
Brown Pelican	•	•				2 sightings: 1 bird in May, 3 in June
Double-crested Cormorant	•	•	•	•	+	5 (June) - 1,100 (Nov); on all counts; highest numbers Sep-Jan; a few nests in 1998
American Bittern				•		1 bird seen 1x in Jan
Least Bittern		•	•		p	1 bird seen 3x in July-Aug; may have nested
Great Blue Heron	•	•	•	•	+	4 (Jan) - 86 (June); on 14/15 counts; 75 nests in snags in '98
Great Egret	•	•	•	•		2-30 (Dec); on all counts; usually <10
Snowy Egret	•	•	•			1-14 (July); on 9/15 counts Mar-Oct; usually ≤5
Cattle Egret	•	•	•			1-33 (July); on 6/15 counts May-Oct; usually <10
Green Heron	•	•	•	•		1-4 birds seen on 7/15 counts May-Oct
Black-crowned Night-Heron	•	•	•	•	+	4 (July) - 50 (Dec); on 14/15 counts; usually ≥10
White-faced Ibis	•	•	•			1-7 birds seen 3x in May, June, July
Turkey Vulture	•	•	•			1-4 birds seen 3x in May, Aug, Sep
Fulvous Whistling-Duck		•				2 birds overhead 1x in July
Snow Goose			•			Flock of 76 birds seen 1x in Nov

	Spr	Sum	Aut	Win	Br	Comments
Brant	•	•				3 sightings: 35 birds in May, 36 in June, 1 in July
Gadwall				•		1 bird seen 1x in Dec
American Wigeon				•		2 birds seen 1x in Dec
Mallard	•			•		1-6 birds seen on 6/15 counts Jan-July
Cinnamon Teal	•	•		•		2-14 (Aug); on 6/15 counts Dec-Aug
Northern Shoveler	•		•	•		1 (May) - 194 (Jan); on 7/15 counts Sep-May
Northern Pintail		•		•		1-55 (Dec); seen on 4 counts in Jan, Jun, Dec
Green-winged Teal	•			•		1-9 birds seen 3x in Dec, Jan, Mar
Redhead	•	•		•		4 sightings of 2-3 birds in Jan, Mar, July
Lesser Scaup	•		•	•		7-55 (Jan); on 7/15 counts Nov-Apr; highest numbers Nov-Jan
Bufflehead				•		7 birds seen 1x in Dec
Ruddy Duck	•		•	•		9 (July) - 882 (Jan); on 11/15 counts
Osprey	•	•	•	•		1-5 birds seen on 12/15 counts
Northern Harrier			•	•		1 bird seen 2x in Jan, Nov
Red-tailed Hawk			•	•		1 bird seen 3x in Oct/Nov
American Kestrel	•		•	•	p	1-4 birds seen on 13/15 counts
Gambel's Quail	•		•	•	+	3-25 birds seen on 11/15 counts; nested locally
Black Rail	•			•		Single birds heard 2x in Jan, Mar 1999
Clapper Rail		•				Single bird heard 1x in July
Sora	•		•	•		4 sightings: 1 & 4 birds in Jan, 2 in Apr, 1 in Nov
Common Moorhen	•	•	•	•		1-11 seen on all counts; juvs in June
American Coot	•	•	•	•	+	2 (Nov) - 56 (May); on 14/15 counts; juvs in June

	Spr	Sum	Aut	Win	Br	Comments
Black-bellied Plover	•	•	•	•		2-11 birds seen on all counts
Snowy Plover	•	•			+	1-7 birds seen on 5/15 counts Mar-Aug; nested on the shore
Semipalmated Plover	•	•				1-9 birds seen on 4/15 counts Mar-July
Killdeer	•		•	•	+	1-3 birds seen on 9/15 counts
Black-necked Stilt	•		•	•	+	11 (May) - 306 (July); on all counts, usually ≥45; highest numbers July/Aug
American Avocet	•	•	•	•	p	4 (July) - 453 (Nov); on all counts, usually >30
Greater Yellowlegs	•	•	•	•		1-4 birds seen on 7/15 counts June-Jan
Lesser Yellowlegs	•	•	•			1-3 birds seen 3x in Mar, Apr, July
Willet	•	•	•	•		1-58 (Mar); on 13/15 counts
Spotted Sandpiper	•					1 bird seen 1x in Apr
Whimbrel	•					1 bird seen 1x in Apr
Long-billed Curlew	•					2 birds seen 1x in May
Marbled Godwit	•	•	•	•		1-113 (July); on 10/15 counts
Western Sandpiper	•	•	•	•		27 (Jan) - 355 (Aug); on 11/15 counts; usually >100
Least Sandpiper	•	•	•	•		2 (Sep) - 41 (Mar); on 6/15 counts
Dunlin	•					1-14 birds seen on 7/15 counts Mar-Nov
Dowitcher spp.	•		•	•		1-124 (Oct); on 10/15 counts; 1 large flock, usually ≤30
Red-necked Phalarope	•		•			2 sightings: 3 birds in Aug, 7 in Nov
Laughing Gull	•	•				1 bird seen 1x in June
Bonaparte's Gull	•		•	•		1-60 (Mar); on 5/15 counts Nov-May
Ring-billed Gull	•		•	•		8 (May) - 725 (Nov); on 14/15 counts; usually ≥100

	Spr	Sum	Aut	Win	Br	Comments
California Gull	•	•	•	•		2-50 (July); on 6/15 counts Dec-July
Herring Gull	•	•	•	•		1 (June) - 79 (Dec); on 11/15 counts; usually <30
Yellow-footed Gull		•	•			1-15 birds seen on 4/15 counts July-Nov
Gull spp.				•		Flocks of 35-685 too distant for speciation; seen on 7/15 counts
Gull-billed Tern	•	•				1-2 birds seen 3x in May, July
Caspian Tern	•	•	•	•		2 (Dec) - 241 (Aug); on 12/15 counts; numbers variable
Forster's Tern	•	•	•	•		6 (Nov) - 62 (Aug); on 8/15 counts Apr-Nov; usually <20
Black Tern	•	•				3-13 birds seen 3x in July/Aug
Black Skimmer	•	•				1-11 birds seen 3x in May, July, Aug
White-winged Dove	•	•			p	1-16 (Aug); on 7/15 counts Apr-Aug, usually <10
Mourning Dove	•	•	•	•	p	1 (Nov) - 39 (Apr); on 12/15 counts Mar-Nov; usually <10
Common Ground-Dove	•	•	•	•	p	1-3 birds birds seen on 5/15 counts May-June, 1 in Dec
Greater Roadrunner	•	•	•	•	p	1-2 birds seen on 7/15 counts
Lesser Nighthawk	•	•			+	1-4 birds seen on 4/15 counts May-July
Vaux's Swift	•					18 birds seen overhead 1x in Apr
White-throated Swift	•					18 birds seen 1x in Apr
Belted Kingfisher			•	•		1 bird seen 2x in Oct-Nov
Ladder-backed Woodpecker	•	•	•	•	p	1-4 birds seen on 9/15 counts Nov-July
Northern Flicker				•		1 bird seen 2x in Dec, Jan
Black Phoebe	•	•	•	•	p	1-5 birds seen on 11/15 counts
Say's Phoebe	•		•	•		1-3 birds seen on 7/15 counts Oct-Apr
Ash-throated Flycatcher	•	•			+	1-2 birds seen on 5/15 counts Apr-July

	Spr	Sum	Aut	Win	Br	Comments
Cassin's Kingbird		•				1 bird seen 1x in June
Western Kingbird	•	•	•	•	+	1-8 birds seen on 4/15 counts Apr-July
Loggerhead Shrike	•	•	•	•	p	1-4 birds seen on 14/15 counts
Common Raven	•		•	•		3 sightings of 1-2 birds; in Apr, Sep, Dec
Tree Swallow	•			•		3 sightings of 3-9 birds; in Jan, Mar
No. Rough-winged Swallow	•					3 sightings of 2-10 birds Mar-May
Cliff Swallow	•	•	•			3 (Sep) - 209 (Mar); on 5/15 counts Mar-Sep
Barn Swallow	•					8 birds seen 1x in Apr
Verdin	•	•	•	•	+	10 (Sep) - 67 (July); on all counts
Cactus Wren	•	•	•	•	+	1-2 birds seen on 6 counts
Bewick's Wren	•	•	•	•	+	1-8 (Jan); on 7/15 counts June-Jan
House Wren				•		1 bird seen 1x in Dec
Marsh Wren	•	•	•	•	+	2 (Aug) - 46 (Apr); on all counts; nested in cattails
Ruby-crowned Kinglet				•		1 bird seen 2x in Dec-Jan
Blue-gray Gnatcatcher	•	•	•	•		1-2 birds seen on 4/15 counts in Jan, May, June, Oct
Black-tailed Gnatcatcher	•	•	•	•	+	1 (Dec) - 26 (July); on 14/15 counts; usually <15
Northern Mockingbird	•		•			1 bird seen 2x in May, Nov
Crissal Thrasher	•	•	•	•	p	1-6 (Apr); on 5/15 counts Mar-Oct
European Starling	•	•				3 sightings of 2-7 birds; in Mar, Apr, Nov
American Pipit			•	•		1 bird seen 2x in Nov-Dec
Phainopepla			•	•		2 birds seen 2x in Nov, Jan
Orange-crowned Warbler	•			•		3 sightings of 1-2 birds; in Jan, Mar, Apr

	Spr	Sum	Aut	Win	Br	Comments
Yellow Warbler	•		•			3 sightings of 1-3 birds; in Apr, Oct, Nov
Yellow-rumped Warbler	•	•	•	•		1 (Apr) - 39 (Jan); on 8/15 counts Oct-Apr
Common Yellowthroat	•		•	•	+	2-21 (May); on 13/15 counts
Wilson's Warbler			•			1 bird seen 1x in Nov
Yellow-breasted Chat		•			p	2 birds seen 1x in June
Spotted Towhee	•			•		1-2 birds seen 2x in Mar, Dec
Abert's Towhee	•	•	•	•	p	2-36 (July); on all counts
Brewer's Sparrow	•					2 birds seen 1x in Mar 1999
Lark Sparrow			•			1 bird seen 1x in Oct
Sage Sparrow			•	•		3 sightings of 2-7 birds; in Nov, Jan
Savannah Sparrow			•	•		3 sightings of 1-2 birds; in Oct, Dec, Jan
Song Sparrow	•	•	•	•	+	2 (Aug) - 40 (Apr); on all counts; highest numbers Mar-July
Lincoln's Sparrow	•		•			1 bird seen 2x in Mar, Nov
White-crowned Sparrow			•	•		2 (Oct) - 18 (Nov); on 5/15 counts Oct-Jan
Blue Grosbeak		•				1 bird seen 1x in July 1998
Red-winged Blackbird	•	•	•	•	p	1-45 (July); on 11/15 counts; usually ≤6
Yellow-headed Blackbird	•					3 birds seen 1x in Apr
Brewer's Blackbird		•				1 bird seen 1x in June
Great-tailed Grackle	•	•	•	•		1-4 birds seen on 5/15 counts
Brown-headed Cowbird	•	•			+	3-22 (Apr); on 6/15 counts Apr-July; usually <10
Bullock's Oriole	•	•			+	3 sightings: 1 bird in Apr, 15 in May, 4 in June
House Finch	•		•	•		2-11 (Oct-Nov); on 7/15 counts Oct-Apr

Wister Unit, State Imperial Wildlife Area

	Spr	Sum	Aut	Win	Br	Comments
Pied-billed Grebe	•	•	•	•	p	1-19 (Nov); on all counts
Eared Grebe	•	•	•	•		1-697 (Dec); on 14/19 counts; highest numbers Dec-Jan
Western Grebe	•		•	•		1-33 (Feb); on 11/19 counts, Oct-May
Clark's Grebe	•		•			2 sightings: 4 birds in May, 1 in Oct
American White Pelican	•	•	•	•		1 (May) - 3,687 (Jan); on all counts; highest numbers Oct-Feb
Brown Pelican	•	•	•	•		1 (Mar) - 152 (Sep); on 12/19 counts
Double-crested Cormorant	•	•	•	•	+	12 (May) - 908 (Jan); on all counts; breeds on Mullet Island, off-shore
American Bittern	•		•	•	p	1-8 birds seen on 11/19 counts; usually 1-2
Least Bittern**		•		•		1 bird seen 2x in Jan, June
Great Blue Heron	•	•	•	•	+	9-121 (Jan); on all counts; nested in snags offshore
Great Egret	•	•	•	•		5 (Jan) - 160 (Sep); on all counts; numbers variable
Snowy Egret	•	•	•	•		7 (Jan) - 314 (July); on all counts; usually <50
Little Blue Heron*			•			1 bird seen 2x in Nov-Dec
Cattle Egret	•	•	•	•		1-14 (June); on 8/19 counts
Green Heron	•	•	•	•	p	1-15 (July); on 13/19 counts; usually ≤4
Black-crowned Night-Heron	•	•	•	•		3 (Feb) - 177 (Sep); on all counts
White-faced Ibis	•	•	•	•		14 (Aug) - 473 (Nov); on all counts; 1 large flock; usually <100
Wood Stork		•	•			4 sightings: 2 birds in June, 20 in July, 17 in Aug, 1 in Sep
Chilean Flamingo**		•				4 seen 1x in July 1999

	Spr	Sum	Aut	Win	Br	Comments
Turkey Vulture	•	•	•	•		1-11 (Apr); on 13/19 counts; usually ≤4
Snow Goose	•		•	•		1 (June) - 5,800 (Nov); on 8/19 counts; Oct-Jan; 1 summer stray
Ross's Goose**			•			46 birds seen 1x in Nov
Brant	•	•	•			1 (Sep) - 64 (May); on 5/19 counts Apr-Sep; usually 1-7
Gadwall	•	•	•	•	+	9 (May) - 1,070 (Aug); on 18/19 counts; 1 large flock; usually <75; chicks in June
Eurasian Wigeon**			•			1 bird seen 1x in Nov 1998
American Wigeon	•		•	•		3-169 (Mar); on 15/19 counts; numbers variable
Mallard	•	•	•	•		2-50 (June); on 14/19 counts; numbers variable
Blue-winged Teal	•	•				2 sightings: 2 birds in May, 5 in June
Cinnamon Teal	•	•	•	•	+	2 (Dec) - 613 (Aug); on 18/19 counts; occ flocks, usually <100; chicks in June
Northern Shoveler	•	•	•	•		5 (July) - 5,300 (Sep); on 18/19 counts; highest numbers Sep-Apr
Northern Pintail	•	•	•	•		5 (June) - 854 (Jan); on 17/19 counts; highest numbers Sep-Feb
Green-winged Teal	•		•	•		1 (May) - 1,300 (Jan); on 16/19 counts; highest numbers Jan-Mar
Canvasback	•	•				3 sightings of 1-2 birds; in May-June
Redhead	•	•	•	•	+	1-161 (Sep); on 15/18 counts; highest numbers May-Sep; chicks in June
Ring-necked Duck			•	•		4 sightings of 1-48 birds Oct-Feb
Lesser Scaup*	•		•	•		2-520 (Feb); on 5/19 counts Nov-Mar
Bufflehead	•		•	•		1-22 (Feb); on 9/19 counts Nov-July
Ruddy Duck	•		•	•	p	1 (Sep) - 4,400 (Nov); on all counts; highest numbers Oct-Apr
Duck spp.			•	•		Distant flocks of 605-2,200 ducks in Jan, Sep, Nov

	Spr	Sum	Aut	Win	Br	Comments
Osprey**		•	•			4 sightings of single birds in July, Sep, Oct
Bald Eagle**				•		1 bird seen 1x in Jan 1998
Northern Harrier	•	•	•	•		1 (Sep) - 23 (Jan); on 12/19 counts Sep-May
Sharp-shinned Hawk**				•		1 bird seen 1x in Dec
Cooper's Hawk**				•		1 bird seen 1x in Jan
Red-tailed Hawk			•	•		1-5 birds seen on 3 counts in Nov, Jan
American Kestrel		•	•	•		1-4 birds seen 4x in Jan, July, Aug, Nov
Merlin			•	•		3 sightings: 1 bird in Oct, 2 in Nov, 1 in Dec
Peregrine Falcon		•	•	•		1-3 birds seen on 8/19 counts June-Jan
Prairie Falcon*			•			1 bird seen 1x in Sep
Ring-necked Pheasant*	•					2 birds seen 1x in May
Gambel's Quail	•	•	•	•	p	1-22 (May); on 14/19 counts
Clapper Rail	•	•	•	•	+	1-22 (Apr); on 16/19 counts; usually ≤10; nested in freshwater marsh
Virginia Rail	•	•	•	•		1-3 seen on 6/19 counts
Sora	•	•	•	•	p	1-13 (Sep); on 18/19 counts; possible breeder
Common Moorhen	•	•	•	•	p	1-10 (Aug); on 14/19 counts
American Coot	•	•	•	•	p	18 (July) - 2,200 (Nov); on all counts; usually >1,000
Black-bellied Plover	•	•	•	•		1-54 (Sep); on 12/19 counts; usually <10; numbers variable
American Golden Plover**			•			1 bird seen 1x in Oct 1998
Snowy Plover	•	•	•	•	+	1 (Mar) - 76 (July); on 12/19 counts; highest numbers Apr-Aug; nested on salt pans

	Spr	Sum	Aut	Win	Br	Comments
Semipalmated Plover	•		•			1-23 (Apr); on 6/19 counts Mar-Oct; usually ≤5
Killdeer	•	•	•	•	+	6 (Dec) - 62 (Aug); on all counts; nests found
Black-necked Stilt	•	•	•	•	+	44 - 1,060 (Nov); on all counts; usually >200; nests observed
American Avocet	•	•	•	•	p	76 (May) - 4,370 (Sep); on all counts; usually >800
Greater Yellowlegs	•	•	•	•		1-21 (Nov); on 16/19 counts
Lesser Yellowlegs*		•	•	•		4 sightings of single birds in Jan, Feb, Aug, Sep
Willet	•	•	•	•		1-125 (June); on 14/19 counts
Spotted Sandpiper*	•		•	•		3 sightings of 1-2 birds in Jan, Feb, Sep
Whimbrel	•	•				4 sightings of 1-2 birds Mar-July
Long-billed Curlew	•	•	•	•		1 (Feb) - 45 (Oct); on 7/19 counts; usually <20
Marbled Godwit	•	•	•	•		1 (Oct) - 216 (May); on 12/19 counts; usually <50
Western Sandpiper	•	•	•	•		1 (May) - 2,000 (Oct); on 15/19 counts; highest numbers Sep-Nov
Least Sandpiper	•	•	•	•		3 (July) - 196 (Mar); on 16/19 counts; highest numbers Sep-Mar
Dunlin	•		•	•		1 (Aug) - 57 (Feb); on 9/19 counts, usually <15
Stilt Sandpiper	•		•	•		2-12 birds seen 4x in Feb, Sep, Dec
Peeps (*Calidris* spp.)	•	•	•	•		Distant flocks of 80-2060 small sandpipers on 17/19 counts
Dowitcher spp.	•	•	•	•		5 (May) - 3,200 (July); on 18/19 counts
Common Snipe	•		•	•		1-8 birds seen on 7/19 counts Sep-Apr
Wilson's Phalarope	•	•	•			1-125 (July); on 7/19 counts Apr-Sep; usually ≤20
Red-necked Phalarope	•	•	•	•		1 (Jan) - 650 (July); on 6/19 counts Apr-July (+ 1 Jan sighting)
Parasitic Jaeger*			•			1 bird seen 1x in Aug
Laughing Gull	•	•	•			1-18 (June); on 6/19 counts, May-Sep

	Spr	Sum	Aut	Win	Br	Comments
Franklin's Gull**	•					3 birds seen 1x in May 1999
Little Gull**	•					1 bird seen 1x in May 1999
Bonaparte's Gull	•	•	•	•		2 (June) - 570 (Nov); on 13/19 counts; highest numbers Nov-Apr
Heermann's Gull**		•				1 bird seen 1x in June
Ring-billed Gull	•	•	•	•		43 (June) - 1,982 (Jan); on all counts
California Gull	•	•	•	•		1 (May) - 631 (July); on 18/19 counts
Herring Gull	•		•	•		5-276 (Jan); on 15/19 counts Sep-May
Western Gull*	•					4 birds seen 1x in Mar
Yellow-footed Gull	•	•	•	•		2 (May) - 141 (July); on 9/19 counts Jan-Sep; usually <50
Gull spp.	•	•	•	•		Distant flocks of 50-1,150 gulls on 17/19 counts
Gull-billed Tern	•	•	•			1-21 seen on 4/19 counts Apr-July
Caspian Tern	•	•	•	•		1 (Jan) - 537 (Aug); on all counts; highest numbers July-Sep
Forster's Tern	•	•	•	•		1 (Jan) - 61 (Nov); on 16/19 counts; highest numbers May-Nov
Black Tern	•	•				4 sightings of 1-6 birds June-Aug
Black Skimmer	•	•				2 sightings: 8 birds in May, 9 in July
Rock Dove**				•		2 sightings: 4 birds in Jan, 50 in Feb
White-winged Dove	•	•			p	2-31 birds seen on 6/19 counts May-July
Mourning Dove	•	•	•	•	p	1 (Mar) - 107 (Aug); on 14/19 counts
Common Ground-Dove	•	•	•			1-15 birds seen on 6/19 counts Mar-Nov
Greater Roadrunner	•			•		1-2 seen on 8/19 counts
Great Horned Owl*	•	•				2 sightings: 2 birds seen in July, 1 in Nov
Burrowing Owl*		•				1 bird seen 1x in June

	Spr	Sum	Aut	Win	Br	Comments
Lesser Nighthawk	•	•	•			1 (Sep) - 25 (May); on 8/19 counts Apr-Sep
Vaux's Swift**	•					2 sightings: 25 birds in Apr, 4 in Sep
Belted Kingfisher	•		•	•		1 bird seen on 5/19 counts Sep-Apr
Ladder-backed Woodpecker**			•	•		1 bird seen 2x in Jan, Nov
Northern Flicker*			•	•		2 sightings: 2 birds in Oct, 1 in Nov
Western Wood-Pewee	•		•			1-2 birds seen 3x in May, Sep
Pacific Slope Flycatcher**	•					2 birds seen 1x in Sep
Black Phoebe	•	•	•	•	p	2 (July) - 27 (Jan); on all counts
Say's Phoebe	•	•	•	•	p	1-20 (Jan); on 13/19 counts
Ash-throated Flycatcher**	•	•				1 bird seen 2x in June, Aug
Cassin's Kingbird*	•					2 sightings: 1 bird in Apr, 2 in May
Western Kingbird	•	•				1-15 (May); on 7/19 counts Mar-Aug
Loggerhead Shrike	•	•	•	•	p	1 (Jan) - 18 (Aug-Sep); on 14/19 counts
Plumbeous Vireo*	•					1 bird seen 1x in Apr
Warbling Vireo**			•			3 birds seen 1x in Sep
Common Raven**			•	•		2 birds seen 2x in Sep, Dec
Horned Lark*				•		1 bird seen 1x in Jan
Tree Swallow	•		•	•		4 (Feb) - 170 (Sep); on 10/19 counts
No. Rough-winged Swallow	•	•	•	•		1 (May) - 200 (July); on 8/19 counts Feb-July
Cliff Swallow	•	•				2 (July) - 96 (May); on 6/19 counts Mar-July
Barn Swallow	•		•			2 (Mar) - 205 (Sep); on 6/19 counts Jan-Sep
Verdin	•	•	•	•	p	1-20 (June); on all counts; highest numbers Apr-Oct

	Spr	Sum	Aut	Win	Br	Comments
Cactus Wren*	•			•		2 sightings: 1 bird in Jan, 2 in Mar
Bewick's Wren*				•		1 bird seen 2x in Dec-Jan
House Wren*				•		4 birds seen 1x in Feb
Marsh Wren	•	•	•	•	+	4 (July) - 105 (Feb); on 18/19 counts
Ruby-crowned Kinglet	•		•	•		1-9 birds seen on 8/19 counts Oct-Mar
Blue-gray Gnatcatcher	•		•	•		1-3 birds seen on 8/19 counts Sep-Apr
Black-tailed Gnatcatcher	•		•	•	p	1-5 birds seen on 13/19 counts
Northern Mockingbird				•		1-4 birds seen 4x in Jan, May, June, Dec
European Starling				•		1-3 birds seen 3x in Jan, Sep
American Pipit	•			•		6 (Mar) - 190 (Nov); on 10/19 counts Oct-May; usually in flocks
Sprague's Pipit**				•		3 bird 1x in Feb
Phainopepla	•	•	•	•		1-3 seen 4x in May, June, Dec
Orange-crowned Warbler**			•	•		3 sightings of 1-5 birds in Jan, Nov
Yellow Warbler*		•				1 bird seen 1x in Aug
Yellow-rumped Warbler			•	•		1 (Sep) - 179 (Nov); on 12/19 counts Sep-Mar
Townsend's Warbler*		•				1 bird seen 1x in Mar
American Redstart**			•			1 bird seen 1x in Sep 1999
Common Yellowthroat	•		•	•	p	1-64 (June); on 17/19 counts
Wilson's Warbler**	•	•				3 sightings of 1-6 birds in Apr, May, Sep
Yellow-breasted Chat**		•				1 bird seen 1x in June
Western Tanager**			•			1 bird seen 1x in Sep
Abert's Towhee	•	•	•	•	p	1-21 (Aug); on 18/19 counts

	Spr	Sum	Aut	Win	Br	Comments
Brewer's Sparrow*	•					1 bird seen 1x in Mar 1999
Lark Sparrow*		•				1 bird seen 1x in June
Sage Sparrow**			•			1 bird seen 1x in Sep
Savannah Sparrow	•		•	•		2 (June) - 27 (Nov); on 6/19 counts June-Jan
Song Sparrow	•		•	•	p	1 (Nov) - 78 (Apr); on all counts
Lincoln's Sparrow				•		1 bird seen 2x in Dec-Jan
White-crowned Sparrow	•		•	•		4-37 (Oct); on 8/19 counts Oct-Mar
Dark-eyed Junco**			•			2 birds seen 1x in Oct
Black-headed Grosbeak*	•					3 birds seen 1x in Apr
Blue Grosbeak**	•	•			p	2 sightings: 1 bird in May, 2 in June; may have nested
Red-winged Blackbird	•	•	•	•	+	2 (Dec) - 751 (Sep); on all counts
Tricolored Blackbird*	•					10 birds seen 1x in Mar
Western Meadowlark	•		•	•	p	2-6 seen on 7/19 counts Oct-May
Yellow-headed Blackbird	•	•	•	•	p	1 (Sep) - 100 (Mar); on 7/19 counts Mar-Sep
Brewer's Blackbird				•		2 sightings: 15 in Jan, 30 in Feb
Great-tailed Grackle	•	•	•	•	p	3 (Sep) - 159 (Feb); on all counts; usually <50
Brown-headed Cowbird	•	•			p	2 (Feb) - 40 (June); on 7/19 counts Feb-July
Bullock's Oriole**	•					2 birds seen 1x in May
House Finch	•	•		•	p	1-34 (May); on 8/19 counts; usually 1-2; 1 flock of 34

Key:
* Species seen only in section of refuge north of the headquarters
** Species seen only in section of refuge south of the headquarters